BIRDS
of
PREY
of the
BRITISH
ISLES

BIRDS
of
PREY
of the
BRITISH ISLES

Brian P. Martin

David & Charles

To Britain's army of amateur birdwatchers, whose
enthusiasm and observations support the
framework of effective conservation

———————

(Page 2) For centuries the spectral barn owl
was better known as the white owl

———————

Paintings by Alastair Proud

British Library Cataloguing in Publication Data
Martin, Brian P.
   Birds of prey of the British Isles.
   I. Title
   598.90941

   ISBN 0–7153–9782–6

First published 1992
Reprinted 1993

Typeset by ABM Typographics Ltd., Hull.
and printed in Great Britain
by Butler & Tanner Ltd
for David & Charles plc
Brunel House Newton Abbot Devon

CONTENTS

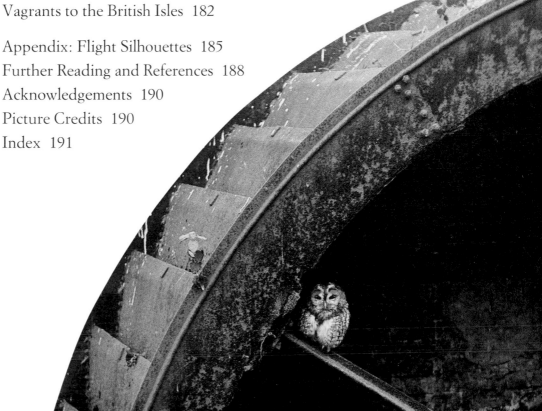

INTRODUCTION

EAGLE OWL

You have only to look into the eye of a bird of prey to perceive that sparkling, wild defiance which has intrigued man for many centuries. There resides that restless spirit which has enthused so many people – poets, artists, sportsmen and naturalists as well as humble country folk. Such beauty, such grace, such power, such freedom – all neatly packaged within one magnificent life form. Surely the ultimate design for living.

Little wonder, then, that these princes of day and night fire my earliest memories of the natural world. As a schoolboy I raised an orphan tawny owl in my bedroom cupboard, later successfully returning it to the wild after encouraging it to hunt for itself. And I am proud that my first-ever printed work was a poem entitled *The Owl*, which appeared in the magazine *Birds Illustrated* when I was just eleven. The fascination and inspiration continue to this day.

In 1799, long before 'curiosity in the feathered tribes' had become the sophist-icated science of ornithology which we know today, Thomas Bewick wrote the following passage in his book *A History of British Birds*:

Rapacious birds, or those which subsist chiefly on flesh, are much less numer-ous than ravenous quadrupeds; and it seems wisely provided by nature, that their powers should be equally confined and limited with their numbers; for if to the rapid flight and penetrating eye of the eagle, were joined the strength and voracious appetite of the lion, the tiger, or the glutton, no artifice could evade the one, and no speed could escape the other.

The characters of birds of the ravenous kind are particularly strong, and easily to be distinguished: the formidable talons, the large head, the strong and crooked beak, indicate their ability for rapine and carnage; their dispositions are fierce, and their nature intractable; unsociable and cruel, they avoid the haunts of civilisation, and retire to the most melancholy and wild recesses of nature, where they can enjoy in gloomy solitude the effects of their depredatory excursions. The fierceness of their nature extends even to their young, which they drive from the nest at a very early stage. The difficulty of supplying a con-stant supply of food for them sometimes overcomes the feelings of parental affection, and they have been known to destroy them in the fury of dis-appointed hunger. Different from all other kinds, the female of birds of prey is larger and stronger than the male: naturalists have puzzled themselves to assign the reason for this extraordinary property, but the final cause at least is obvious, – as the care of rearing her young is solely intrusted to the female, nature has furnished her with more ample powers to provide for her own wants, and those of her offspring.

This formidable tribe constitutes the first order among the genera of birds. Those of our own country consist only of two kinds, viz the falcon and the owl.

Though quaint and stylish, this extract is in part misleading and inaccurate, and perpetuates the popular anthropomorphic image of these birds which had evolved in the absence of hard science. For a start, the reasons for sexual di-morphism are complex, the female's sometimes pronounced greater size being re-lated to territorial defence and the pair's ability to take wide-ranging prey – thus reducing competition – as well as caring for the young.

The peregrine has been a favourite with falconers for many generations

Theoretically, any species of bird that feeds or preys upon other living creatures is a bird of prey, even including the tiny wren seeking spiders in the hedgerow. But such hunters have been excluded and over many years the term 'bird of prey' has come to mean a species which hunts and kills higher vertebrates – mammals, birds, reptiles, amphibians and fish – using specialised beaks and claws. A few concentrate on carrion or larger invertebrates.

These species are generally either diurnal or nocturnal, neatly dividing available hunting time between them, but the fact that hawks and owls share some characteristics is due to convergent evolution – through which similar structures can evolve for special purposes in unrelated groups of animals – rather than close relationship. Indeed, the owls (*Strigiformes*) are more closely related to the *Caprimulgiformes*, including the nightjars. Their ancestry is great, a single bone of a primitive owl being known from the late Paleocene of Colorado, from 54–57 million years ago.

Sometimes a bird of prey is referred to as a raptor, but this is generally applied to the day-flying species only. The term 'raptor' comes from the Latin for 'plunderer', *raptare* meaning 'to seize and carry away'.

Because they are not closely related, owls are classified in a separate order, their evolutionary path being traced through detailed studies of biochemistry, anatomy and behaviour. As a result, most specialist books have confined their coverage to either owls or diurnal raptors. Indeed, there is so much to say about both groups of birds that most scientific works must choose between them to produce a marketable book. Nevertheless, to the layman it must seem silly to differentiate and that is why I have chosen to include both owls and day-flying raptors in this book. However, with a limited number of words available I have been forced to leave out some detail. Thus I have chosen to omit much of the material chiefly of interest to professional biologists – notably the fine points of antagonistic behaviour, courtship, calls, moults and plumage – and concentrate on wider interests.

Since Bewick said British birds of prey consisted of two kinds – 'the falcon and the owl' – the science of classification has moved forward rapidly, and yet taxonomists still disagree. Until quite recently, all diurnal raptors were classed in a single order; in 1977, however, K.H. Voous put them in three: the *Cathartiformes* (New World vultures), *Accipitriformes* (kites, vultures, harriers, hawks, buzzards and eagles), and *Falconiformes* (falcons). These three orders contain about 290 species which are distributed throughout the world, except in Antarctica. However, their distribution is uneven. The Tropics hold the most – about 130 residents and 125 visitors, with a total of some 210 (72 per cent of the world total) breeding regularly. In contrast, the Arctic tundra raptor list comprises only four truly adapted species plus four regular breeders.

The order of owls, *Strigiformes*, contains two families: the typical owls, *Strigidae*, and the barn owls, *Tytonidae*, together embracing some 133 species. The barn owl differs only in minor osteological details from the typical owls. However, although owls are easily distinguished from other birds, family and sub-family relationships within the order are less certain.

Britain's raptor list is small – only twenty-three species are described in detail here, and although it is tempting to blame man's impact for this, I doubt whether the list was ever much larger. But what spectacular species we do have! Today many people are only familiar with the kestrel, whose habit of hunting motorway verges has made it an everyday sight, yet few are completely unaware of national treasures such as the kite and golden eagle because the birds' rarity and subsequent vulnerability constantly put them in the news.

The harriers and falcons are among the most widespread bird families in the world, and the barn owl, peregrine and osprey are among the few non-passerines which are virtually cosmopolitan. However, this does not necessarily mean they are abundant as many widespread species are restricted to small pockets of suitable habitat across the world.

The *Falconidae* is the world's most widespread landbird family, with 60 species in 10 genera, but the most widespread genus is *Falco*, with 37 species. Representatives are found in all continents except Antarctica, ranging from the tiny 15cm (6 in) Philippine falcon to the spectacular 50–60cm (20–24in) gyrfalcon, which is a rare visitor to Britain. *Falconidae* occur in a wide range of habitats from arctic tundra (gyr) to desert (North African sooty falcon). Some species, such as the common kestrel of Britain and Europe, have proliferated in recent years, making good use of man-made habitats, but others have failed to adapt and now include some of the world's rarest birds, such as the Mauritius kestrel. Many falcons have great dispersive abilities, 13 species breeding on two or more continents, and the peregrine is notable for having a worldwide breeding distribution virtually as wide as the entire genus.

In any work, the use of Latin names is important for they are used by scientists worldwide to avoid confusion between the many local names for single species. Indeed, they are also useful in tracing a species' history in just one country as the most popular names for many birds have varied considerably over the last few centuries.

The order of the species in this book does not follow any scientific system, other than grouping closely related species together. It is merely a personal choice, partly influenced by general public interest.

While every effort has been made to consult the best sources, measurements given are only approximate as there is considerable variation between individuals within a species, and some recorders are less accurate than others. Generally, the length is taken with the bird on its back — from bill-tip to tail-tip — and is normally only possible with a dead specimen, when inadvertent stretching is easily done. But the wing length is more accurate, indicating the distance from the wrist joint of the wing to the tip of the longest primary (flight feather). The wingspan is less reliable, being the distance between the two wing-tips when the bird is on its back and the wings fully stretched. The tendency for the female to be larger is most marked among bird-eating species. It has been suggested that this helps to establish the dominance that causes the male to bring food during incubation and much of the fledging period. Another idea is that this pronounced sexual dimorphism safeguards the female during courtship, as the male's aggression is so strong. Weights given are the range for healthy adult birds of all ages all year, females generally being significantly heavier, especially at the start of the breeding season. Starvation weights are not included.

It is regretted that descriptions of range cannot be too specific because birds of prey still suffer through man's persecution. Also for reasons of security, some observers prefer not to disclose breeding records. This means that some of the rarer species are almost certainly under-recorded, and even recorded population levels may be inaccurate because lack of map grid references can lead to duplication. Finally, it must be remembered that, with far fewer observers, early estimations of rarity were far less reliable, but remain valuable in assessing trends. The important thing is that we strive to build on what we have now.

BRIAN MARTIN, BROOK, SURREY

FEMALE HORNED OWL

DESIGN FOR LIVING: SPECIAL ADAPTATIONS

Having been hunters and killers for millions of years, birds of prey have evolved certain common features to make the capture and consumption of prey easier. Most of these characteristics are found in both diurnal and nocturnal species and are reason enough to put both owls and hawks in the same book, even though they are not closely related.

A casual glance might suggest that all birds of prey have the same 'weapons', but closer examination reveals that even within the flesh-eaters there is marked specialisation. Each species is adapted to exploit particular food sources, at the same time being equipped to live in the particular habitats where the prey lives. In the diet of most birds of prey there is an overall predominance of birds and small mammals but secondary food sources include reptiles, fish, insects, amphibians and carrion. The few examples of extreme diet specialisation in Britain are dealt with under the species accounts, notably the honey buzzard and osprey.

Shape and Plumage

Obviously, prey is going to try its best to avoid capture, so the hunter must have the physical capability to out-perform its victim. Some raptors rely on greater speed to catch prey, while others concentrate on stealth or surprise. Others use both methods in pursuit of a wider variety of victims. The individual species' life-style and preferred habitat determine its shape and plumage.

Of special importance is the shape of the wing, which facilitates the mode of hunting. For example, the goshawk needs a relatively short wing for great man-oeuvrability in hot pursuit of prey through woodland, whereas the speedy peregrine has a relatively long wing for open chasing and diving. However, the raptor's wing is of the same basic construction as those of other birds, having 9–11 primary wing feathers attached to the hand. But some species have the outermost primaries narrower than the others and separated like fingers — especially among the eagles. These 'fingers' act like the flaps of an aircraft in regulating the up-draught, and can even be adjusted individually.

The eagle's rather long and narrow wing is a compromise, facilitating both sustained soaring in searching for food over wide areas and considerable man-oeuvrability near the ground. Thus it can exploit many food sources, ranging from carrion found largely through luck, to agile hares jinking to avoid capture. Other raptor wings are similarly compromised, according to the degree of food specialisation.

The secondary feathers on the inner part of the wing also vary — in length with the width of the wing, and their number varies much more than that of the primaries. Hawks, for example, have an intermediate condition, with short, broad and rounded wings to enable swift turns among trees and bushes.

Some raptors need neither great speed nor great agility to kill small, easily caught prey such as voles. For example, the kestrel and roughlegged buzzard commonly 'hover', taking up an aerial station in open country where prey abounds but perches do not. However, this is not true hovering in the manner of

hummingbirds. These larger species cannot sustain the high power output this would entail to remain stationary relative to the ground. So they must fly into the wind at the same speed they are being blown back. If the wind is strong enough, the bird can almost 'hang' in the sky without flapping its wings at all.

Common buzzard alighting near a dead rabbit – the species' most important food item in Britain before myxomatosis

Generally, slow flight is difficult for large birds to maintain, and some of the large raptors have very slow flapping rates. However, this is relatively unimportant for species such as buzzards, which save on energy by utilising updraughts generated by warm air-currents to soar in search of carrion.

The harriers are perhaps the most adept raptors which employ slow flapping flight in systematic food searching; they have also developed a characteristic buoyancy, but this is used in conjunction with exceptional hearing for a diurnal raptor. Such hunting is further enhanced by low wing-loading — the weight supported relative to the wing area — and harriers are extremely light for their size, achieving remarkable manoeuvrability.

Just as in an aircraft, the shape of the tail is important, too, and relative to the particular wing design. While the particular shape purpose is not always clear, it is certain that a long tail facilitates manoeuvrability, being an excellent steering mechanism. The sparrowhawk, for example, uses it to weave between trees.

Among British birds of prey, the kite's long, forked tail is the most spectacular, comprising up to 62 per cent of the body length. Not only does this make the kite our most graceful raptor, but also extremely manoeuvrable, twisting and canting the tail this way and that in delicate response to air currents.

As well as rudders, tails are also used as extra aerofoils, being spread by the hovering kestrel or soaring eagle. They are used as air brakes when landing on prey and subtly raised or lowered to alter the angle in a dive.

Being hunters of the night, owls have little or no need for speed. Instead, they rely on silence to come upon their prey before there is any chance of escape, and for this their plumage is specially suited. Most owl wings are short and broad, with a large surface area relative to the weight of the bird (low wing-loading); this facilitates buoyancy and manoeuvrability, particularly important in woodland species.

The owl's low wing-loading also means that vigorous, rapid wingbeats are unnecessary; this helps the bird to fly quietly, thus avoiding disturbance of prey and interference with the owl's own hearing. In addition, the body plumage is deep and soft, many of the feathers having a fur-like covering and special construction. There is a soft fringe on the leading edges of the primary wing feathers, where the ends of the barbs do not interlock, and similarly, the barb tips on the trailing edges are free, producing a narrow, fur-like margin. However, these sound-deadening adaptations increase drag or air resistance.

The owl's striking facial disc is thought to enhance hearing sensitivity, probably serving to direct sound to the ear openings, the marginal ruff of the disc being especially significant. To facilitate this the owl raises facial feathers as required.

Some birds of prey number among those species which have special types of down feathers which break off at the tips and break down into a fine powder. In many hawks these powder-down feathers are randomly scattered throughout the plumage. They grow continuously to keep up with fragmentation and are designed to soak up the blood, water and slime with which the birds are in constant contact.

Vision

The keen eyesight of raptors is legendary and has given rise to common expressions such as 'eagle-eyed'. Indeed, good vision is one of the hunter's most important attributes, especially among diurnal raptors, but mythology has misled us. When it comes to the ability of birds to see detail, visual acuity or resolving power (keenness) appears to be best developed in species which need to see tiny, moving, or distant prey, for example hawks. But it is now thought that the old claim of diurnal birds of prey having visual acuity 8–10 times greater than man's is widely exaggerated. Biologists have found that the foveae (parts of the retina) of raptors have about one million cones per square millimetre compared with a mere 200,000 in man. Thus the eyesight of raptors is probably at best five times 'sharper' than man's, but three times is more likely. That of other birds varies from three times poorer to one times better than man's.

Studies have shown that a bird of prey's ability to see into the distance varies with both the contrast and brightness of stimuli. Examination of the wedge-tailed eagle's (*Aquila audax*) eye revealed structures approaching theoretical limits, and as the eye of that species is, in absolute terms, among the largest known, it is unlikely that maximum spatial resolution (ability to pick out detail at extreme distance) in any other bird will be much greater. It was also shown that the eagle's eye is specialised for vision at the highest natural light levels. Once these start to fall, the eagle's spatial resolution deteriorates more rapidly than that of man, which also explains why few raptors hunt at or after twilight. There are exceptions, including the letter-winged kite (*Elanus scriptus*) of central Australia, which

The tawny owl rarely nests on the ground in southern England

hunts mice by moonlight. No doubt there are examples of diurnal raptors spotting tiny prey at great distances, but it now seems that the extreme cases have been greatly exaggerated.

Raptor eyes are positioned so that they have forward binocular vision over a field of some 35–50°, whereas the monocular vision of each eye covers about 150°. The retina contains two image-making centres, one functioning mainly when binocular vision is used, the other particularly in monocular vision. Because of these adaptations the raptor eye is proportionately very large (for example, a buzzard's is fifty times as large relative to the bird's body compared with that of man) and must be protected by a nictitating membrane and (in some species) by a prominent eyebrow. More significantly, such huge eyes are almost immovable in their sockets, being capable of only minor adjustments to enhance binocular vision. To get round this, raptors have specially flexible necks so that they can constantly crane in every direction. Even so, they can achieve 360° vision with greater economy of movement than can a human.

How well a bird can see at night is determined by light-gathering ability or 'visual sensitivity', and this is obviously greater in nocturnal hunters, notably owls. Most owls rely heavily on acute hearing as well as sight in prey location, but controlled experiments have shown that they can spot dead (and therefore silent) prey 1.82m (6ft) away at a light intensity as little as one hundredth of what man would require. But owls cannot see prey in total darkness and by night their resolving power (ability to see detail) is often only slightly better than that of man.

Fortunately, even on moonless nights absolute darkness does not occur, illumination rarely being less than about 37,000 lux, and both tawny and long-eared owls can see with less than seven lux illumination — close to total darkness. Owl eyes are large and pear-shaped with comparatively wide corneal and lens surfaces which allow a maximum amount of light to reach the retina. Concentration of light-sensitive rods is very high, but cones are proportionately few so that owls have low visual acuity compared with the day-flying raptors.

Owls are certainly not 'blind' by day, as was once popularly thought (little and short-eared owls frequently hunt by day, as must other species during summer when nights are short and families must be fed. On the contrary, some species have greater visual acuity than man both by day and night. But there are disadvantages for nocturnal hunters. Night vision in birds, though generally superior to that of humans, usually takes longer to 'switch on' — perhaps an hour compared with about ten minutes in man. And like those of the diurnal raptors, owl eyes are so large and tubular they cannot turn in their sockets at all, although owls have exceptionally flexible necks to compensate; the head can be turned through 270° in some species. Behavioural studies have shown that in the eye of the tawny owl (which has been studied more than any other owl species) both absolute visual sensitivity and maximum spatial resolution at low light levels are close to theoretical limits.

Owls are the only birds to have an opaque nictitating membrane — the third eyelid that protects the eye during the day. It is also thought that pigment moves into the owl's retina during daylight to protect it from excess light. Like other birds, owls also have a structure on the retina known as the pecten. Close to the optic tract, it is rich in blood vessels and probably supplies the eye with food and oxygen. However, the owl pecten is small, whereas in other birds (including diurnal raptors) it is large and thought to aid the pinpointing of small or distant moving objects as well as having a nutritive function.

With the eyes so well to the front of the head, owls have an unusually wide field of binocular vision — 70° in a total field of view of around 110°. And the hooked bill curves more steeply downward than in diurnal raptors, to keep it out of the visual field. Notwithstanding their great visual ability, it seems that territory-holding is especially important for owls because, among other things, it enables the birds to become very familiar with obstacles and thus avoid them more easily in the dark.

Hearing

Although diurnal raptors do have acute hearing, as a hunting aid it is generally secondary to acute vision, though some rely on it in certain situations such as when detecting prey in woodland. However, the harriers have partially evolved the hearing aids brought to perfection in owls. They have large, external ear openings, sometimes with a pronounced concha, and their partial facial discs are quite owl-like when facing the observer. It is assumed that this extra-keen hearing benefits the harrier in prey detection while it flies slowly over dense vegetation. On hearing a sound it checks in flight, hovers briefly, then drops when the prey's precise position is determined.

The hearing of owls is extraordinary and for most species is the most important characteristic in prey detection. For example, the great grey owl (*Strix nebulosa*) can pinpoint the sounds of mice under snow. But owls do not have the fleshy, ex-

The short-eared owl's true ear flap probably has nothing to do with the erectile tufts

ternal ears so prominent in mammals; their ear holes are totally concealed under the feathers called ear coverts. (The so-called 'ears' of the long-eared owl are merely tufts of feathers for display.) However, some have a flap of skin called an operculum or concha along the front edge of the ear hole, which can be closed over the opening or raised to catch sounds from behind. To minimise obstruction of sounds, birds' ear coverts lack barbules and can be erected from the sides of the head, though this is rarely witnessed. The ruff of feathers around the facial disc is thought to help direct sounds to the vertical ear slits.

Owls have an astonishing high-frequency hearing limit around 12kHz, which, as already mentioned, enables them to catch prey in the wild in almost complete darkness. Indeed, experiments have shown that owls can catch prey in the *total* absence of light, using sound only. In such artificial conditions barn owls were able to strike at rodents to within an accuracy of 1°; but if frequencies above 5kHz· were filtered out, the birds refused to attack. Infra-red photography revealed how an attack in darkness involved moving the head from side to side to enable a three-dimensional 'audio pattern' to be built up.

Owls' ears are unique among birds. Not only are the holes of different size and shape on each side of the head, but they are also in different positions (asymmetrical). And owls' heads are relatively wide so that the sounds reach one ear a tiny fraction of a second before the other; coupled with the asymmetry of the ears, this permits precise location of sound source. In some owls the entire skull is asymmetrical. For example, in the tawny owl the right side of the skull is slightly larger than the left when viewed from behind.

Nonetheless, location of prey through hearing is dependent on that prey moving so that it emits sounds. And as with vision, high performance of owl hearing seems to be linked to familiarity with the local environment. This helps to explain the great territoriality and sedentary behaviour of most owls.

A barn owl weighing about 300g (10½oz) has some 95,000 nerve cells in the auditory centre of its brain, whereas that of a 600g (1lb 5oz) crow has only about 27,000 cells. Although some owls have about the same auditory spectrum as man

— approximately 20 hertz (vibrations per second) to 20,000 hertz (20kHz) — in others the range is narrower. For example, the lowest pitch audible to the tawny and long-eared owls is only about 100 hertz, so they cannot hear the lowest notes on a piano (down to 27 hertz). But within the range 2–6kHz the hearing of these two species is at its most sensitive — about ten times more acute than man's.

Sense of Smell

Until very recently, it was assumed that because birds generally have good vision and hearing they had little need for even a moderate sense of smell. And because birds of prey are among the species with the most acute vision and hearing, it was thought that their need for other senses was minimal. But new research, although in its infancy, suggests otherwise. On the contrary, the sense governed by the olfactory bulbs may be rather more sophisticated than anyone suspected. It could be that the olfactory system serves a wider function than simply processing information about odorous stimuli. For example, after removal of their olfactory bulbs, pigeons lost the ability to detect x-rays (gained through simple training) and they were generally considered slower to adapt to new situations.

Although not involving a British species, it is interesting that of the few birds in the world known to be specially dependent on a sense of smell, one is a raptor. Turkey vultures (*Cathartes aura*) of the Americas appear to have the ability to home in on carrion using their sense of smell over considerable distances, whereas other vultures concentrate on visual signs. With large, nerve-rich nasal organs, they have been seen to gather above upcurrents of the chemical ethyl mercapton released from hidden sites in a canyon. This heightened sense of smell has enabled these vultures to exploit the forest habitat, vultures of open plains habitat having concentrated on visual acuity. In view of this, it would be interesting to study British raptors with significant dependence on carrion.

In diurnal raptors, the nostrils are located on the cere (function unknown), the fleshy, often yellow swelling at the base of the upper mandible, while in most birds, including owls, they are usually separated by a cartilaginous or ossified medial septum. The osprey can close its slit-like nostrils to exclude water.

Feet

Birds of prey use their feet both in catching prey and killing it. Any victim not killed by the initial strike is usually killed quickly and efficiently by the exceptionally long, pointed talons. But these killing tools vary with the diet specialisation of each species. Short legs with short, powerful toes characterise a species which concentrates on ground prey, such as snakes and lizards, while long legs and long, slender toes with more pointed talons are better for snatching birds in flight. The latter often have a long middle toe. A powerful hind toe indicates that the species kills larger mammals. Raptors generally have strong, grasping feet which minimise the chances of prey escaping.

While diurnal raptors generally adopt the common avian characteristic of three toes forward and one behind (the outer toe is reversible in the osprey), all owls have a reversible outer toe, and when perched usually have two toes in front and two behind.

The particular degree of foot specialisation among raptors is discussed in detail within the species' accounts.

Headless, part-plucked blackbird – the work of a kestrel

Beaks

Contrary to popular belief, raptors do not generally use their beaks for killing prey, the foot being the prime tool of execution. Instead, the downcurved, pointed beak, with the upper mandible longer than the lower, is ideal for ripping carrion and prey animals apart and tearing off chunks of flesh small enough to swallow. Thus, the bigger the prey, the bigger and more powerful the beak required. Eagles, for example, need massive, stout beaks for ripping apart the tough skin of sheep and deer, while species such as the sparrowhawk, which catch generally small birds in flight, have relatively short beaks.

However, the beaks of falcons do assist in killing. To facilitate this, on the upper mandible they have a notch or toral 'tooth' which is thought to help in breaking the neck of prey caught alive. Falcons which are partially insectivorous have more delicate beaks. Owls have relatively short beaks and a wide gape so they can swallow prey whole. Enhanced beak specialisation is discussed within the species' accounts.

Digestion

Although at least 330 bird species can regurgitate the indigestible parts of their meals in the form of compact pellets, this facility is most commonly associated with raptors, notably owls. Hard materials such as bones, beaks, claws, teeth, scales and chitin are enveloped by softer substances such as feathers and fur and ejected through the mouth rather than evacuated as faeces. They vary considerably between species, in size, shape, colour and content.

Most pellets are elongated and oval, with the long, hard food fragments such as mammal long-bones and birds' beaks and legs aligned longitudinally to permit comfortable ejection. As owls usually swallow prey whole, their pellets generally contain most bones consumed as well as good evidence of most invertebrates eaten. Because digestion needs to be rapid to release sufficient energy, owl pellets are formed in as little as 6 – 8 hours from the time the prey is eaten, twice per day, just before the bird sets off to hunt.

While analysis of pellets is a useful way to determine diet variety, it is unreliable in assessing proportions by weight, because different parts and different prey are absorbed at different rates and analysis is biased towards less digestible species.

17

*Selection of raptor pellets:
left – barn owl; centre –
short-eared owl; right –
little owl; below – kestrel*

The pellets of diurnal raptors are especially unhelpful to the analyst in that these species generally tear their prey to pieces so that the record is incomplete.

However, pellets can be an important source for the recovery of bird rings, especially those of regular small-bird feeders such as the short-eared owl and kestrel. Others are useful indicators of the presence of scarce or rare species and help to indicate the relative abundance of prey. More specialised diets make pellet identification easier. For example, those of the honey buzzard are dominated by wax from the wasp and bee nests which they raid.

Apart from bony items such as rodent skulls, pellets can contain some surprising remains, such as the external skeletons of insects, fish scales, and even earthworm bristles.

Further pellet details are given under individual species' accounts. Unlike the *Falconiformes*, owls do not have a crop and the caecum (blind end of the large intestine) is large, to accommodate the swallowing and digestion of whole prey.

Other Adaptations

Although laying one egg every 24 hours is most common among birds, a two- or three-day interval is more common among diurnal and nocturnal raptors, for whom varying prey supply is linked to survival. When food is short the older and larger birds get the lion's share and are more likely to survive. Otherwise, entire broods would be at risk during lean times.

The voices of some raptors — notably the hooting of woodland owls — have special penetrative qualities suited to habitats such as dense forest. This is essential in establishing territory and courtship. Owl territories are generally retained throughout the year, not only to safeguard sufficient feeding but also because tree-cavity nest-sites are relatively rare.

Owls are not colour blind and probably have white eggs so they may see them more easily in their dark nest-holes. On the other hand, the owls themselves are well camouflaged, mostly in mottled browns, to protect them when they roost by day.

Owls have an especially high degree of pneumatisation (honeycombing of bone structure) to increase power/weight ratio and facilitate silent flight.

RELATIONS WITH MAN

female
KESTREL

For thousands of years man has revered birds of prey, drawing on their many admirable attributes to enhance his sport and illustrate his literature, legend and mythology. But at the same time he has persecuted them — directly through sport and collecting, indirectly through the destruction and pollution of habitat. Today we realise what valuable indicators of the countryside's health these top-of-the-food-chain species are.

Legend and Literature

Much of our legacy of language is derived from birds of prey, some based on superstition and ignorance in early times, the rest on widely admired characteristics. For example, the popular saying 'eye like a hawk' is based on the excellent eyesight of raptors, as are the opening lines to Geoffrey Chaucer's *Parlement of Foules* (late 14th century):

> There mighte men the royal eagle find,
> That with his sharp look pierceth the sun.

Five centuries later, the eagle was still seen as the epitome of perfection in a wild creature, when Lord Tennyson wrote:

> He clasps the crag with crooked hands;
> Close to the sun in lonely lands,
> Ringed with the azure world he stands.
>
> The wrinkled sea beneath him crawls;
> He watches from the mountain walls,
> And like a thunderbolt he falls.

But birds which fed on carrion, such as buzzards and kites (both once much commoner and familiar to many more people) were constantly maligned. The word kite is still used to describe a rapacious person.

Owls have frequently been associated with doom and disaster, birds of ill omen and messengers of woe; since earliest times they have been connected with the black arts in both hemispheres. Among the ancients, only the Athenians seem to have been free from this popular prejudice, regarding the owl with veneration rather than abhorrence, considering it the favourite of Minerva and the image of wisdom. The Romans, on the other hand, regarded the owl with detestation and dread. By them it was held sacred to Prosperpine; its appearance foretold unfortunate events and, according to Pliny, the city of Rome underwent a solemn lustration as a result of an owl accidentally straying into the capital.

In the ancient pharmacopoeia, whose main ingredient was magic, the owl was regarded as powerful medicine. Ovid said the bird was used wholesale in the composition of Medea's gruel:

> Et strigis infames ipsis cum carnibus alas.

Even Shakespeare freely perpetuated the owl's unfortunate image. In Macbeth (Act IV Sc I) the 'owlet's wing' was an ingredient of the cauldron wherein the witches prepared their 'charm of powerful trouble', and when Richard III (Act IV

Sc 4) was irritated by the ill news showered upon him, he interrupted the third messenger with:

> Out on ye, owls! nothing but songs of death?

But as the mysteries of the owl's nocturnal life were unravelled, the bird attracted many admirers, among them Tennyson, who penned the famous lines:

> When cats run home and light is come,
> And dew is cold upon the ground,
> And the far-off stream is dumb,
> And the whirring sail goes round,
> And the whirring sail goes round,
> Alone and warming his five wits,
> The white owl in the belfry sits.

Today few people in Britain believe that white owls are reincarnations of bad men, any more than they suspect eagles of carrying off children. Some of the more popular myths and legends are considered within the species' accounts.

Falconry

Long before guns were invented, birds of prey were trained to catch and provide game for the table. But it was such an attractive pastime that even those who did not need to hunt their own food became ardent followers of falconry, in the name of sport. As early as AD760, Ethelbert II, King of Kent, wrote a letter requesting a falcon suitable for flying at local cranes; and in 1212 King John flew gyrfalcons at cranes in Cambridgeshire.

Such was the early importance of falconry that books were written on the subject long before we had the first works on the natural history of birds. The first falconry book in English was George Turbevile's *Book of Faulconrie or Hawking* published in 1575, pre-dating the first natural history of birds in English — *The Ornithology of Francis Willughby* — by 103 years. But the world's first real book about birds was by the emperor Frederick II and entitled *De Arta Venandi cum Avibus* (The Art of Hunting with Birds). It was written in about 1240, but existed only in manuscript for over three hundred years; it was printed for the first time in 1596.

In Shakespeare's time birds of prey were an everyday sight. Wild birds were much more common than they are now, and there were also plenty to supply potential falconers. Indeed, everybody who could afford one kept a 'hawk', and the social rank of the owner was indicated by the species he carried.

> To a king belonged the gyrfalcon; to a prince, the falcon gentle; to an earl, the peregrine; to a lady, the merlin; to a young squire, the hobby; while a yeoman carried a goshawk; a priest, a sparrowhawk; and a knave, or servant, a kestrel.

As a result, the works of Shakespeare are littered with quotes and terms from falconry.

But already the notion of falconry as a provider was ludicrous, social distinction apparently being more important. For example, the idea of a knave getting much food from a kestrel, which feeds largely on small rodents and songbirds, was farcical. Yet the sport carried on, generation after generation producing a small band of dedicated enthusiasts, as it does today. Unfortunately, despite legal protection now, and the caring control of responsible clubs, there is still a selfish minority which continues to rob nests of eggs and young. Some take birds for themselves, but the main threat comes from those who satisfy the international market. Arabs, for example, will pay huge sums for British peregrines, the licensed breeding of cheaper, captive birds apparently being insufficient to satisfy demand.

Falcon flying remains the highlight of many country shows, and it would appear that bird protection bodies are happy for the activity to continue in a well-organised and legal manner. For example, only a few years ago the Royal Society for the Protection of Birds decided to boycott the Game Fair, Britain's biggest country show, because of raptor-flying there, but now they, too, have revised their opinion. It cannot be denied that exhibitions before such large audiences may sometimes attract an irresponsible element, but they do have great educational value and their promoters have done much to improve the status of some of Britain's most endangered species. Some falconers have contributed greatly to our knowledge of raptors, and have helped threatened populations to recover through rearing and release schemes as well as habitat protection and improvement. They have also helped indirectly in that at least one population — that of the goshawk — now owes its existence in Britain almost entirely to escaped and released birds. With this in mind, raptor crosses — such as the so-called perlin, a female merlin/peregrine tiercel hybrid — ought to be outlawed.

Sport Shooting

When guns were still relatively inefficient and quarry shooting the casual, walk-about pastime of a few country folk, the impact on bird populations was negligible. But when the rapid-fire breechloader was introduced in the mid-19th century the position changed dramatically. Well-organised driven gameshooting became possible, attracting many city people who demanded plenty of sport to fire the new social scene; indeed, many of them vied jealously with each other to be top Gun on each and every occasion. Thus it was necessary for hosts to employ large numbers of gamekeepers to ensure that there were enough birds for their

Illegal and vicious persecution – pole trap on a golden eagle eyrie

guests to shoot, and whether they relied on wild game stocks or the increasingly popular rearing-and-release schemes, predator control was central to their management. Consequently anything with a hooked beak was seen as a competitor and all birds of prey were killed without question, through indiscriminate poisoning of baits and trapping as well as shooting.

There had been some significant slaughter of raptors in the previous two centuries; for example as early as 1684–85, one hundred kites were killed in Kent, with the encouragement of a bounty scheme. But that was for an entire county and palls into insignificance when compared with local efforts in the 19th century. For example in Glen Garry 1837–40, the destruction included 98 peregrines, 78 merlins, 462 kestrels, 285 buzzards, 3 honey buzzards, 15 golden eagles, 27 white-tailed eagles, 18 ospreys, 63 goshawks, 275 kites and 68 miscellaneous harriers — totalling no less than 1,372 diurnal raptors. Owls were treated similarly, and this is but *one* of the many dismal records from the time.

The depressive effect of this toll first came to notice when keepering lapsed during World War I — with the keepers away at the front, many raptor populations soared again. Sadly, when peace returned, although many landowners could no longer afford to entertain in the old way and employ so many keepers, the syndicate shoot was born and the still-large army of game preservers was required to provide value for money. Thus the killing continued, until World War II provided further respite.

Eventually, bird protection legislation put the brakes on the slaughter, as did advice from more enlightened game researchers, though many keepers were unfortunately too old to change their ways and 'hook-beaks' continued to appear on gibbets in the 1960s and 70s. Lone voices condemned the secret slaughter, but it was not until well into the 1980s that gameshooters generally realised that the future of their sport was in jeopardy unless they made greater efforts to eradicate this evil. Yet some keepers have been threatened with the sack if they do not continue to remove all predators, while other employers simply turn a blind eye. Now the pressure is on to make all employers take a greater interest in their keepers' activities, and from 1991 it became an offence for a person to 'knowingly cause or permit' the illegal killing of any wild bird or animal. Nevertheless, the good intentions of the vast majority of shooting folk cannot be doubted.

Much of the persecution stems from ignorance as to the degree of predation on game by individual raptor species, and there is no doubt that some interests have widely exaggerated these levels. In particular, there have been recent calls from some shooters to permit limited culling of hen harriers on grouse moors: nothing, however, could be more disastrous for both the image of shooting and harrier conservation.

Eagles, too, are still harassed on some moors. Yet it can be confidently predicted that a moor with two pairs of eagles will have more grouse than one with a single pair. It is the prey population that controls the number of predators, not vice versa. Unfortunately, because raptors are relatively large and conspicuous they give a false impression of abundance and are more vulnerable to persecution.

The RSPB has produced some figures which point up the problem — though it must be said that the culprits include sheep-rearers, especially in upland districts. Between 1971 and 1989 at least 400 buzzards, 110 peregrines, 95 sparrowhawks, 70 golden eagles, 70 hen harriers, 30 goshawks, 30 red kites and 6 ospreys were illegally shot, trapped or poisoned in a sad list of 15 raptor species also including merlins, hobbies and kestrels. In some cases these losses represent high propor-

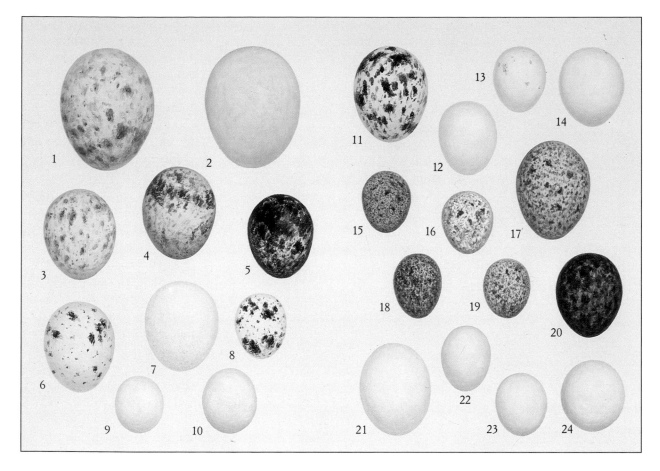

EGGS

1 Golden eagle (*Aquila chrysaetos*)	9 Little owl (*Athene noctua*)	17 Gyrfalcon (*Falco rusticolus*)
2 White-tailed eagle (*Haliaeetus albicilla*)	10 Long-eared owl (*Asio otus*)	18 Hobby (*Falco subbuteo*)
3 Roughlegged buzzard (*Buteo lagopus*)	11 Osprey (*Pandion haliaetus*)	19 Red-footed falcon (*Falco vespertinus*)
4 Common buzzard (*Buteo buteo*)	12 Hen harrier (*Circus cyaneus*)	20 Peregrine falcon (*Falco peregrinus*)
5 Honey buzzard (*Pernis apivorus*)	13 Montagu's harrier (*Circus pygargus*)	21 Snowy owl (*Nyctea scandiaca*)
6 Red kite (*Milvus milvus*)	14 Marsh harrier (*Circus aeruginosus*)	22 Barn owl (*Tyto alba*)
7 Goshawk (*Accipiter gentilis*)	15 Merlin (*Falco columbarius*)	23 Short-eared owl (*Asio flammeus*)
8 Sparrowhawk (*Accipiter nisus*)	16 Kestrel (*Falco tinnunculus*)	24 Tawny owl (*Strix aluco*)

tions of the British populations. There is little doubt that there were many other victims, too, as much persecution takes place on remote, private land.

It is hard to believe that in a so-called civilised country some villains still use devices as gruesome as the pole trap, which was outlawed as long ago as 1904. Equally savage is the use of poison, yet the number of incidents reported each year has shown no sign of sustained decrease. That said, it could be that the number of people bothering to make reports has increased, thus masking the fact that the true number of bird deaths has decreased.

Overall, the depressive effect on raptor populations of deliberate killing has become less significant than indirect killing through use of chemicals on the land and destruction of habitat. But there is no excuse whatsoever for any sportsman worthy of the name to condone the continuing senseless slaughter by this very selfish minority. On the contrary, Britain should be setting a supreme example to the many other countries where raptors are still slain in alarming numbers. Some of the migratory birds which visit Britain regularly face a fusillade on more hostile, foreign shores.

Collecting

In an age of unprecedented discovery, it is not surprising that the Victorians were keen collectors, especially of natural objects. Anything beautiful and occurring in great variety became the subject of innumerable collections, from rocks and fossils to butterflies and beetles. But above all, wild birds held the greatest attraction, not only among serious naturalists who still lacked sophisticated cameras to record their findings, but also ordinary householders who liked to display their trophies as ornaments.

The precedent was set in the late 18th and early 19th centuries, when famous naturalists such as Gilbert White of Selborne and artist Audubon wrote openly about killing specimens for description or painting. Eventually, almost every large country house had its display, not only of the birds themselves, but also their nests and eggs. The keenest had specimens of male, female and juvenile as well as unusual plumages such as albinos, and entire nests with complete clutches of eggs. Sadly, because they are so handsome and awe-inspiring, birds of prey were among the most keenly collected. And the more they were shot by gamekeepers, the rarer they became and the greater was the price collectors put on their skins. It was a vicious circle of decline.

Fortunately, the fashion for skin-collecting faded even without eventual protective legislation. Much earlier this century, most households cleared out the dusty accumulations of their grandfathers, and more recently, increased concern for the natural world decreed that collecting was anti-social. Nonetheless, a small demand for skins continued, largely centred around the game-trophy business, and it became necessary to introduce new laws requiring taxidermists to account for all birds handled. However, although it is illegal to kill a raptor, it is still legal to mount a bird found dead and properly registered.

Much more serious is the unbelievable continuance of egg-collecting. Many of us can remember how this was still a favourite pastime among small boys as late as the 1950s, although most did little harm with their removal of single eggs from the clutches of common species. Now children are better educated; but the hard core of serious and ruthless collectors is another matter entirely, and they have never let up. This is particularly serious for birds of prey, which include some of Britain's rarest species.

For the period 1971–88, the RSPB has 344 definite egg-collectors and 143 suspect egg-collectors on record, and they come from a wide variety of backgrounds. Although it has been illegal to take the eggs of wild birds since the passing of the Protection of Birds Act 1954, their possession was not effectively controlled until the Wildlife and Countryside Act 1981. There has been an increase in the number of reports since 1971, but then, the level of vigilance of RSPB staff, volunteers and the public has increased, too.

Although the impact of egg-collecting on common species is probably insignificant at its current level, the effect on rare raptors is serious. In the case of the osprey and red kite, both highly vulnerable species, it has been shown that egg-collecting reduced annual population growth by 1 per cent. And had it not been for the rigorous protection given to their nests, the incidence of collecting would almost certainly have been much higher and its impact disastrous for the survival of small breeding populations in the British Isles.

Despite sophisticated surveillance equipment and round-the-clock watches, the thefts continued in 1990. In Scotland, 7 osprey clutches were taken, and in Wales 8 of only 71 kite nests were robbed.

Pesticides

In the 1950s and 1960s a range of new agro-chemicals was introduced to boost food production. Unfortunately, some of these were very persistent and they accumulated in those species at the top of the food chain, notably birds of prey. This secondary poisoning occurred chiefly through eating prey which had ingested pesticides, fungicides, herbicides and fertilizers and caused direct death when sufficient toxins accumulated in the body; it also reduced fertility, and diminished breeding success because of the resulting egg-shell thinning and weakened offspring.

DDT was in widespread agricultural use as an insecticide from 1948 and was an unforeseen major problem, working its way through the food chain to cause insufficiently thick egg-shells, easily broken by sitting raptors. Peregrines, sparrowhawks, merlins, golden eagles and marsh harriers suffered most.

However, it was the group of chemicals called cyclodienes (aldrin, dieldrin and heptachlor), introduced in 1955, which had the most devastating effect on birds of prey. These were used heavily in arable areas — especially the South East — as seed-corn dressing to protect against wheat-bulb fly, and to kill soil pests of crops. In Britain, the sparrowhawk, kestrel, peregrine, marsh harrier and Montagu's harrier were most affected. Their populations crashed in the late 1950s and early 1960s, when the sparrowhawk almost disappeared from most of eastern England — the area where it remained under greatest threat from intensive shooting. But even in the less intensively farmed areas of south-west England, Wales and west Scotland, numbers were hit hard.

Most raptors accumulated the toxic organochlorines from live prey; golden eagles, however, were mainly contaminated through feeding on sheep carrion, because dieldrin was used as a sheep dip between 1960 and 1965. When the practice was stopped the golden eagle enjoyed a big increase in breeding success.

Dieldrin and the other cyclodienes were withdrawn as seed-dressings for spring-sown cereals in 1962, but it was not till 1975 that restrictions were imposed on their use in dressing autumn-sown seed. Much less persistent chemicals have taken their place and the recovery of raptor populations has been excellent, sometimes dramatic. But it was not till 1985 that DDT was finally withdrawn from all agricultural uses.

While these successes are to be applauded, the need for vigilance in the use of chemicals within the natural environment remains. The effects of many compounds are yet to be fully assessed. For example, PCBs (polychlorinated biphenyls), which have numerous industrial uses, are much less toxic than DDT but are so stable they have a very worrying cumulative effect. Large residues have been recorded in many birds. Organophosphate insecticides also cause bird deaths, while herbicides to control weeds cause malformed young. Then there are accumulations of heavy metals such as mercury and lead. And we must not forget the little-known indirect effects of pesticides on birds. For example, there is evidence that low numbers of barn owls and kestrels in some areas are due not only to habitat loss, but also to lack of food caused by pesticides. There has also been the deliberate misuse of pesticides such as alphachloralose, mevinphos and strychnine in poison baits to kill many raptors.

Habitat Loss and Abuse

Compared with most other countries, Britain does not have a rich raptor population because there is insufficient variety of habitat, and much of what remains has been radically altered. Neither do these tiny, overcrowded islands have much space for these generally wide-ranging birds. Yet there is much we can do to halt the decline of both nest-sites and food supplies; in particular we must fight the removal of wetlands, the replacement of lowland deciduous forest and upland moor with blanket conifers, and other loss of habitat to agriculture.

Very recently, raptors have been at the forefront of our fight to save the uplands, where Britain's last substantial tracts of open space are found. The RSPB has warned of 'the dawn of an ecological disaster' through the encroachment of forestry and farming — although this is one area in which shooting has done much to save the day. There is no doubt that without the incentive of grouse-shooting,

Despite rigorous protection, Britain's red kites are still being poisoned

landowners would have allowed vast acreages of the internationally important heather habitat to be lost to other uses. The value of heather moorland to some raptors cannot be overstated.

Traditional sheep farming on impoverished uplands has provided much carrion, to the benefit of red kites in central Wales and golden eagles in Scotland. Now, however, many of the sheep walks are being lost to more profitable forestry, and although initially the upsurge in vole populations benefits hen harriers, kites and kestrels, once the plantations become thickets a wide range of raptor prey disappears. Grouse, hares, rabbits, small mammals, small birds, earthworms and beetles vanish along with the sheep carrion. One of the hardest-hit areas is the south-west Highlands, where the replacement of sheep by forestry has reduced suitable hunting ground for eagles by a third and the population has declined by 30 per cent. The threat to the merlin is even more serious.

In some cases there is no doubt that diurnal raptors and owls have recaptured lost territory through recent lowland afforestation, but generally this has been fortuitous, rather like the kestrel's exploitation of motorway verges. What we desperately need is a much more co-ordinated countryside policy, with the state arm of conservation giving more substantial backing to the overburdened voluntary bodies.

Among the most promising of recent developments has been the Hawk and Owl Trust's interest in sensitive forest design, which could be the salvation of many birds of prey. As an extension of its three-year merlin research programme, the Trust began a forest raptor project (sponsored by the Country Landowners Association) in association with the Forestry Commission, private forestry companies and moorland owners. It was not long before eleven species of raptor were identified regularly within the fifty-five study areas, and it became clear that properly designed commercial woods can provide a network of refuges where birds of prey can live free from disturbance. Such fine examples of land-user cooperation must be the way forward in a land where every acre is precious, and conservation but one ingredient in the cake of life.

At the same time we must seek to minimise disturbance of raptors and all forms of wildlife. It is not only fieldsportsmen and ramblers who venture into the outback in ever-increasing numbers: nature photographers and birdwatchers pose a threat, too, especially when they focus on scarce or endangered species, stressing birds and perhaps causing the desertion of eggs or young. Channelling such interests through honeypot sites such as the osprey eyrie at Loch Garten and the honey buzzards at the Forestry Commission's Haldon Hills viewpoint are steps in the right direction.

The environment must be made a safe place, too. There must be greater awareness of hazards such as high-tension wires with which raptors often collide, barbed wire which entangles their wings, uncovered water butts in which owls drown, and speeding traffic which constantly kills large numbers of both diurnal and nocturnal raptors. Of course we will never eradicate all these problems and many people will regard some of them as trivial, but together they add up to a substantial drain on our already impoverished wildlife. The good news is that much of the harm can be remedied, and we have enough goodwill in this country to make further expansion of 'green' education well worthwhile. With any luck the kite will return regularly to grace the skies of southern England in the next century, and space-age poets will follow Shakespeare's example in drawing on raptor character to expand out literary heritage.

GOLDEN EAGLE
(*Aquila chrysaetos*)

GOLDEN EAGLE
Once known as the erne, black eagle, ringtailed eagle and mountain eagle

ALTHOUGH in Britain it is now virtually confined to Scotland, the magnificent golden eagle remains the epitome of wildness for most people, representing freedom and strength even for those who have never seen one. It is a creature of fable and legend, with a magnetism matched by few other birds. The Reverend F.O. Morris called it the bird world's 'equivalent of the tiger among mammals — both noble and majestic and supreme predators'. But although one of the better-informed Victorian naturalists, he too was beguiled by the bird's charisma into perpetuating much of the mythology surrounding it:

> It assails with characteristic resoluteness even roebucks and other deer. It is said to fix itself on the head of the victim and to flap its wings in the animal's eyes, until in distraction it is driven over some precipice or into some morass, where it then becomes a secure and easy prey.

Thomas Bewick, too, was spellbound by the erne. In 1799 he wrote: 'The eyes are large, deep sunk, and covered by a projecting brow; the iris is of a fine, bright yellow, and sparkles with uncommon lustre.' And for many generations before him the wing feathers of these grand birds were in great demand for the bonnets of those of high rank: three pinion feathers formed the badge of a Highland chief, two of a chieftain, and one of a gentleman.

History and Conservation

The word eagle is known from 1385, going back to the Middle English *ēgle*, deriving from the Old French *egle* or *aigle*, which came in with the Normans and originates in the Latin *aquila*. The present spelling is known from 1555: 'erens or eagles'. The term 'golden eagle' originated with Ray in 1678 and derives from the Greek *chrysaetos* (*chrys* being golden), chosen by Aldrovandi in 1603 to designate this bird. Before Ray the species was called simply the 'eagle' or 'erne'.

Until quite recently it had always been supposed that the golden eagle was much more common in the British Isles when wilderness areas were far greater and human disturbance minimal. But now it seems that it probably always had a range largely restricted to mountain areas, where density is governed by very considerable territory requirements and a limited number of suitable nest sites. In parts of the range — notably in coastal districts — there would also have been competition with the white-tailed eagle, which was once commoner than the golden, the two species often being confused by early writers.

The only very early remains in the South are from a Cheddar cave, and date from about the end of the Ice Ages, or early Holocene, but there is no evidence that it bred there. In the North, there are records from the Pennines and Derbyshire from the same period. Leslie Brown estimated that carrying capacity never exceeded about 500 pairs in Scotland, 150 in Ireland and 50 in England and Wales.

Like most raptors, it was killed from early times but persecution probably had little effect on its population until upland sheep farming became popular in the 18th century. From then on, right up to recent times, ignorant shepherds would destroy it in the mistaken belief that it commonly took healthy lambs, rather than predominantly sick or weak animals. The slaughter intensified in the 19th century, when gamekeepers shot many eagles, ostensibly to protect grouse and other gamebirds. Yet in 1928 T.A. Coward remarked: 'Sport, not sentiment, has saved the eagle from extinction, and on some of the Scottish deer-forests it is almost common; had the shepherd had his way he would have harried it out of existence.' Many stalkers welcomed the eagle because it cleared up the gralloch after a kill.

However, there is no doubt that the golden eagle did benefit to some degree from the introduction of sheep, in that a new and important source of carrion was provided. The Highland Clearances probably helped as well, removing people from the upper glens and leaving them more secluded for deer and sheep.

The effect of collecting was also significant, both of skins and eggs, as an increasingly mobile public began to explore the high hills. The eagle was a sought-after centre-piece for innumerable displays, and as early as 1850 A.E. Knox expressed concern over eyrie-robbing: 'The eggs fetch, on the spot, from a pound to 30 shillings each; indeed, I have known a larger sum given.' The problem is still with us: during 1976–86 the RSPB reported at least twenty-one nests robbed.

The species ceased to breed in Wales in the 19th century, though nobody knows exactly when and, as elsewhere, the position is confused by the wanderings of non-breeders. In the late 18th century, Pennant said they bred, though rarely, in the 'Snowdon Hills', and in 1850 Morris believed that some still bred in the Welsh highlands.

Extermination in England was probably complete with the disappearance of the last few birds from the Cheviots in the mid-19th century. Breeding in Lakeland, Cumbria, the Peak District and Pennines probably ceased in the 18th century. Birds shot in other areas up to 1850 were rare enough to warrant writing up and were almost certainly stragglers. Admiral Mitford's keeper bagged one in Yorkshire, and one shot in 1847 at Littlecott, near Hungerford 'had glutted itself on a dead deer and was unable to fly away at the approach of the keeper, who fired six times before he killed it.'

In 1969 a pair nested in England, in the Lake District, for the first time this century, and it has bred successfully in most years since. Not surprisingly, its productivity has attracted much media attention, so it is equally unsurprising that rumours of at least one other English pair have been vigorously denied for security reasons.

Quieter Ireland clung on to its eagles much longer, the species still being widespread there at the beginning of the 19th century. Between 1828 and 1832, fourteen were killed in Donegal alone, where Ireland's last definite breeding was recorded in 1910, a 1912 County Mayo record not being verified. Other last stands were on the island of Achil, around Killarney, at Rosheen, near Dunfanaghy, about Tralee and Monasterevan, and in western Mayo.

From 1953 to 1960 one pair returned to breed on Northern Ireland's Antrim coast, and more recently a pair has taken food from Ireland to an eyrie on the Scottish coast.

Even in the Scottish stronghold, the golden eagle was eliminated from some areas, notably the southern uplands, and greatly reduced in others, especially the eastern Highlands. Fortunately there was some respite during the 1914–18 war when keepering lapsed, allowing former territory to be regained. Similarly, there were gains during World War II.

During the 1940s there were substantial gains in the Hebrides, and south-west Scotland was recolonised from 1948. A pair bred in Orkney in the mid-1970s for the first time since about 1844.

During the 1960s many areas reported poor breeding success, but a 1964–68 survey showed marked regional variation, reflecting the variable quality of food supply — live prey being superior to carrion — and the degree of persecution.

The first overall census in 1982–83 revealed 424 pairs and 87 single birds hold-

ing territories. In 1982 at least 182 pairs bred successfully, fledging 210 young — an average of 0.52 per home range, comparing well with the theoretical figure of 0.5 thought necessary to stabilise the population.

Loss of rabbits with the introduction of myxomatosis in 1954 was a setback, but much more serious was the contamination of carrion in the 1960s, when organochlorines — notably dieldrin — were used in sheep dip. When the chemicals were withdrawn, breeding success improved markedly, especially in western Scotland. In the east, where eagles concentrate on wild prey, dieldrin accumulations were generally insufficient to affect breeding success.

Illegal persecution includes the despicable burning of nests, use of poison baits, and shooting and trapping of adults and young. Also, a few skins are still taken, prices of £600–800 having been mentioned in recent years. There is also increasing disturbance from hill walkers, tourists, rock climbers, skiers, birdwatchers and other outdoor enthusiasts. However, the main threats are from changes in land use. Vast areas of eagle habitat have been lost to forestry — mainly blanket conifers, reducing wild prey availability. At the same time sheep husbandry has become more efficient, resulting in less carrion, notably during the critical winter period, when there is an increasing tendency to move sheep to lower ground. So far, market forces have generally determined the fate of eagle country, but the current debate between government, landowners and environmentalists over the future of the uplands could result in strategic policy decisions which may improve the situation.

Distribution, Habitat and Population

The golden eagle is a bird of the northern hemisphere, of the Old and New Worlds, ranging widely over Europe, Asia, the Middle East, North Africa and North America. Although it is the most numerous and widespread large eagle in the northern hemisphere, nowhere is it very common. The British population is probably stable, possibly slightly decreasing. It is most abundant in the western, central and north-west Highlands and the Hebrides. There is just one pair outside Scotland, in the Lake District, which can be seen at long range from the RSPB viewpoint at the head of Haweswater. It failed to breed successfully in 1990 but a chick was fledged in 1991.

With about 420 breeding pairs and 90 single birds holding territories, Scotland harbours some 15 per cent of the European (excluding the USSR) and 25 per cent of the European Community populations.

Some former white-tailed eagle territory has been taken over during expansion this century, during which time the number of home ranges has been remarkably constant, leading to the estimate that there is room in Scotland for about 600 pairs. A pair's home range is about 30–100sq km (according to prey density) of mostly open moorland. Although breeding densities are highest in west Scotland, where carrion is more abundant, birds rear most young in the eastern Highlands, where live prey is abundant. In 1990 bad winter weather affected production, many birds being unable to find enough food to attain good breeding conditions. With emigration and immigration virtually absent in Britain, the population changes little the year round, being about 1,000–1,200 including immatures.

The preferred habitat is open, mountainous country, the wilder the better, ideally with hunting over forest edge alternating with moorland and rocky areas, providing a variety of prey. There must be access to several alternative nest-sites, either in large, old trees or on cliff faces with overhangs, and with freedom from disturbance. Commanding look-out posts — on crags, trees, etc — are important in prey detection and security. Generally, territories overlap.

OPPOSITE
The golden eagle – now virtually confined to Scotland

The sexes are similar, but the female is up to 20 per cent heavier and 10 per cent larger than the male. Length 75–88cm (30–35in), tail 28–36cm (11–14in), wing 56.5–68.5cm (22.2–26.9in), wingspan 204–220cm (80–87in), weight 2.8–6.7kg (6.2–14.7lb).

The voice is seldom used, even during breeding. The main calls are variously described as loud yelping, yapping or barking, and screeching or mewing reminiscent of the common buzzard. Said to be more talkative when several birds overwinter together.

Observations in parts of Scotland showed that immatures comprised about 34 per cent of the population July–September, but only about 16 per cent – October–June, 75 per cent probably dying before reaching sexual maturity at about four years old. Each year some 10–25 per cent of pairs may fail to breed, the higher figures apparently related to areas where the food supply is poorest. The oldest ringed bird recovered to date was 25 years 8 months.

Field Characters and Anatomy

When a shaft of sunlight falls on the golden crown and neck feathers of this generally dark-brown bird it is easy to see how it acquired its name. In Britain there is little chance of confusing the species with any other, the legs feathered down to the toes distinguishing it from the less elegant, larger, still very rare and recently reintroduced white-tailed eagle. It exudes power, with noticeably protruding head, large bill, long, wide tail, and long, quite broad wings whose trailing edges have a distinctive 'S' curve due to bulging secondaries. The primaries are spread like fingers. Despite the power, it is remarkably graceful — the most elegant of all large raptors, soaring with wings raised in a shallow V and extended slightly forward, gliding with wings lower, sometimes flat. Wingbeats are powerful and deep, a short series of 6–7 strokes being interspersed with glides. When hanging on the wind the head is held down, but on the ground it is up as the eagle adopts a somewhat horizontal stance, and waddles rather than walks.

The dark-brown juvenile has a conspicuous white panel along the bases of the inner primaries and outer secondaries, and a white base to the tail (visible from above and below), which causes confusion with the white-tailed eagle. The white markings begin to disappear after 4–5 years and full adult plumage is acquired over 6–8 years. The roughlegged buzzard is the only British raptor with plumage similar to that of the juvenile.

Breeding

As befits its image, the golden eagle generally remains faithful to just one mate for many years, and probably for life. Indeed, they frequently occupy their territories throughout the year. However, a lost mate is replaced, sometimes during the same season. They generally breed for the first time when the adult plumage is acquired, at about five years old. However, in some areas it is common to find successful breeding between an adult and a bird still in juvenile plumage; this is perhaps an indication that human persecution and disturbance has interfered with the age structure of the population. It is likely that most pairs are formed after the establishment of territory.

Like other large raptors, the eagle generally displays only in fine weather, resident birds frequently showing their great aerial agility on sunny days in late winter and early spring, their activity diminishing as the breeding season advances. Birds usually have favoured spots, and display alone or in pairs, soaring and sometimes flapping to a great height, ascending in great circles. Then they wheel around each other and may indulge in flight-play, swooping close or the higher bird diving towards its mate below, which rolls over to ward off the mock attack, but without the talons interlocking. Sometimes the game is played with prey or some inanimate object such as a twig, which is dropped from a height and caught by either bird. Intruding eagles are soon driven out of the territory.

Each territory generally has several nest-sites, but up to eleven have been recorded. The chosen eyries are usually about 3–5km (2–3 miles) apart so that displaying neighbours can see each other easily and thus avoid conflict. It is thought that sites are changed according to disturbance or weather conditions, or when a nest becomes so bulky that it starts to attract attention.

Most Highland nests are on cliffs, tree-nests rarely being found outside the old pine forests in the east, except on a few islands. Cliff nests are up to about 2m (6.5ft) high and 1.5m (4.9ft) wide. The untidy mass of twigs and branches, interlaced with oddments ranging from stags' antlers to a coil of wire, may grow to enormous size over many seasons. The tree-nests are the biggest — as much as 5.2m (17ft) deep and in use for fifty years. As with some other raptors which build in high, inaccessible places, the eagle's nest is commonly called an eyrie or eyry, which probably derives from the Saxon *eghe* ('g' sounding like 'y') for an egg. Therefore the modern English form of the word should be eggery, but in about 1400 Chaucer set a precedent when he wrote *ey* for egg.

Most nests are shaded by an overhanging rock or tree, and steep bank sides or gulleys are used where cliffs or trees are absent. It is untrue that there is *regular* rotation of nest-sites. Sometimes the choice is restricted, for example when there is lying snow at high sites. Building occurs at any time of year, with concentrated activity in late February or early March. The amount added each year varies greatly, but most nests are decorated with green sprigs and the cup is commonly lined with woodrush (*Luzula sylvatica*), which grows profusely on neighbouring ledges, as well as heather, moss and grass. Both sexes build, at altitudes ranging from 16m to 900m above sea level.

Incubation is mostly by the female for 43–45 days per egg, and begins with the first egg; the nestlings are therefore of varying sizes, and the bigger one often kills its weaker sibling within the first week. After about three weeks it is safe, but

GOLDEN EAGLE

The two (sometimes one or three) eggs have an average size of 70–89mm (2.75–3.5in) × 51–66mm (2–2.6in) and are mostly laid from early March to early April (according to altitude), often when there is snow on the ground, at intervals of 3–4 days. If the single clutch is lost, replacement is rare.

The golden eagle remains faithful to just one mate for many years, probably for life

33

Golden eagle chick a few hours old; another about to hatch

about four out of five chicks are killed in this way. The adults do not interfere, and such deaths occur even where food is plentiful. Some die through food shortage. In Scotland, the average number of young reared in each successful nest varies from scarcely more than one where the food supply is poor, to about 1.2 where it is good. During incubation the female usually hunts for herself, leaving the nest unattended.

Until about two weeks old, the chicks are brooded almost continuously, chiefly by the female. Although both parents bring food to the nest, it is mostly the female which tears it up and feeds the young bill to bill. Chicks can feed themselves at about 30 days, they fledge at 65–80 days, and become independent after a further 90–100 days. However, in non-migratory populations such as that in Scotland, the young seem reluctant to leave the nest area, and even when driven away by their parents in the following year, they do not move far.

Diet and Feeding Behaviour

As one of our largest predators and an inhabitant of wild places, the golden eagle has always been the subject of great speculation as regards its prey. However, tales of very large animals and even children being carried off are to be viewed with scepticism as the maximum weight most golden eagles can lift is 4–5kg (8.8–11lb). Yet even an authority of the stature of the Reverend Morris (1850) wrote: 'There are at least three authenticated instances of their having carried off children in this country – those in Orkney and Skye were rescued'. More interestingly, he commented: 'The numbers of animals and birds destroyed by eagles must be very great . . . and it is on record that a peasant in Kerry, and another in Antrim, supported their families for a considerable time by means of the animals brought by parent eagles to their nests.' Exceptional loads may be tackled when a bird is disturbed at a kill, and prey is generally killed before being carried off.

34

The diet varies according to locality, the principal items being mammals and birds, with smaller numbers of reptiles taken and occasionally fish and invertebrates. Larger prey is generally taken only if injured or sick, or as carrion, although specialist individual eagles or inexperienced birds may attempt to kill large, healthy animals such as deer. Sometimes pairs hunt co-operatively, for example one flying directly over a hare, the other following near the ground.

In Scotland, mammals taken include rabbit, hare, fox, squirrel, weasel, hedgehog, wild and feral cat, rat, voles, mole, sheep, badger, pine marten, roe and red deer. Birds include red grouse, black grouse, ptarmigan, capercaillie, ducks, geese, swans, cormorants, gulls, buntings, pipits and larks. Snakes and lizards are sometimes taken, and fish include salmon, trout, pike and lumpsucker. Amphibians and insects are recorded, but are generally of little importance.

Scottish birds concentrate on the red grouse, ptarmigan, mountain hare, rabbit, and dead — mostly young — sheep and red deer, though coastal pairs take many seabirds. In one study (Stephen 1957), 94 per cent of 577 prey items were rabbits and hares; in another (Lockie and Stephen 1959), out of a total of 198 prey items, 68 per cent were mammals (mainly hare and rabbit, 49.5 per cent), and 31.5 per cent birds (mainly grouse family, 26.5 per cent). However, several studies have shown the importance of carrion, especially in the west Highlands where live prey is scarce. For example Lockie (1964) showed that in the north-west Highlands in winter the diet consisted of 38 per cent sheep and deer carrion (by weight), 32 per cent hares and rabbits, and 30 per cent grouse family. More recent studies have shown an even greater winter dependence on carrion in areas where hill sheep farming is still widespread. Indeed, the availability of sheep and deer carrion is probably crucial to the winter survival of golden eagles in much of the south-west Highlands and islands. Daily food requirements for wild Scottish birds have been estimated at about 230g (½lb) per bird per day, equivalent to about 84kg (185lb) per year. But with wastage, the estimate is 214kg (472lb) killed or utilised.

Sometimes prey is spotted from a perch on a branch or cliff, from which the eagle will strike, but only rarely does it stoop from a great height after prey. Most prey — hares and grouse for example — is taken from the ground, the eagle flying low, at tree-top height, quartering the ground methodically for hours at a time and suddenly appearing in surprise attack, striking with the talons in a swift pounce. Larger mammals are usually chased, but the eagle is often unsuccessful. Indeed, a falconer's eagle may take a hare at only every twentieth attempt, but acquires more skill over the years. Birds are rarely taken in mid-air, but those put up are pursued.

The eagle's mastery of the air makes its pursuit of prey seem effortless, with all manner of graceful glides and side-slips, soaring ascents and spectacular dives in excess of 160kph (100mph), all with scarcely a sign of wing movement. Eagles also make great use of the thermals which abound in hilly country. Seton Gordon watched one bird rise 200m up a vertical cliff in less than 30 seconds. Flight attitude varies with the wind direction, speed of gliding being controlled by wing flexing. These skills, plus great endurance, enable the golden eagle to hunt over long distances — up to 22km (14 miles), which is especially important in the random search for carrion.

GOLDEN EAGLE

Migration, Movements and Roosting

In western and central Europe the adults are largely resident, though young birds drift south from most northern areas. The small number of ring recoveries confirms that Scottish birds are very sedentary, adult pairs being resident all year and remaining in contact with the nesting territory even in winter. Directions are random and the maximum distance recorded is 120km (75 miles). However, daily movements may be considerable, the hunting range being extended in severe weather or when food is scarce. A pair which bred on Rathlin Island, Northern Ireland regularly crossed 22km (14 miles) to Kintyre, Scotland, to feed. Birds which occasionally turn up outside the breeding range are mostly immatures, though some unpaired adults are nomadic. Congregation at a food source is rare and most unpaired birds are solitary, though small gatherings have been reported.

In winter the night roost is often near the eyrie, on a rock ledge or in a tree (commonly Scots pine), the spot with the best shelter being chosen each day. A site may be identified by the fresh droppings and small downy feathers. A pair will arrive at dusk, either together or separately. During periods of rain, mist or low temperatures, birds may loaf all day on a perch with a good outlook, male and female separate, each having its favoured places, generally far apart. However, there are records of fast flight through fog with visibility under 20m. It is thought that birds detect air currents accurately enough to avoid hitting the ground. Like eyries, roosts are traditional and may be used for many years.

WHITE-TAILED EAGLE
(Haliaeetus albicilla)

WHITE-TAILED EAGLE
Once known as the sea eagle, erne, great erne and cinereous eagle

A THOUSAND years ago the white-tailed eagle was a familiar British bird. It is mentioned in the Angle-Saxon poem *The Seafarer*, in describing the lonely scene of savage rocks and seas, with only calling seabirds for company:

> Storms there, the stacks thrashed, there answered
> them the tern
> With icy feathers; full oft the erne wailed round
> Spray feathered . . .

But this poet's descendants cared little for the erne, and by the beginning of the 20th century they had killed the last one. Now a more enlightened generation seeks to redress the balance, restoring this, the largest of the British raptors to its rocky throne through an exciting reintroduction scheme.

History and Conservation

Whether or not the white-tailed eagle was ever more common than the golden eagle — as has been suggested — is a matter for speculation, but there is no doubt that it was still relatively widespread in 18th-century Britain, where the species found plenty of its preferred rocky-coast habitat. But even relative isolation could not save it, and it disappeared from most of its European range in historic times.

The earliest British record is from a Devon site and dates towards the end of the Wolstonian glaciation. Bones found there, together with those of likely prey species, suggest that caves might once have been used for nesting or roosting. There are also remains from Bronze Age and Iron Age settlements, where this long-revered bird was probably used in burial rituals. As late as 1799 Bewick wrote: 'It is equal in strength and vigour to the common eagle, but more furious.' Harting (1864) noted that it had always been associated with great powers of endurance and longevity: 'One captured in Caithness died at Duff House in February, 1862, having been kept in confinement, by the late Earl of Fife, for 32 years.'

Although primarily a scavenger throughout its range, the sea eagle does occasionally take healthy lambs, and with the arrival of sheep farmers and crofters in its ancient haunts, the bounty on its head soon rose sharply, reaching the very considerable sum of ten shillings on Skye. In Britain its eventual extinction was a result of direct and sustained persecution by shepherds, gamekeepers, fishery owners, skin-collectors and egg-collectors. For once, its demise was not the result of significant habitat loss.

The last English breeding record is from 1794, from the Lake District, though birds were still seen there up to 1835. In the 18th century there were also nests near Plymouth and on Lundy, and the last nest noted in southern England was that on Culver Cliffs, Isle of Wight, in 1780. There are no English records from the 19th century.

With extensive ideal habitat, Wales undoubtedly had many pairs, but they all seemed to have disappeared by the early 19th century, leaving no record except for where the name occurs in some place-names.

Ireland probably still had at least fifty breeding sites in the 18th century, but the birds were soon shot out, the last record being from the north Mayo coast in 1898. The Isle of Man's last was in 1818, and those on St Kilda and Fair Isle went in about 1830. In 1825 there were still enough on Rhum for a man to kill five in a single day, and even in 1866 a gamekeeper shot eight in the year.

Very gradually the birds were forced north and west, the process accelerating throughout the 19th century with the general movement of crofters towards the coasts in the wake of the Highland Clearances, the rising popularity of shooting and collecting, and the spread of sheep farming. Although about two-thirds of the one hundred known Scottish sites were still in use in the early 19th century, the species was lost to southern Scotland in 1866, and to the entire mainland in 1901. Britain's last breeding record is from 1916, when an English vicar took the eggs from a nest on Skye. A solitary female — a white-plumaged bird said to be thirty years old — remained till 1918, when it was shot, perhaps the last British-bred bird. After that there were only the occasional young Scandinavian birds which wandered to the east coast of England in winter, more rarely elsewhere.

Fortunately, it was not long before ornithologists realised that reintroduction from Norway's still healthy population was viable. Indeed, it was advisable because natural recolonisation was most unlikely. It was noted that the habitat had changed little and, as the bird often eats carrion, imported juveniles could easily be provisioned until they learnt to fend for themselves. Also, its proven suitability for falconry training techniques meant that it was amenable to 'hacking back' — getting acclimatised to the wild.

Unfortunately, the first small-scale attempt, by a private individual in 1959, failed through capture, killing and loss of the three birds. The next effort was in

WHITE-TAILED EAGLE

The name 'white-tailed eagle' dates back to 1743, to G. Edwards, who was inspired by Gesner, who in 1555 used the term *Albicilla*, coined by Gaza in 1476 from the Latin *albi* for white and *cilla* for tail. Some 17th-century naturalists called it the osprey, but Bewick applied the present name in 1801 and this was effectively standardised by Yarrell in 1843. The term 'sea eagle', which is still common as an unofficial pseudonym, was introduced as 'sea egle' by Merrett in 1667. It is a translation of the Greek *haliaetos*, derived from *hali* for (salt) sea and *aetos* for eagle.

WHITE-TAILED EAGLE

Eighty-two young sea eagles were released on Rhum 1975–85, survival being encouragingly high (estimated at 60–89 per cent). Breeding since 1983 has been erratic (first fledging in 1985, and only two pairs raised a total of two young in 1990), but some of the birds have been ranging quite widely throughout the Scottish islands and mainland and there is every reason to hope for steady improvement. Up to eleven pairs have held territory in one year (1988).

1968, but the RSPB's choice of Fair Isle was a poor one: of the four birds released, three disappeared and the other was last seen smothered in fulmar oil and barely able to fly. Apparently it had taken to attacking young fulmars, but they defended themselves in the usual way with jets of stomach oil, which ruined the eagle's plumage.

The Nature Conservancy Council's long-term scheme, established in 1975, was a much better prospect, the chosen site being the National Trust reserve on the Isle of Rhum, where breeding had continued till 1907. Subsequently, food has been provided at special dumps and includes fish, venison offal and gulls, the young Norwegian eagles quickly learning to kill gulls for themselves. Considerable patience was necessary as sea eagles take some five years to reach maturity.

Eggs were first laid in 1983, but failed, as did those in 1984. However, in 1985, four pairs made serious attempts to breed and one was successful. Since then, with regular importations of birds, there have been further breeding attempts, admittedly with mixed success, but as the birds become more experienced and more numerous the population's viability will increase. Security remains good, but the threat of egg collecting continues and is potentially disastrous for such a tenuously established bird. Furthermore, at least two birds have been poisoned. Between 1975 and 1984, eighty-two young eagles were introduced to the Inner Hebridean island, and since 1981 they have been protected and monitored by RSPB wardens. Some birds have dispersed as far afield as Shetland, Northern Ireland and Inverness-shire. Like the RSPB's Operation Osprey, this reintroduction scheme has done a great deal to foster public support for birds of prey, and to further the conservation movement in Britain; and in 1991 four pairs raised 7 young, the highest number since the scheme began.

Distribution, Habitat and Population

Very tolerant of climatic variation, the white-tailed eagle is distributed right across Eurasia, being mainly resident in subarctic to temperate or warm temperate zones. Throughout much of its range it has been the subject of intense persecution over the last two centuries, disappearing entirely from many areas. With recent habitat loss, and further mortality caused by pesticide use in some countries, increased protection has had little effect. Only northern Norway retains a healthy population — recently estimated at over 600 pairs, from which birds have been taken for Britain's reintroduction scheme on Rhum. The Greenland population is regarded as a separate subspecies.

This eagle is a vagrant rather than a migrant — that is, young birds without territories may temporarily wander beyond the usual range — and so few birds have drifted into Britain this century (only seven records 1957–81); natural recolonisation would therefore be extremely unlikely. However, between 1982 and 1989 there were at least a further eleven vagrants, all in south and east England and one bearing an East German ring. All were immatures, and continued the welcome trend towards greater regularity.

Although it is primarily a coastal bird, the sea eagle also occurs near large lakes and rivers, and in some countries inland pairs nest as far as 10km (6.25 miles) from their main food sources. It takes a wide range of prey, and changes quite happily from a diet of colonial seabirds to sheep and deer carrion. The environment in west and north Scotland has changed in few ways which would seriously affect the sea eagle. On the contrary, some prey species, such as gulls and eiders, have in-

OPPOSITE
White tailed eagle –
recently reintroduced
to Britain

38

WHITE-TAILED EAGLE

This is the fourth largest eagle in the world, and has the greatest wingspan of any British bird – to 2.4m (7.87ft). Individuals with spans of 3m (9.75ft) have been claimed, but the normal range is 2–2.4m (6.5–7.87 ft), females being up to 25 per cent heavier and 15 per cent larger than males. (The golden eagle is less bulky and its wingspan generally a centimetre or two shorter). The body length is 68–90cm (27–36in) but despite the massive, vulture-like appearance, the sea eagle is not as cumbersome as it appears. The weight range is 3.1–6.9kg (6.8–15.2lb); tail 25.4–33.0cm (10–13in); wing 55.2–71.5cm (21.7–28in).

A more vociferous bird than the golden eagle, it is often heard during the breeding season. The main call consists of a series of 15–30 variable, screeching yaps, generally increasing in rapidity and pitch, and often rendered as *kee* or *klee*. The female's call is lower than the male's.

White-tailed eagle being ringed prior to release on Rhum

creased, and the species is ready to accept some human settlement and activity where it is not associated with persecution. Should the happy day come when it is widespread again, I do not believe it will compete significantly with the golden eagle because it is primarily a coastal bird.

Field Characters and Anatomy

In flight silhouette the long, broad wings have parallel front and rear edges and are deeply fingered; the short tail is wedge-shaped, the huge bill deep, the head protruding unusually far forward.

The sexes are similar, with almost uniform brown plumage, distinguishing white tail and unfeathered legs at all ages. The yellow bill and adult dress are acquired at 4–5 years, but even then there may be brown feathers in the white tail.

Wingbeats are slow, stiff and fairly shallow in long series with only the occa-

sional short glide. In soaring, the wings are either held flat or slightly raised, but are always slightly arched. In gliding they are horizontal, again slightly arched.

Breeding

Although the monogamous, probably life-long pair-bond is generally formed when the sea eagle attains maturity at 4–5 years, on Rhum there has been a wide age-span (3–9 years) at first breeding, perhaps linked to the period in captivity. Though slightly less territorial than the golden eagle, it generally lives on or near its territory throughout the year. Courtship, generally from late December to mid-March, mostly involves one or both birds circling over the nest-site to about 200m, with some flight-play and much excited calling.

Most nests — one to eleven sites per territory recorded — are on cliffs, crags and skerries, or in crowns of tall trees, but some are on the ground. Of twenty Rhum sites located to 1987, five were in trees and fifteen on largely inaccessible cliff ledges. Nests are often used in successive years or alternated with others in the territory. An Icelandic site was in use for over 150 years. Most nests are less than 3km (1.9 miles) from the main foraging area and at least 1–2km (0.6–1.2 miles) apart. These huge structures of twigs, heather, driftwood and seaweed, about 1.5m (5ft) across, are usually very shallow, arranged in a slovenly manner, and with a shallow cup lined with grass, wool, feathers, moss and lichens. They are built by both sexes, the male mostly bringing material for the female to incorporate, and as they are added to each year they may reach immense proportions.

Incubation, mostly by the female, starts with the first egg and averages 38 days (34–46 days reported), the fourth longest of any British bird.

Hatching is asynchronous, and during the first two weeks one of the parents — mostly the female — is always brooding. After about 20–25 days the female joins in the hunting and the young may be left by themselves for long periods. At 35–40 days the eaglets feed themselves in the nest. From 55 days they perch on nearby rocks and branches, and fledge at 70–75 days, but remain near the eyrie for a further 35–40 days. Up to 1987, all chicks on Rhum fledged at 77–84 days. In the nest, the young are less aggressive towards each other than are those of the golden eagle. Productivity is better than the golden eagle's, averaging 1.6 young per nest in Norway.

The single clutch (replacement is possible after egg loss) of two (sometimes one or three) eggs is generally laid in March or April, at intervals of 2–5 days.

Observations on Rhum indicate that age and experience influence egg-laying, which becomes progressively earlier with each attempt. The earliest Rhum laying has been 9 March. There is some geographical variation in egg size, Norwegian and British being similar at an average of 76 × 59mm (3.0 × 2.3in).

Diet and Feeding Behaviour

Surprisingly agile for a big bird, the sea eagle has a variety of hunting methods to cope with the diversity and wide range in size and weight of its food items. It is a scavenger and kleptoparasite as well as a predator, taking waterbirds, fish, mammals and carrion.

Diving birds such as eider ducks, auks and shags, are harried to exhaustion (for coots, 43–65 attacks have been recorded over 35–45 minutes before success), two eagles — mates or unrelated birds — sometimes working together. It can easily catch birds in level flight too, especially the more clumsy species, although it rarely does so. Surprise is the main weapon in catching prey other than fish. Prey may be spotted from a perch on a rock or tree or on the ground; while soaring at 200–300m; or when flying low over the ground or water. Sometimes the eagle will hover or glide before attacking with legs outstretched and talons extended.

Immature white-tailed eagle. The species has been reintroduced to Britain following extinction in 1918

The diet varies with the locality and the time of year. In many areas fish is the most important item in spring and summer, especially species which move close to the surface to spawn, and there is no doubt that overall, the value of fish has been underestimated as their remains are difficult to identify. In Norway, where cod and lumpsucker are commonest among 24 fish species taken, fish generally comprise 60 per cent of the diet (to 90 per cent in some areas). Equally at home on fresh or salt water, the sea eagle prefers to fish in calm conditions, approaching low or hovering before striking at surface-feeders; nor does it plunge-dive in spectacular fashion like the osprey. Sometimes it stands still in the water or wanders about the shallows in search of stranded or dying fish. A fish too big to lift may be towed to land by rowing with the wings. However, this habit may be the bird's undoing: Morris recorded a salmon found dead on the shores of Moffat Water, 'and an immense erne lifeless also beside it, having met its fate by being hooked by its own claws to a fish too large and powerful for it to carry off'. Other fish taken include trout, pike, perch, eel and herring.

There are many fanciful stories concerning the erne's ability to carry large prey. Most concerning children and even adults have been discounted by ornithologists, but there is at least one case which appears to be fully authenticated. In 1932 a four-year-old Norwegian girl is said to have been carried off by a sea eagle when

she was playing in her parents' farmyard. The huge bird tried to carry the girl (apparently small for her age) back to its eyrie 224m (800ft) up the side of a mountain more than 1.6km (1 mile) away, but the effort was too great and the poor child was dropped on a narrow ledge about 15m (50ft) from the nest. Fortunately, a search party pinpointed the eagle soaring above the eyrie and the girl was found asleep and unharmed save for some scratches and bruises. One theory is that the bird had the advantage of a powerful upcurrent of air. But whatever the truth, the girl, Svanhild Hansen, grew up happily and kept the little dress she wore that terrible day, with the holes made by the eagle's talons.

The largest prey seen taken in flight is the greylag goose, which rarely has a weight above 4.25kg (9.4lb). Colonies of seabirds are a major attraction, eggs, young and adults being taken. Other birds eaten include swans, ducks, grebes, divers, herons, cormorants, gulls and crows. In Norway birds commonly account for about 40 per cent of the diet. An East German study revealed a breeding-season diet of 56 per cent fish, 37 per cent birds and 7 per cent mammals, changing to 79 per cent birds, 15 per cent mammals and only 6 per cent fish in winter.

Mammals taken range from small rodents such as the water vole, to sheep and red deer calves, though predation on larger mammals is insignificant in most areas. Carrion is especially important in winter and may include seals, porpoises and even man, as well as sheep and deer. Morris noted that some Hebridean people lived partially on the abundance of food taken to erne nests. The species' daily requirement has been put at 700g (1.5lb), of which some 500g (1.1lb) is pure meat.

Other prey includes snakes, frogs, molluscs, cuttlefish, hares, rabbits, dogs and goats, though ascertaining which was taken as carrion and which incapacitated is always difficult. Birds which are frequently robbed of food include the osprey, red kite, buzzard, peregrine, snowy owl and gulls. The eagle will also take fish left by otters or gulls, and offal from gralloched deer and fishing boats, which it follows.

The feet have sharp spicules on their undersides, to assist in taking slippery prey.

Migration, Movements and Roosting

Apart from birds in northern Russia, which are forced to migrate wherever fresh waters freeze up and waterfowl prey are absent in winter, most adult pairs in the Western Palearctic are strictly resident. However, young birds wander extensively, on the track of waterfowl prey rather than in true directional migration. Sometimes these birds are seen in small loose parties, but British records are few, most occurring in eastern England from November to March.

At night, adults roost alone or in pairs, in secure, sheltered roosts near the sea, or inland in crevices, on ledges below rocks, in dense trees or even on the ground. Tree perches are usually on living branches, not dead ones as used by the golden eagle. A pair usually roosts together, often at the nest, during the early part of the breeding season. When the female starts to incubate, the male usually roosts nearby, but sometimes they spend the night together on the nest. They also spend long periods during the day loafing on favourite perches, or even on the ground or in shallow water.

Most sightings of birds released on Rhum have been within sixty miles, though one bird turned up a hundred miles to the north after prolonged south-easterly gales.

OSPREY
(Pandion haliaetus)

OSPREY
Once known as the bald buzzard, sea eagle, leaden eagle, fishing eagle, water eagle, fishing hawk, mullet hawk and eagle fisher

Pliny mentioned the word osprey in its Latin form *Ossifraga* (bone-breaker) to denote a lammergeier, and in 1460 there is the first English reference, as 'ospray'. With such an inappropriate Latin derivation, the name must have been a folk corruption of an earlier form, borrowed from the Old French *osfraie*, becoming *orfraie* in 1491. Turner took up the present spelling in 1544 and this has continued to the present day, despite some naturalists applying the name to the white-tailed eagle in the 17th and 18th centuries.

O NE of the few birds which regularly make the headlines, the osprey has probably done more than any other species to stimulate interest in birdwatching and conservation in Britain. Although it is one of the most widespread of all birds of prey, it was harried to temporary extinction in Britain; however, since it was coaxed back to breed in 1959 over one million people have visited the hide at Loch Garten. The visitors are not all hardened 'twitchers' either: this masterly RSPB public-relations exercise has attracted many complete beginners to the joys of birdwatching, and this most famous of eyries still entices over 70,000 people a season.

History and Conservation

Apart from a possible record from the end of the last glaciation in Derbyshire, there is little fossil evidence of the osprey in Britain. But there is no doubt that it became widespread, though perhaps not in Ireland, and it was commonly shot as a pest which took fish. Records are scant from Ireland and Wales, but some of the last-known English breeding dates are: 1570 on the Solent, 1678 in Lakeland, 1757 in South Devon, 1838 on Lundy and 1847 in Somerset. It is not clear whether many birds killed in England during the 19th century were breeding or passage migrants, but eyries in Devon and Cornwall may have been used beyond 1850.

There was a marked decline throughout its range in the 19th and early 20th centuries, largely through fishermen and collectors of skins and eggs; by World War II even Norway had only 3–4 known pairs. In Scotland it was still common in 1800, but with new interest in sport and commercial fishing and improved guns it was soon shot out in many areas, especially where bounties were offered. Then along came the egg thieves, who went to extraordinary lengths to obtain British eggs for their English customers, and the rarer the clutches became the more they were sought after. Sadly, the handsome osprey also made a fine display for Victorian cabinets.

The species was eliminated from southern and central Scotland in the early 19th century and gradually pushed back into the wilder north, and by 1850 there were only two major strongholds — Speyside and Sutherland. The last nesting in northern Perthshire was in 1886; in Cromerty in 1901; and in south Inverness in 1908, on Loch Arkaig in an island oak protected by the laird, Donald Cameron of Lochiel. He placed the nest under police protection and put barbed wire around the tree and the island, but to no avail. After that the only British nesting recorded was that on an island in Loch Loyne till 1916, though other birds may have bred at Loch-an-Eilean in the Spey Valley till the same year.

Fortunately, when the Scandinavian population began to recover in the 1940s, following protection, more ospreys found their way to Britain and there were rumours of Scottish breeding in the early 1950s. Then in 1954, a pair built at a secret site on Speyside and it is said that two young were fledged. In 1955 the eyrie was occupied again, but this time the eggs were stolen and the birds moved on to Loch Garten, where the clutch suffered the same fate. Astonishingly, they then tried again in the Sluggan Pass, but it was too late in the season and the birds soon drifted away. The RSPB planned to protect this site in 1956 but the birds never returned, instead choosing Rothiemurchus and Loch Morlich for further abortive attempts. No nesting pair was located in 1957, but in 1958 the RSPB got 'Operation Osprey' into full swing with round-the-clock protection. Despite this, eggs were taken again, being smashed as the robber was chased away, and two further nesting attempts by the same pair were fruitless.

Thus it was not until 1959 that ospreys were definitely fledged in Britain for the first time since 1916. The site, at Loch Garten, was then declared a bird reserve; the lower, climbable limbs were lopped off the nest tree which, along with the replacement tree, was swathed in barbed wire. With security improved, no less than 14,000 people were admitted free to view that first successful nest. Since then the stream of visitors to Loch Garten has included three prime ministers and most members of the royal family.

Slowly, other parts of Scotland were colonised, though the egg thieves have continued to take incredible chances, and in 1986 vandals actually tried to cut down the Loch Garten tree with a chainsaw. However, the osprey now seems well established in Britain, and a steady influx of Scandinavian birds continues to augment the stock; with luck, its range may one day extend south into England once again. There is no doubt that the building of artificial nest foundations in selected trees has done much to encourage the settlement of new pairs, enabling some to breed a year earlier than they would have done, as the first season together is usually taken up by nest construction.

Every year more and more people visit osprey country for leisure purposes such as climbing, walking, skiing and pony-trekking, quite apart from birdwatching. Obviously such pressures must be carefully monitored and controlled if the osprey is to continue range-expansion. Ironically, although fishermen contributed much to the demise of the osprey, the growing interest in sport angling and in fish for food is now helping the bird's recovery; increased demand for salmon and trout has led to the establishment of numerous fish farms, and the osprey is able to feed at most of these without receiving a blast of buckshot — most managers are prepared to put up with losing a few pounds in the knowledge that they are furthering the conservation movement. Southern fish farms and 'stew ponds' are helping too, in providing easy feeding for passage birds, though sadly, many of these birds are shot or fly into overhead wires on their migrations abroad.

Some cases of infertility in Scotland have been attributed to high levels of pesticides and other chemicals, though accumulations have been generally lower in British-bred birds than in Swedish ospreys which died in this country.

Distribution, Habitat and Population

The osprey is found worldwide, except in the Arctic and Antarctic. It breeds in North and Central America, parts of the Mediterranean, northern and eastern Europe, much of Asia, sporadically in Africa, and along much of the Australian coast. In Europe prolonged persecution has led to severe range-contraction. The re-establishing British breeding population is confined to Scotland, where it is concentrated in the central and eastern Highlands, with only a few western records. Passage migrants occur chiefly in eastern Britain, though reservoirs and other fisheries are attracting increasing numbers to the Midlands and southern England.

As such a specialised feeder, the osprey is restricted to areas with plenty of

Through prolonged and effective protection, the British stock has grown steadily. In 1990 the largest number of ospreys in more than a hundred years arrived in Scotland to breed in the spring, and 62 pairs raised 87 young, more than in any year this century. This figure would have been even higher had not poor weather in May and June caused many young to die in their nests. In addition, egg-collectors robbed seven nests. In 1991 there were some 70 pairs.

OSPREY

The female is 5–10 per cent larger than the male. Length 55–58cm (21.6–22.8in), wingspan 145–170cm (57–70in), wing 44.8–51.8cm (17.6–20.4in), tail 18.7–23.2cm (7.4–9.1in), weight 1.1–2.0kg (2.5–4.5lb).

Calls are almost exclusive to the breeding season, mostly a variety of whistling and whining screeches, generally in short rhythmic series and rather feeble for a bird of this size.

medium-sized fish which live close to the surface in clear, unpolluted water — fresh, brackish or salt. Thus it is found near lakes, reservoirs and rivers as well as along the coast, wherever human disturbance is minimal. In its winter quarters, in Africa, it normally lives near the coast or large rivers, but passage birds will use almost any water where fishing is possible.

Field Characters and Anatomy

Despite its wide range, the osprey shows little geographic variation in size or plumage, but because its anatomy has many differences from other raptors — indicating only distant relationship with most of them — it is placed in a family of its own, *Pandionidae*. It is particularly well adapted to catching fish, the back of the tarsus and lower surfaces of the toes being covered with sharp spicules for holding slimy, wriggling prey. The outer toe is reversible and the claws are strongly curved and very sharp, also useful features in clutching awkward prey. The strongly curved upper mandible of the broad-based bill tapers to a sharp point well beyond the lower mandible. The plumage is dense, oily and imbricated.

Confusion is unlikely with any other British raptor, although at long range it can be mistaken for a large gull as it has long, narrow wings and glides with the inner wing raised and primaries lowered, the wing joints protruding noticeably. The relatively small head is extended well forward, and the tail is rather short. The sexes are similar, with a very noticeable black stripe through the staring eye and dark-brown upperparts contrasting well with the white underparts. Young birds are similar, though up to about one year may be distinguished in the field by their paler and more variegated upperparts.

The wingbeats are powerful but quite shallow, interspersed with long periods of gliding; hovering is frequent over water in search of fish. The osprey is also well known for its practice of head-scratching and heavy panting to lose heat. It also bathes quite frequently, for up to 15 minutes, and in flight will drag its feet in the water, presumably to clean them or keep cool. It spends much time preening and oiling its plumage, and cleans its bill and claws meticulously, flicking away fish scales with a shake of the head.

Breeding

Although it shows strong attachment to its mate and eyrie, the osprey normally has only a seasonal pair-bond, unlike the non-migratory golden and white-tailed eagles; bigamy is very rare. Birds first breed from three years old. The male generally arrives a few days before the female and displays both to assert territorial rights and to attract a mate, usually from late March to late April. In dramatic show he rises to about 300m, flutters his wings with his body momentarily almost vertical, then tilts over into a short dive, repeating the performance and gradually losing height till he alights on the nest, screeching *pyeh-pyeh-pyeh* the whole time. Once paired, the birds may sky-dance singly or together, the male sometimes carrying nest material or a fish.

A new nest averages 120–150cm (47–59in) in diameter and 50–60cm (20–24in) in height, but with re-use can grow enormously. Coward described it as being 'Like that of the kite, a rubbish heap. A huge pile of sticks, turf and seaweed, which has included in one the skeleton of a pheasant, the wheel of a child's mail-cart and many corks; it was lined with seaweed and cow-dung'. Moss, bark and

The migrant osprey is a specialist fish-eater

grass are also used for lining. Both sexes build for about 14–21 days before laying. The most frequent natural sites are in the crown or on the stout side-branches of a tree; indeed, recent Scottish eyries have all been in trees (some with artificial platforms), although former British sites included cliffs, rocks, ruins, low bushes and even the ground. Overseas the species is more adaptable and surprisingly tolerant of urbanisation, some even nesting on telegraph poles, buildings and pylons. Material is added throughout the breeding season, mostly by the female.

The 34/40-day incubation (average 37) is mostly by the female and begins with the first egg, so hatching is asynchronous. The young are fed by the female with fish brought entirely by the male. Fledging is at seven or eight weeks, but independence is not for a further month or two. In Scotland, in the good season of 1988, the mean brood size was 2.23, productivity of young per nest being about average at 1.53.

In Scotland the single clutch is normally of two eggs for a female laying for the first time, and thereafter three (sometimes one or four), average egg size being 62 × 46mm (2.4 × 1.8in) laid at 1 to 3-day intervals mostly in April and May.

Diet and Feeding Behaviour

The osprey is primarily a fish-eater, catching a variety of species according to availability, up to a maximum weight of about 2kg (4.5lb). Frequently hunting like a kestrel, the osprey quarters the surface of fresh- or saltwater at a height of about 20–30m, gliding, flapping or hovering according to the wind and diving out of a mid-air 'stop'. The wings are half-folded and the feet thrown forward at the

Often using a spectacular crash-dive, it sinks its long talons deep into a fish, and there have been cases where the bird drowned because its claws became embedded in the scales or bones of prey too big to lift. Sometimes the osprey is almost completely immersed, but most dives are no deeper than 1m and the technique employed varies with the species of fish.

Ospreys are capable of sustained flapping flight, which means that they do not have to concentrate at favoured, relatively narrow crossing-points, as predominantly soaring species do. Both seas and deserts are crossed with ease.

last moment. Some dives are from perches, others from soaring flight over 70m up; not all are successful. One Scottish study found that 65 per cent of dives at flounders succeeded. A search can take up to an hour.

The fish is mostly carried with the head forward, but sometimes as it was caught — sideways or by the tail. It is usually taken to an established feeding perch such as a bare, horizontal branch, rock or mudflat. There the bird generally waits briefly till the fish is dead before commencing to eat it, starting with the head but usually leaving the gut.

Long ago, it was known as the mullet hawk in Hampshire because it concentrated on that surface-feeding fish in Christchurch Harbour. In Scotland the main prey species are brown trout and now rainbow trout, pike and flounder, brown trout having declined in recent years while pike have spread and rainbow trout have been introduced to many more waters. Since 1970 the proportion of trout in the diet at Loch Garten has almost doubled, to 80 per cent. Because the flesh is torn off the fish, species with barbs or spines, such as bass, are not excluded from the diet, but obviously only surface feeders are taken. Passage migrants in southern England also take perch and garfish. The osprey's average daily requirement has been estimated at 300g (0.66lb).

A wide variety of other prey has been recorded, including small mammals, birds, reptiles, amphibians, crustaceans, beetles and other invertebrates. Such species may be taken when locally abundant and easy to catch, or when ice, fog, rain or cloudy water make fishing difficult, especially for young, inexperienced ospreys. On rough days, when waves make assessing the position of a fish awkward, even old birds may be forced to hunt in quiet bays and creeks.

In former times, when both species were more abundant, white-tailed eagles apparently sometimes robbed ospreys of their food; at the moment, however, it looks as if it will be a very long time before their British ranges overlap significantly again.

Migration and Movements

Almost all the ospreys breeding in Europe winter in Africa south of the Sahara. The few Scottish-ringed birds which have been recovered abroad have all been on passage in Iberia or on the west coast of Africa. Adults start to leave their African winter quarters in March, mostly arriving in Scotland during late March and April. Many young birds stay in the wintering grounds for their first summer, or only venture north as far as the Mediterranean. More rarely, second-summer birds also stay south. Young returning for the first time generally follow about a month behind the experienced breeders, and on arrival they wander around a lot as they do not normally have time to settle and breed. Breeding grounds are usually vacated from mid-August, adults heading between south-west and south-east on a broad front, generally preceding the juveniles. They arrive in their winter quarters from late September to early October.

Passage birds often stop off at a suitable reservoir, lake or river for several days, the immatures for even weeks. There has been an increasing tendency for passage birds to halt at certain reservoirs in southern England, even in suburbia, and especially in autumn when their progress is more leisurely. Ringing recoveries show that a considerable number of passage birds are from Scandinavia, where a revival of the species' fortunes has helped re-fuel Britain's breeding stock.

Ospreys usually migrate singly, but sometimes in small groups. Although they can be highly gregarious overseas, concentrations are unusual in Britain. Up to eleven have been noted on certain Scottish waters, during July and August.

RED KITE
(*Milvus milvus*)

SCOTLAND might have the osprey, but in Britain Wales alone can claim the red kite as a breeding species. The fact that it never quite became extinct in these islands is partly a matter of luck, but also a tribute to the efforts of a small band of caring people. For most of this century they have encouraged and protected this tiny, remnant population against many enemies. But now there is new hope that the species will become common again as, encouraged by the sea-eagle success, conservationists have recently introduced Spanish- and Swedish-bred kites to the English and Scottish countryside.

History and Conservation

This species is now listed among the twenty-nine most at risk in Europe, and it is hard to believe that in mediaeval times it was probably the most familiar bird of prey in lowland Britain. Indeed, it was so well known in Shakespeare's time that it was easily absorbed into popular literature. In *Macbeth* (Act III, Sc 4), the Bard showed that he was well aware of the kite's habit (in common with other raptors) of casting pellets.

> If charnel-houses and our graves must send
> Those that we bury back, our monuments
> Shall be the maws of kites.

He also freely alluded to the bird's habit of scavenging the streets of London, which he called 'a city of crows and kites'. From its association with carrion, the name 'kite' became a term of reproach: 'You kite' (*Anthony and Cleopatra* Act III, Sc 13) and 'Detested kite' (*King Lear* Act I, Sc 4), and 'I should have fatted all the region kites with this slave's offal' (*Hamlet* Act II, Sc 2). But at the same time the kite was valued in helping to keep the cities clean, and for a long time it was a capital crime to kill them in London. Indeed, along with its fellow scavenger, the raven, this was the first bird to be protected for any reason other than hunting.

However, in the countryside the kite soon had a price on its head, as it commonly took free-range fowls. In *Henry VI Part II* (Act III, Sc I) Shakespeare wrote:

> Wer't not all one, an empty eagle were set
> To guard the chicken from a hungry kite,
> As place Duke Humphrey for the king's protector?

In the 15th century kites were so common in London that travellers commonly remarked on them, mentioning how the birds were so tame that they took bread and butter from the hands of children. But it could be that the kite population was at its peak in the squalor of mediaeval England, temporarily encouraged by the rich pickings.

The earliest record of British kites is from South Wales, from cave bones dating back to the last inter-glacial period, about 120,000 years ago. Subsequently, when some 60 per cent of Britain was covered by forest, the kite's range was probably quite restricted because it is mainly an open-country bird, relying on woodland only for nesting and roosting. Thus gradual deforestation for agriculture, coupled

RED KITE
Once known as the gled, glead, greedy gled, glead hawk, glade, fork-tail, crotch tail, puttock, scoul, baegez, forky-tailed kite, bod, boda wenol, barcud, bascud, bascutan, bodfforchog, crotchet-tailed puttock, barend and whew

The name 'kite' derives from the Middle English 'kyte' and Old English 'cyta', once also applied to the buzzard and related to the mewing or whistling call common to both species. Indeed, the term was probably first applied to the buzzard, the kite originally being more commonly known as the 'glcdc', which derives from the Saxon word *glida*, being descriptive of the bird's gliding flight. 'Glede' gradually gave way to 'kite' in the late 17th and early 18th centuries. As applied to the toy, the word 'kite' is known from 1664.

with greater availability of carrion through animal farming, must have encouraged the species. The refuse, excrement and animal carcases in and about towns were a bonus.

The kite's decline started when the cities were cleaned up, the London streets paved with cobbles and drained, and household refuse disposed of more hygienically. And from 1532 a series of Acts of Parliament were passed requiring parishes to pay bounties for the destruction of an ever-extending list of 'noyfull Fowles and Vermyn', to which the kite was added in 1566 as a predator of farmyard poultry and the then more highly esteemed rabbit. The number of kites killed in the 16th and 17th centuries was enormous, records revealing the volume of bounties paid: 411 in only twelve years at Tarporley in Cheshire and 428 over a similar period in the parish of Tenterden, Kent.

After that the kite suffered the same fate as most other British raptors — relentless persecution by gamekeepers and egg and skin collectors. Middlesex was probably the first English county to lose the kite completely as a breeding species, in about 1777, and the last probably Shropshire in 1879, though there are records of a Devon nest in 1913 and one in Cornwall in 1920. No doubt there were other isolated nests at about this time.

The extermination was probably even faster in Scotland. In 1875, 105 were killed on the Callander Hills alone, and by about 1890 they had been eliminated from the whole country. However, there may have been a temporary recovery during the 1914–18 war, when keepering was in abeyance; the kite was said to have bred in Glen Garry in 1917, as well as being seen in other counties.

It is said that the kite was only ever a vagrant in Ireland, though some writers, such as Smith in his 1749 history of Cork, maintained it was once common there. So it was in Wales alone that it struggled on as a breeding species, though even there it had been eliminated from most areas by about 1850. In 1905 there were perhaps nine, certainly no more than twelve kites left in Britain, in the upper Towy Valley, and it is only because of huge effort by private individuals who first provided protection, then later the RSPB with sophisticated electronic equipment, that the bulk of egg-thieves have been kept at bay. There have been many setbacks, such as poor breeding due to loss of rabbits through myxomatosis in 1954–5 and toxic chemicals in 1963–4; but by the mid-1980s there were 46 pairs, and in 1991 a record 76 pairs fledged 62 young.

Egg-collecting remains a serious problem: between 1900 and 1947 21 (23.6 per cent) of 81 known nests were robbed. For 1960–9 this fell to 9 (5.5 per cent) of 165 nests, rising to 23 (8.2 per cent) of 281 during 1970–9, and up again to 40 (10 per cent) of 401 during 1980–9. This represents a very serious setback, as Welsh kites have a particularly low productivity rate, probably related to poor spring weather. In addition, it could be that isolation has led to loss of vigour through inbreeding. An increase in kite numbers in the 1960s coincided with major afforestation of the Welsh uplands, perhaps because of the concomitant increase in vole numbers; in the long-term, however, the spread of mature forestry may be bad for kites because it precludes sheep carrion, the most important winter food in Wales.

In the mid-1980s the Kite Committee was increasingly concerned about continuing poor productivity — only 25–30 per cent of all eggs laid resulted in fledged birds. So in 1986 they decided to take some wild eggs for artificial incubation, the young produced being returned to kite nests at about ten days old. This has had limited success.

To try to overcome the many problems associated with isolation of the Welsh

OPPOSITE
The red kite is distinguished by its long, forked tail

RED KITE

kites, and to encourage natural recolonisation of former parts of the species' range, in 1986 the Nature Conservancy Council and the RSPB also decided to attempt reintroduction of the kite to more suitable areas of Britain. Thus on 13 June 1989, ten young Swedish kites were flown to Kinloss, Grampian, by the RAF. Six were released at a Scottish site and four at an English site, along with a single chick from Wales. After 35 days in quarantine cages, the ringed birds, fitted with radio transmitters, were released. For two weeks the birds relied on food placed in and around the cages, but then they started to venture further afield and feed independently. It was hoped to release minimum batches of ten birds annually at each site for the following five years. Thus in July 1990, nineteen young Swedish kites were released in Scotland, while eleven Spanish and two Welsh birds were released in England. The birds have been closely monitored and at the time of writing their survival rates have been encouraging.

Sadly, one of the first birds released was poisoned by a gamekeeper, but conservationists were pleased with the heavy fines that this evil man and four of his colleagues received, an outcome which reflects the growing public concern for one of our most threatened species. If the kite is to stand a sporting chance in Britain, then landowners generally must take a greater interest in their employees' activities.

Distribution, Habitat and Population

A world-endangered species, the red kite has a remarkably small range, breeding in only small numbers outside Europe, in North Africa and on the Canaries and Cape Verde Islands. In 1984 the Western Palearctic population was estimated at 5,500–15,000 breeding pairs, the great variance due to disagreement over the size of the Spanish population. Despite persecution, numbers are increasing in parts of Europe. Britain's breeding population, for long confined to a remote part of central Wales (some 3,000sq km within Dyfed, Powys and Gwynedd), has more than trebled in the last three decades, perhaps through better weather conditions.

Vagrants are rare and mostly occur in eastern and south-west England, where isolated breeding attempts have been rumoured. In Wales the Gwenffrwd and Dinas reserves were established specifically for the kites, being central to their distribution. The kite is a very rare vagrant to Ireland; a pair was present there in 1976 but did not nest.

Though tolerant of wide climatic variation, the kite seems hampered by Welsh weather, where the small surviving population is centred on fragments of ancient oakwoods in undisturbed upland valleys, up to about 400m. These woods provide roosts and breeding places, but hunting is mainly over nearby heath, rough grassland, relapsed farmland and higher moorland, especially where sheep are carried. Lowland pastures, wetlands and meadows divided by hedgerows and spinneys are used mainly in mid-winter. Rubbish tips and main roads with wildlife fatalities also attract them, especially in winter.

In 1988 there were 67 pairs (48 laid eggs and fledged 38 young) plus at least 40 unmated individuals; the April population was about 174, and in August at least 210.

In 1990 63 pairs raised 70 young despite eight nests being robbed. In 1991 a record 76 pairs nested, but only 62 young fledged in difficult weather conditions. In addition there are the survivors of the release scheme.

Field Characters and Anatomy

Easily identified by its cruciform silhouette and long, forked tail, one of the longest of any British bird; also, with its long wings, relatively slender body and great flying skills, it is one of the most elegant hunters. In Britain there is little likelihood of confusion with any other species. Sexes are similar and there is no seasonal variation. The juvenile resembles the adult, but with more boldly patterned upperwing, paler body and less contrasting underwing. Full plumage is acquired at two years.

The flight is buoyant and effortless, tail and wings being used freely and independently to catch every nuance of wind. Soaring is frequent, usually with the wings slightly raised and held forward, but in gliding the 'hands' are slightly drooped and the wings angled back. Wingbeats are deep, elastic and slow, with noticeable body movement like that of a tern. It also hovers. In contrast, it is awkward on the ground, with a shuffling, bouncing walk or hop. Perched birds are upright, the tail depressed.

Breeding

In migrant populations, the monogamous pair-bond is probably mainly of seasonal duration, but among resident birds, such as those in Wales, the attachment is loosely maintained in winter, especially when the breeding territory is still occupied. First breeding is at 2–3 years. Display begins with high circling over the nest area during fine weather in January or February, but more commonly in March and early April. Sometimes a flock may circle together (in spring or autumn), but it is not known if this relates to pair formation. Pairs may also indulge in flight-play, chasing each other, tumbling with closed wings and occasional cartwheeling with interlocked talons. There is also a slow pursuit flight with

RED KITE

The female is only slightly larger than the male (up to 5 per cent). Length 60–66cm (23.6–26.0in), wingspan 175–195cm (69–77in), wing 44.8–53.5cm (17.6–21.0in), tail 28–32cm (11–12.6in), weight 0.76–1.6kg (1.7–3.5lb) with significant seasonal variation.

Most red kite pairs have several nest-sites which are re-used according to success in previous seasons

exaggerated wingbeats. In courtship feeding the male places prey on a branch or even the nest, and the female moves across to take it.

In Wales the nests are usually well dispersed — about 3–5km (2–3 miles) apart — mostly in the hanging woodlands of the valley sides, and built in the main fork or the fork of a main side branch of a tree (92 per cent of 228 nests in hardwoods). Sometimes the base of an old buzzard's or raven's nest is used. Most pairs have between one and five nest-sites, some of which can be in use for a very long time: one was used for seventeen successive seasons, although interrupted tenancies can exceed a century. Re-use is related to success in the previous year. A new nest measures about 45–60cm (18–24in) across, and up to 30cm (12in) high, but with re-use can become massive. The male brings most of the sticks for the female to do most of the building, chiefly in the early morning and evening. The nest is an untidy affair and long ago, when the species was common about towns, it was renowned for incorporating all sorts of oddments. In *The Winter's Tale* (Act IV, Sc 2) Shakespeare wrote: 'When the kite builds, look to lesser linen', indicating that the bird was a great nuisance to the washerwoman. J.E. Harting gave a good example in a Huntingdonshire nest: 'the lining consisted of small pieces of linen, part of a saddle-girth, a bit of harvest glove, part of a straw bonnet, pieces of paper, and a worsted garter'. Today the lining is more likely to be sheep's wool, and the decoration scraps of polythene — but not greenery, as is the habit of other raptors.

Incubation, mostly by the female, begins with the first egg and takes 31–32

The single clutch of 1–3 (rarely 4 or 5) eggs — average size 57 × 45mm (2.2 × 1.8in) — is usually laid in early April at 3-day intervals. Of 92 clutches, 76 per cent were of two eggs, 18 per cent three and 6 per cent one, but four and five have been recorded. Replacement of lost clutches is mostly complete by the first week of May.

days, a typical clutch of three taking 38 days. Hatching is asynchronous. During the early part of the breeding cycle, kites are very susceptible to disturbance by unfamiliar intruders, so the eggs are often deserted or eaten by crows.

Recent RSPB research using small video cameras has revealed that nestlings do sometimes kill each other, probably as a result of insufficient food. Others die through the wet and cold which characterise Welsh spring weather, or succumb to infections through eating putrid meat at this vulnerable stage. During the first fourteen days the male provides for the whole family, his mate tearing the food to pieces for the young. Fledging can be very long — anything from 48 to 70 days, according to food supply and disturbance. Once airborne, the young become independent in about a month. Welsh kite productivity is disappointingly low — averaging only 0.5 young per territorial pair each year, and less than half that in mainland Europe. Fortunately kites are relatively long-lived birds — one of 26 years has been recorded — and this has aided their survival in Wales.

Diet and Feeding Behaviour

The kite takes a wider range of foods than any other European raptor, and it is not particularly fussy whether they are dead or alive. Birds, mammals, reptiles, amphibians, fish, invertebrates and carrion are taken in varying proportions according to local abundance and availability, varying with the seasons and among individuals. Birds include chickens (live and dead), starling, thrushes, partridge, pheasant (live and dead), doves, skylark, sparrows, magpie (including nestlings and eggs), crows, lapwing, and even rooks and blackheaded gulls which come too near. It is also fast and agile enough to steal prey from other birds, including peregrine, goshawk, osprey, white-tailed eagle, hobby, heron and crows. Most vulnerable are young birds and those feeding in open country. Mammals taken include voles (mainly short-tailed), mole (twenty-two were found in one nest), hares (mainly young), mice, brown rat, shrews, rabbit, and as carrion, sheep, deer, cow, pig, horse, fox, dog, squirrel, polecat, stoat, weasel and hedgehog. Reptiles include lizards, snakes and slow-worms, and amphibians frogs and toads. Fish taken are mostly dying or injured, if not dead, and include trout, eel, perch, pike, carp, tench and roach. Invertebrates include earthworms, grasshoppers, beetles and butterflies, some insects being taken in flight, but more commonly on the ground. Country rubbish dumps are favourite foraging grounds, and offal from slaughterhouses was an attraction before regulations were tightened up. Roadside fatalities are often taken.

Hunting is mostly by soaring in circles over open ground at widely varying heights, or low gliding. The approach to carrion is cautious, descending in tightening circles or walking slowly, and most prey is caught by surprise rather than in a chase, generally in a steep dive and landing with feet outstretched. Sometimes it hovers briefly or drops from a perch. Small prey may be plucked and eaten in flight, but most food is taken to the nest or a plucking station. Unusually, most kills are made with the beak rather than the talons: yet the beak is weak for a scavenger, and in fact the kite has to rely on other predators such as foxes and ravens to open the carcases of larger mammals.

Welsh studies have found that the single most important item throughout the year is sheep carrion, especially in late winter and early spring, when food is scarce. This is very different from the pattern among other European kite populations, probably because mid-Wales is the most intensive stock-rearing area in Europe.

RED KITE

A very quiet bird, generally heard only near the nest or at assembly places outside the breeding season. The commonest call is a shrill, buzzard-like mew, quickly repeated; this gave rise to its old name, 'whew'.

RED KITE

Migration, Movements and Roosting

In some parts of its range the red kite is migratory, but the Welsh breeding population is largely sedentary. Only young birds sometimes move for the winter, mostly south-east into England, but they generally return in the spring, though a few may wander around for a year or two before going back to Wales. In addition, a small but increasing number of Continental vagrants visit Britain, from Devon to Scotland. One German bird was recovered in the Welsh breeding area. The birds liberated in the reintroduction scheme since 1989 have wandered extensively, north and south. Some dispersed birds may settle in small areas for long periods before returning to the breeding area.

Like their Continental cousins, Welsh kites are gregarious, often forming groups (up to twenty-two have been reported) to exploit food sources or roost, mainly outside the breeding season. All known night roosts are in trees, the male near the nest during the breeding season, and they prefer those near woodland edge or close to breaks in the canopy. Hedgerow trees and spinneys are also used. Some roosts are used throughout the winter and over many years. The approach to a roost is often very cautious, birds slipping from tree to tree in the deep dusk. In poor weather they may remain in their roosts all day, sometimes in special loafing places.

HEN HARRIER
Once known as: *from male plumage* – blue hawk, blue kite, blue sleeves, white hawk, white aboon gled, grey buzzard, miller; *from female plumage* – ringtail, brown gled, brown kite; *various* – faller, katabella, moor hawk, dove hawk, dove-coloured falcon, furze kite, vuzz kite, gorse harrier, seagull hawk, hen driver, hen harrow(er) and flapper

HEN HARRIER
(*Circus cyaneus*)

Perhaps more than any other British raptor, this species has suffered very mixed fortunes at the hand of man in recent centuries. After decades of destruction and decline, it responded well to protection and fortuitous habitat changes, but even now it is the focus of conflict between conservationists and a tiny minority of gameshooters. Yet this is one of the world's most fascinating raptors, the males having acquired an extraordinary taste for many 'wives'.

History and Conservation

The hen harrier has not been found in prehistoric deposits and its early status is uncertain, but there is little doubt that it made steady gains as widespread forests were cleared to make way for large areas of rough grazing and heathland. Innumerable references in literature and the wide variety of local names indicate that it was widespread and common enough to be regarded as vermin over much of the British Isles from the 16th to 18th centuries.

Major decline started in the late 18th and early 19th centuries, with enclosure of fields, loss of 'wastes' to agriculture, and drainage of much suitable habitat in southern England. In the north and west this harrier was shot and trapped mercilessly as yet another 'hook-beak' competitor of sheep farmers and grouse keepers, whose numbers and range increased every year. By the 1860s it was gone from much of lowland England and the Scottish lowlands, but it was still abundant in the Highlands and Scottish islands, parts of southern Ireland and a small area of Antrim. Thereafter it was all downhill as agriculture intensified and pushed its uniformity north and west and sportsmen with more efficient guns 'tamed' the last wildernesses. In mainland Britain, some of the last recorded breedings were in 1893 in Devon, in 1899 in Northumberland, and in 1902 in Wales. By 1900 the only viable breeding populations were in Orkney and the Western Isles, places where there was no significant sport, though in Kintyre and Arran there may have been a nucleus up to the 1914–18 war. Small numbers continued in south-west Ireland and Antrim, and there was sporadic breeding in many other counties, though eastern England was virtually deserted.

With keepering and heather burning largely suspended during World War II, and increased afforestation of the uplands, the species was able to recolonise much of mainland Scotland in the 1950s. In the 1960s a few pairs started to breed in northern England and Wales, but subsequent spread there has been limited, unlike in Scotland, where there were further sharp increases in the 1970s with continuing controversial afforestation of uplands. It is remarkable that there were significant gains during the 1950s and 60s when other raptors were declining through use of chemicals.

More recently there appears to be stability or even decline in some areas, and there is considerable disagreement over numbers. There is no doubt that many of the young plantations which once encouraged the hen harrier have now matured into forest blocks with — for the birds — little hunting value. Even in Orkney numbers have declined, as the drainage and re-seeding of heather moorland with grass has destroyed much prime habitat.

Hen harriers continue to be persecuted on some grouse moors, where they are shot and poisoned or have their nests stamped on. Clearly this is illegal and inexcusable as no amount of extra game in the bag is worth the life of even one harrier. It must be said, however, that the great majority of gameshooters adopt a positive, custodial attitude towards harriers and, indeed, many sporting estates offer the relative seclusion and suitable habitat which are increasingly hard for birds of prey to find. Just as some birdwatchers exaggerate harrier persecution, so some shooters exaggerate harrier predation on grouse. But whatever the truth, calls for legalised culling of this threatened bird must be stoutly resisted. The RSPB has said that it is not opposed to grouse shooting, but it has quite rightly stressed that the short-sighted killing of a few harriers, which is unlikely to have any significant impact on local grouse bags, will only bring the whole of shooting into disrepute. Sadly, a 1988 RSPB survey revealed the seriousness of this problem: on moorland managed for grouse, which is probably the preferred habitat, only about one harrier nest in four is successful in producing young birds. Elsewhere the figure is three out of four.

Sensible heather burning on a rotational basis should benefit harriers as well as grouse, in that it ensures the continuance of patches of tall, rank heather in which harriers like to nest. But the heather is also threatened by farming, being overgrazed and even eradicated in many areas. Yet the latest research is showing that by managing heather as a valuable crop, sheep and grouse can co-exist happily and leave room for harriers, too. Instead of being castigated for not being zealous in their duties, perhaps gamekeepers and shepherds should be paid a bonus for every raptor spotted by their bosses.

Even the Forestry Commission, whose plantations have both helped and hindered harriers, is now making more of an effort in their conservation. In 1988 they opened a special Harrier Watch centre twenty miles north of Inverness, and in the first two years over 10,000 people visited the hide to view the birds.

HEN HARRIER

In 1544, Turner stated that the 'hen harroer gets this name among our countrymen from butchering their fowls', 'harrower' and 'harrier' being variants of the same word. Thereafter a very wide variety of names developed, because many naturalists believed that the male and female were different species on account of their contrasting plumages, a conviction which persisted even into the 19th century.

HEN HARRIER

The number of breeding pairs varies considerably, with the rodent population, from year to year. In 1977 the British Isles breeding population was put at 750–800 pairs, but this may well have since declined to about 500 pairs. In the mid-1980s the number of UK breeding females was estimated at 450, a more useful gauge because some males practise polygyny. The most recent winter estimates are: England 300 individuals, Scotland 400, Ireland under 150 and Wales 50; together a significant part of the total European population.

Length 44–52cm (17.3–20.5in), wingspan 100–120cm (39.4–47.2in), wing 32.3–39.2cm (12.7–15.4in), tail 17–19cm (6.7–7.5in), weight 0.3–0.7kg (0.66–1.56lb).

Silent for much of the year, this species is often heard during the breeding season, in the course of display and about the nest. The most common calls are of a chattering type and include a rapidly repeated *kee-kee* uttered at intruders, and a high-pitched, plaintive *pee-you* in display.

OPPOSITE
The male (upper bird) and female hen harriers have such contrasting plumage they used to be considered separate species

Distribution, Habitat and Population

The hen harrier occurs throughout North America and Eurasia and is resident and migrant in boreal to temperate zones, wintering in temperate to warm temperate zones. Decline has been widespread, largely through habitat loss, even though it is quite tolerant of man unless it is deliberately persecuted. It is flexible in its habitat requirements, which are governed by seasonal availability of prey, but it has a distinct preference for open, low-lying country such as rough grazing and heathland, moorland, marshes and boggy areas with high rodent populations. It has adapted well to young conifer plantations and cultivated areas. In winter it is more likely to be seen near inhabited areas and to use coastal marshes and sand-dunes. Rank heather provides ideal nest-sites, but new coniferous forests are also commonly used. The breeding distribution is centred on upland Scotland, Ireland and Wales, and bears no resemblance to the winter map which gravitates heavily towards the coasts, especially south-east England, the Midlands being shunned the year round. Since the mid-1970s it has become much commoner as a winter visitor to East Anglia and south-east England, especially on coasts. In southern Ireland recent decreases following major spread since 1950 have been linked to widespread maturation of coniferous forests and loss of moorland and bog to agriculture. The spread into northern England has been severely hampered by shooting interests.

Field Characters and Anatomy

When viewed clearly, the male's white rump and beautiful grey plumage, contrasting sharply with the black primaries, are unmistakable, though at a distance it is easily mistaken for a gull. The female (5–10 per cent larger) is harder to identify, but the white rump and banded tail (hence the old name 'ringtail') contrast well with the dark-brown upperparts and yellow-brown underparts. Old females may be very pale in the spring. The juvenile is very similar to the female, but the plumage is warmer, with an orange wash on the underparts, darker secondaries and noticeably pale edges to the upper wing coverts. Males differ until they are about three years old, but young females cannot be distinguished after about two years. Observation of habits and locality should always aid identification.

The adult male is sometimes confused with the male Montagu's harrier, but the more slender Montagu's has a longer tail, narrower, longer wings and darker plumage with more mottled upperparts, two long, dark bands on the underwing and no white rump. Separation of the females is very difficult as they have the same proportions and plumage, but in optimum conditions comparison of the head patterns is useful, the hen harrier lacking the pale throat of the Montagu's in both adult and juvenile. In typical harrier fashion, it flies close to the ground with wings raised high in both soaring and gliding, in a shallow V. More rarely it glides on flat or slightly drooping wings. With bursts of 5–10 wingbeats interspersed with glides, flight resembles the marsh harriers, but the slightly smaller hen harrier seems lighter. Sometimes it hunts with constant wingbeats and no glides.

Breeding

First breeding is usually at 2–3 years, though one-year-olds sometimes breed, especially in years when food is abundant. Most pair-bonds are monogamous,

The single clutch (replaced after loss) is generally laid in April or May and is partly governed by prey availability, 4–6 eggs being average, but eight not unusual in vole-plague years. In at least some cases, nests with up to twelve eggs are the result of a second clutch being laid about ten days after completing the first. Eggs are laid at 2 to 3-day intervals (sometimes up to eight) and the average size is 46 × 36mm (1.8–1.4in).

particularly where isolated, but bigamy and polygamy are common in areas where nests are close, or even semi-colonial. Polygamy has been associated with achievement of peak numbers, but such activity is in fact bad for the population in that the successful fledging rate drops as polygamy increases. But as only older, more experienced males are involved, perhaps this is a classic example of the survival of the fittest.

The display sky-dance is both spectacular and impressive, the male climbing steeply to a considerable height in tern-like flight, whereupon he flys backwards, side-rolls or somersaults, and then enters into a steep dive, pulling out only just short of the ground. The sequence may be repeated as many as twenty or thirty times. At first the female mostly watches passively from a perch, but later the pair may soar together and she might roll over and show her talons to ward off the male's dives.

The nest is always on the ground, mostly in tall vegetation such as reeds and rank heather, occasionally in low scrub and rarely in the open. It is a low pile of sticks and available vegetation constructed mainly by the female, though the male gathers a little material from the surrounding area. On dry sites the nest may be as shallow as 5cm (2in) with a diameter of 30–50cm (12–21in), but in wet situations it may be up to 45cm (18in) tall with a 90cm (35in) base tapering to 50cm (21in) at the top. The shallow cup is lined with finer vegetation, often after laying has begun. Nest material is carried in the bill or feet, and the project may take anything from a few hours to about fifteen days.

Incubation is by the female alone (the male may exceptionally take over in her absence) and begins with the first, second, third or fourth egg; it takes 29–39 days per clutch. Hatching is mostly asynchronous and results in a considerable size difference between the chicks. During incubation the female is fed by the male in an unusual way: in response to his arrival call, she flies towards him, begging loudly, but just before they meet he drops the prey and she turns elegantly on her back to

Four-week-old hen harrier chick. Pre-fledgling mortality is relatively high

seize it in her talons before landing nearby to eat it or return to the nest to feed the young.

After about two weeks the young may leave the nest to crouch in surrounding vegetation, when the female may start to help with the hunting, but she alone continues to feed the young. Fledging usually takes 32–42 days, the male chicks mostly earlier than the females. Thereafter the female is left alone to feed the young up to independence, within a further 2–4 weeks. Pre-fledging mortality is relatively high, many deaths attributed to cold wet weather, especially where the female is paired with a bigamous or polygamous male. The young are not particularly aggressive towards each other and there is no evidence of fratricide, but age differences between chicks confer obvious advantages during periods of food shortage, when cannibalism occurs. In addition, many clutches are deserted due to polygyny and disturbance by man and stock, and losses through infertility can be as high as 36 per cent. Not surprisingly, production is very variable, the best investigated on Orkney being 0.7–2.2 (mean 1.3) young per clutch started in a comparatively dense population with much polygamy.

Diet and Feeding Behaviour

Although the most agile of harriers and able to take a wide variety of prey, the hen harrier is also the most specialist, with a marked preference for small mammals and birds overall, proportions varying with local and cyclical abundance. Voles are especially important, followed by mice, but in Scotland relatively few rodents are taken, young rabbits and young hares being prime targets in some areas. Birds taken are chiefly ground-nesting species in open countryside, including meadow pipit, skylark and buntings as well as starling, warblers, thrushes and the young of waders, pheasant, partridges and ducks. Reptiles, amphibians and insects are relatively insignificant.

In hunting rodents the flight is slow, the harrier often gliding for considerable distances with only the occasional wingbeat, systematically searching every tussock. When prey is spotted, the bird can turn on a sixpence, tail fanned, before dropping like a stone with outstretched talons. The slow flight enables it to make the best of its highly developed hearing, a feature of all harriers. Only rarely does it hunt from a perch.

When hunting for birds, the flight is lower and faster, though even then, flying birds are mostly ignored. The emphasis is always on surprise and the harrier uses every scrap of cover to best advantage, manoeuvring around bushes and hedges with the utmost dexterity. It also has the skill to rob Montagu's harriers, kestrels and short-eared owls of their kills. Generally it is a solitary feeder, but sometimes harriers form loose groups to exploit a food source.

Migration, Movements and Roosting

This is the least migratory of Palearctic harriers, few leaving Europe in winter, and in autumn it withdraws only from the northern parts of its breeding range. Most move south to south-west, the longest recoveries including a Finnish bird in England in March. The Scottish population is dispersive rather than migratory, the breeding distribution being loosely maintained in winter while there is general gravitation towards lowlands and coasts, some birds reaching England and Ireland as well as the Continent. However, these movements are complicated by

HEN HARRIER

surplus birds from recent increases ranging widely to colonise new areas. Winter visitors from the Continent are mostly found in the fens, river valleys and coastal areas of eastern and central-southern England. There was an exceptionally large influx during the snow and easterly winds of early 1979, when it was estimated that England alone held 753 hen harriers. It is interesting to note some differential movement of the sexes, probably related to size difference, in turn leading to differences in prey and habitat preferences. For example, eastern England winter records show a preponderance of 'ringtails'. In Wales most birds move to the coast during winter, but in milder Ireland there is little seasonal movement. The partially migratory North American race *hudsonius* is said to have occurred in Britain as a vagrant.

Night roosts are always on the ground, in grass or rushes, or on small mounds, though for a time after the eggs hatch the female generally roosts on or near the nest and the male sometimes uses one of several purpose-built platforms — small, circular grass mats. In winter, however, hen harriers often forsake their solitary roosts to gather in communal dormitories which always create a buzz of excitement among birdwatchers. These often contain ten or so birds, but up to fifty have been recorded (maximum thirty-one in Britain), the birds flying in singly from about 45 minutes before sunset to 30 minutes afterwards, leaving for their hunting areas (up to 16km [10 miles] away recorded in Scotland) within half an hour either side of sunrise.

MARSH HARRIER
(*Circus aeruginosus*)

MARSH HARRIER
Once known as moor buzzard, bald buzzard, duck hawk, snipe hawk, marsh hawk, moor hawk, brown hawk, bog gled, dun pickle, white-headed harpy, harpy, puttock and kite

Once persecuted to extinction in Britain, the marsh harrier has recently made remarkable gains, though it is still one of our most vulnerable breeding birds. But much of its new success is no mere accident, being largely due to the caring protection of sympathetic landowners.

History and Conservation

The marsh harrier's story typifies the sorry raptor saga of habitat loss plus persecution equalling major decline, but in this case there is a fairly happy ending. However, while the 'bald buzzard' has been saved in Britain, more recently it has been exterminated in other countries.

This is the only British harrier for which there are very early British records, from the Iron Age settlements of Somerset. A bird of fen and marsh, it must have been very common in the once extensive wetlands of lowland Britain before serious drainage got underway in the 17th century. By the late 18th century it was already relatively scarce as a breeder, despite remaining widely distributed, and gamekeepers and collectors would soon finish off the fragmented population remaining.

Scotland probably lost its breeding stock as early as 1800, and there were only a few records from Wales after this date. Nesting still occurred in many English counties in the mid-19th century when the harrier was still common on the Norfolk Broads, but regular breeding had ceased in much of northern and south-western England (the bird having been common in Devon in the 1830s) by about 1860. By 1870 it was restricted to one area of Broadland, and by 1878 the egg-collectors had sealed its fate in England. Only in Ireland, where there was a greater abundance of suitable habitat, did it linger on, in central and western areas. But even there it was rare by 1900 and the last recorded breeding was in 1917.

There were sporadic breeding attempts in the Norfolk reedbeds in 1908, 1915, 1919 and 1921, but it was not till 1927 onwards that several pairs attempted to breed annually, first under the protection of landowner Lord Desborough and subsequently the budding Norfolk Naturalists Trust. These Hickling and Horsea birds managed to hold their own, and then in 1939 the deliberate wartime flooding of coastal marshes for defence also created the ideal habitat for the species, and so it was able to spread into Suffolk for the first time in a century. Thus a painfully slow recovery began, with subsequent nestings in Anglesey (1945), Kent (1946), Hampshire (1950) and Dorset (1951). But there were many setbacks, too, notably in the 1960s when for several seasons Minsmere in Suffolk was Britain's only breeding site. The most likely reason for the reversal of trends was toxic residues in prey.

The species was greatly helped by the passing of the 1954 Protection of Birds Act, which did much to deter egg-collectors, and also by the severe east coast flooding of 1953, which fortuitously extended the suitable habitat. Behavioural changes may have helped, too. In 1942 polygyny was first recorded in this species in Britain and gradually increased, perhaps therefore allowing more females to breed. Also, from 1937 there were records of overwintering, especially among females — this meant they would avoid the hazards of migration, which included being shot in more hostile countries.

The setbacks of the 1960s were followed by recovery and expansion in the 1970s and 80s after the withdrawal of the persistent organochlorines which had caused eggshell thinning and reduced life expectancy. Britain's extremely low population (down to one pair in 1971) must also have been helped by immigration from north-west Europe — notably the Netherlands, where huge numbers are found on the reclaimed polders of the former Zuider Zee. But this infiltration of foreign birds was not possible till the Dutch harrier population, too, had recovered from the 1960s chemical blitz, and it was a similar story in Denmark and Sweden. At the same time protection improved throughout Europe.

The marsh harrier's future now looks bright: it has bred in seven English counties since 1973, and from 1983 the breeding population has increased at an average annual rate of 17 per cent. For the second time in a century the 'dun pickle' has come back from the brink, and it has broken out of its East Anglian stronghold to recolonise northern England, Scotland and Wales. Britain had twenty nests in 1980, thirty-two in 1984 and at least sixty in 1989, and although further expansion will probably be limited by shortage of suitable *Phragmites* reedbeds, some pairs have taken to nesting in arable crops, a practice they have followed for some time overseas. However, reserves such as Minsmere will remain crucial to the survival of this shy species, as the formerly quiet environment on many marshes has been transformed into a hostile and noisy one because of the increased mobility of the public and the demand for aquatic recreation areas. Where once only the occasional angler cast his line, now speedboats, water-skiers and yachtsmen shatter the peace; even the weight of birdwatchers and photographers can be a major problem. The species' tendency towards gregariousness

MARSH HARRIER

Yarrell suggested that the name harrier 'has probably derived from their beating the ground somewhat in the manner of a harrier dog hunting for game'. In 1843 he made the name 'marsh harrier' acceptable in adopting it from Selby, who in 1825 had altered the term 'marsh hawk', created by Edwards in 1760.

In 1988 at least 145 young fledged from fifty-six nests in seven counties, and the total British summer population was estimated at 160–185 adults.

MARSH HARRIER

may also be a limiting factor in the exploitation of suitable, but relatively small and isolated breeding sites. Finally, the persistent shooting of migrant harriers in southern Europe remains a threat to the species' continuing expansion.

Distribution, Habitat and Population

The marsh harrier is found throughout most of the Old World except in the far north, being resident and migrant in warmer boreal to temperate zones, wintering in warm temperate to tropical zones. It has disappeared from much of western and central Europe this century, although it has recovered in some areas. The small British population is centred on coastal marshes of East Anglia, summer and winter, with recent outposts in the Welsh Marches, Scotland and northern England.

For breeding it requires large, dense reedbeds around lakes, marshes and rivers, with good foraging nearby, though exceptionally it nests in cornfields, scrub and young plantations. There is a strong preference for shallow, standing, fresh, or brackish waters with extensive *Phragmites* reed, reedmace *Typha* and other dense emergent vegetation. Lower densities occur on fens, peat bogs, irrigated fields, floods, rough grazing and saltings, especially outside the breeding season. Where wetlands are limited it hunts more extensively over farmland, but it is very sensitive to disturbance.

About ten individuals remain to overwinter after the breeding season, many of the recent records coming from South Wales and a few from south-east Ireland as well as East Anglia. Most birds winter near the coast.

Field Characters and Anatomy

Length 48–56cm (18.9–22.0in), wingspan 115–130cm (45.3–51.2in), wing 37.2–42.6cm (14.6–16.8in), tail 18–20cm (7.0–7.8in), weight 0.4–0.8kg (0.89–1.76lb). The female is 5–15 per cent larger than the male.

The voice is rarely used outside the breeding season, and even then the adults are remarkably quiet, except in courtship flight, when there is a wailing or peewit-like call. The female receives prey with a high-pitched piping, and intruders are threatened with a chattering *kekekeke*.

This is the largest of the British harriers, about the size of a buzzard but more slender and with longer wings which have more parallel front and rear edges. Characteristic of the genus, the male and female are very different, the male striking, and readily identified from below by his black wing tips and pale-grey wings which contrast with his rufous thighs and dark-chestnut body. The much darker female and juvenile are uniform brown, mostly with a distinctive creamy head and inner forewing. The males vary a great deal from dark to very pale, reminiscent of a hen harrier, but they are always dark on the belly and vent. First-plumage juveniles do not usually have the pale forewing, and can be distinguished from completely dark adult females because they lack the pale area on the breast. The sex difference is clear after about two years, when the females acquire a full plumage, but the young males remain distinguishable for about three years. Young birds have the outer web of the fifth primary notched.

In typical harrier fashion, the bird soars and glides in low flight with the wings held in a distinctive V, and the light, elegant wingbeats are in short series of 5–10 interspersed with glides; the flight is similar to that of the slightly smaller hen harrier, but observation of habitat should help to identify.

Breeding

A few one-year-olds breed when food is plentiful, but first breeding is usually at 2–3 years. The mostly monogamous pair-bond is generally of seasonal duration, though some pairs nest together for several years in succession. Some of the oldest, brightest males are polygamous but this is mostly confined to bigamy, and where monogamy and polygyny occur within the same breeding group, fledging success differs little.

In courtship the male performs spectacular aerobatics over the nest territory and surrounding area, mostly on sunny days. He soars in high circles, sometimes flying with exaggerated, jerky wingbeats, calling occasionally. Sometimes he is joined by his mate, whereupon he dives down at her and she rolls over to present her talons.

Nesting is frequently solitary, although loose groups are relatively common now owing to the often restricted habitat; in areas of high density nests have been as close as 20m, but attempting to breed within about 60m of an established nest generally results in failure. In Britain there appears to be a preference for nesting near others, and the same areas — but not usually the same sites — are used in successive years. Only a small area around each nest is defended against the bird's own kind.

The nest is usually well hidden in the densest part of a reedbed or other thick vegetation in shallow water, and very occasionally on top of a coot's or moorhen's nest. The female takes about 7–10 days to build the substantial pile of sticks, reeds and grass that serves as a nest — its average diameter is 50–80cm (20–30in), height 25–30cm (10–12in) and cup 15–20cm (6–8in) across. Nests over water are considerably bulkier and taller, up to 70cm (28in) above the surface. Meanwhile, the male makes one or more platforms for resting and feeding. Both parents add material to the main nest during fledging.

The female generally incubates alone for 31–38 days per egg, usually starting

MARSH HARRIER

In Britain the average clutch of 3–6 eggs – average size 50 × 39mm (2.0 × 1.5in) – is laid in late May at 2 to 3-day intervals, but layings also occur in April and are commonly of up to eight eggs, though rarely as many as twelve. Replacement of the single clutch is usually restricted to five eggs.

The marsh harrier has a buoyant, elegant flight and occasionally hovers

Marsh harrier: the female is on the left (note the buff head), and the male is on the right

with the first, but sometimes the second or third, during which time the eggs are often stained by damp vegetation. The male provisions the female near the nest, but only rarely does he cover the eggs in her absence. Loss of clutches is very high: 19–34 per cent.

For the first 4–10 days the chicks are brooded by the female, who feeds them bill-to-bill, but later they feed themselves in the nest, often with considerable ferocity, especially if the female is not very attentive. During lean times the bigger chicks may kill and eat their smaller siblings. The male brings food in the characteristic harrier way, dropping it for the female to catch in the air or, more rarely, onto the nest. As the young develop, the female helps with the hunting, and she can rear the brood on her own if her mate is killed or deserts. After a month or so the chicks may scatter into the surrounding vegetation. They fledge at 35–40 days, whereupon the male soon leaves, but they usually remain with the female for a further 15–25 days.

In 1988 there were forty-six successful nests in Britain, with an average productivity of 3.11 young per nest. The fourteen females mated to bigamous males were not markedly less successful than the paired females, achieving 2.36 young per nest (compared with 2.55 for a total of 56 nests) and 3.0 young per successful nest, with three failures. During the period 1978–88, breeding females outnumbered breeding males by an average of 19.8 per cent.

Diet and Feeding Behaviour

Being larger than the hen harrier, the marsh harrier is able to take a wider variety of prey, but it shows a more marked degree of specialisation during the breeding season, when the ranging area is reduced and it must take advantage of local abundances. The concentration is on marsh birds and small mammals which are easily caught, the main hunting techniques relying on surprise rather than speed. The bird usually quarters flat areas at a height of only a few metres, always taking advantage of cover, sometimes hovering or performing impressive aerobatics before dropping with claws outstretched. Some prey is spotted from a low perch.

Few birds are taken in open flight and unsuccessful attacks in tight corners are quickly aborted, but over open water the harrier might pursue a quarry for some distance or exhaust it by forcing it to dive repeatedly. Birds taken include poultry, ducks, waders, coot, moorhen, water rail, gulls, young pheasants and partridges, and songbirds, especially their young.

Mammals include voles, mice, rabbit, mole, rat and leveret. Less important foods, though sometimes seasonally or locally significant, are birds' eggs and nestlings, fish, frogs, snakes, lizards and insects. Larger prey animals are usually sick or wounded or taken as carrion. Local prey preferences between sexes have been recorded.

Migration, Movements and Roosting

Apart from a small number of British birds and those in countries bordering the Mediterranean, regular wintering in Europe appears to be restricted to Holland and Austria. Most northern and eastern populations are mainly migratory, wintering in the Mediterranean and Africa — chiefly south of the Sahara, where some British birds have been recovered. Generally, overwintering in the breeding range is related to mildness of climate and thus prey availability, Britain's winter distribution (first record 1937) reflecting this. Migrants show little concentration at narrow sea-crossings, as typifies the *Accipitridae*. British birds migrate only through France and Iberia, and the period of adult departures is protracted, though mainly in September and October; some linger into November. Juveniles disperse in all directions from early August. Immatures often return to Europe for the summer but wander about a lot, as evidenced by the Dutch, Danish and German birds which have been recovered in Britain between April and September. Migrating groups may be of one sex.

Outside the breeding season the species is mostly solitary, except when roosting, though Britain's population is still too small to attract any significant gatherings. Like the other harriers, it always spends the night on the ground, but probably spends more of the day loafing than they do. Favourite loafing/look-out posts include fences, tree-stumps, haystacks and low trees. During the breeding season the female usually roosts on or near the nest, but the male often spends the night on one of his special platforms. Communal winter roosts are usually in tall vegetation, especially reedbeds, rushes and long grass. Such sites may be used for many weeks where undisturbed, and each bird has its own hare-like 'form'. The birds are silent at roost — they come in singly about half-an-hour after sunset, often having travelled considerable distances from their hunting grounds; they leave according to how far they have to travel, but it is generally before sunrise.

MONTAGU'S HARRIER
(Circus pygargus)

THE Montagu's harrier is the rarest of our breeding raptors and for a long time has been close to extinction in Britain, the north-western limit of its range; but its prospects have suddenly improved as the species has unexpectedly adapted to a new habitat.

History and Conservation

Unfortunately, there are no very early bone records of this species in Britain, nor are there reliable records in the early ornithological literature because of the confusion with the hen harrier. We can only assume that it suffered through extensive habitat loss to agriculture and development in the last few centuries. However, as it is at the limit of its range in Britain, we can also surmise that it is sensitive to relatively minor climatic variations and that it has never been common in these islands. Indeed, study of weather records appears to confirm this.

In 1850, Morris's statement fairly reflected the opinion of the day:

> Different views seem to have been taken as to the numbers of this bird among us. Mr Hewitson's account seems to me to be the correct one, that 'although at one time more abundant than has been supposed, it is now becoming rare, and exceedingly difficult to procure.' It has been met with in the southern and south-western counties . . . It becomes still less frequent towards the north, but appears to be known in Scotland, in Sutherlandshire, where it breeds near Bonar Bridge, and doubtless in other counties also. In Ireland it is believed that one if not more specimens have occurred, but none have been preserved.

From then on the species was destined to become increasingly rare as serious egg collectors sought the few birds left by raptor-hating gamekeepers.

At the beginning of this century there were generally only three or four nests each year, mainly on the Norfolk Broads. Oddly, just when it was almost persecuted to extinction in Britain, its range was expanding northwards. For example, it first bred in Denmark in 1900 and three years later there were 200 pairs there. By the 1930s there were 15–25 pairs breeding in England and Wales. Cessation of most keepering during the 1914–18 war undoubtedly helped, too, but the main encouragement probably came through climatic amelioration in north-west Europe during the first half of the 20th century.

Further abeyance of keepering during World War II gave another boost, and in the 1950s there was a sudden upsurge in numbers to at least 40–80 pairs as the centre of population shifted from East Anglia to south-west England. But from then on it was all downhill, and in 1974 and 1975 not one breeding pair was found, although a small trickle of passage migrants continued in most years. As well as habitat loss and increased disturbance, ringing recoveries implicated hunting pressure on passage birds in France during the 1950s, and in the following decade further decline was probably related to widespread use of toxic chemicals.

Ironically, it was farmland that saved the harrier from ultimate disaster: from 1976, English birds started to nest in growing crops, as Continental harriers had done for some time. However, this has brought new problems, as since that time virtually all the nests have been in autumn-sown cereals which are vulnerable to disturbance and destruction. Because Montagu's harriers breed relatively late, the nests suffer from crop fall (wind or rain causing the corn to smother eggs or chicks), spraying with toxic chemicals, and destruction by farm machinery. Sadly, in an instinctive effort to defend themselves when the combines approach, the young lie on their backs and often get their feet chopped off.

Fortunately, these problems can be overcome with the assistance of sympathetic landowners and farmers. When a nest is located, the RSPB endeavours to contact those reponsible for the land to arrange a care programme. In particular, about 7–14 days after the female is judged to be sitting tightly, the crop immediately surrounding the nest is very carefully trimmed back, taking great care not to leave the site unduly exposed. Drivers involved in spraying are warned about nest-sites, and when lethal sprays are used a request is made to avoid the immediate surroundings. (Exceptionally, suitably aged young have been temporarily removed from nests). Finally, when harvesting commences, arrangements may be made so that the areas of crop around nests are left standing, or recently fledged birds may be flushed into adjacent fields before cutting begins. Similar precautions may be necessary to save nests with eggs when grass is cut for silage in June. However, such measures have met with less success than was hoped for, because the small, uncut areas often have to be left for a long time, and so increasingly attract predators and are more vulnerable to crop fall.

Successful French conservation methods have involved removing chicks from nests prior to harvest and either placing them in nearby field margins or returning them to the nest-site and surrounding them with a few straw bales when the field has been cut. It is ironic that in the same country the fight to stop British migrants being shot has been difficult, and poisoning is still common in winter quarters, where the birds commonly roost on paddy fields sprayed with dieldrin.

Internationally, the Montagu's harrier population is declining and it is obvious that as the species increasingly uses agricultural land in lieu of vanished habitat, there will be greater reliance on the vigilance and goodwill of farmers.

Distribution, Habitat and Population

The breeding range of Montagu's harrier, in the temperate to warm temperate zones of Europe and Russia, has long been subject to frequent change, with much sporadic nesting outside the main areas. The species winters in subtropical to tropical zones in the Mediterranean, Africa and India. Unlike our other two harriers, it is exclusively a summer migrant to Britain, where its distribution has varied considerably in modern times, its breeding habitat overlapping with that of the marsh and hen harriers. Once largely confined to Norfolk, it now has a stronghold in south-west England. Basically a lowland species, it will breed in drier situations such as gorse-covered heaths, young forestry and sand-dunes, as well as marshes, and more recently it has concentrated on nesting in arable crops. In winter, wetlands hold less of an attraction. Intensively disturbed and densely settled areas are avoided at all times.

Field Characters and Anatomy

A very elegant and lightly built bird, Montagu's harrier is slimmer than the hen harrier, with a longer tail and narrower, more pointed wings, not unlike a falcon.

MONTAGU'S HARRIER

In 1990 the British breeding population had its best season for over thirty years. Thanks to co-operation from arable farmers in East Anglia and the South West, twelve nests produced a record twenty-two young. But in 1991 there were only five pairs as poor weather kept birds away.

Length 43–47cm (16.9–18.5in), wingspan 105–120cm (41.3–47.2in), wing 34.6–39.3 cm (13.6–15.5in), tail 16–18cm (6.3–7.0in), weight 0.23–0.44kg (0.5–1.0lb).

This is an exceptionally quiet bird, even during the breeding season, and is generally only heard around the nest. The calls associated with alarm and food are similar to those of the marsh harrier, the female uttering a piping *psee* when prey is delivered or the nest threatened. The displaying male has a rather hoarse, clipped and very shrill *kyek-kyek-kyek*, and when diving out of his sky-dance his wings produce a humming which is similar to, but louder than, the drumming of snipe.

Montagu's harrier feeding young. The species has a wide-ranging diet

The male's ash-grey underparts contrast with the black primaries and distinguishing bands on the secondaries, both above and below. Unlike the other grey male harriers, its upperparts are almost always mottled rather than uniform, but the darker male Montagu's differs greatly in shade of grey. The female is very similar to the female hen harrier, with pale yellow-brown underparts, longitudinal stripes on the belly, spotted wing-coverts, two distinct bands on the greyer primaries (compared with the hen harrier's three), and three conspicuous bands on the tail. In the rare melanistic form the male is brownish-black with a black head, tail grey-brown above and grey below, sometimes banded, primaries with a silvery-green sheen and secondaries pale-tipped. The melanistic female is dark brown, without a white rump, underside occasionally spotted orange-red, the secondaries, primaries and tail grey, the latter banded as usual. The normal juvenile resembles the female but the underparts are not striped, the bands on the darker underwings are scarcely visible and the head pattern shows more contrast. At two years old juvenile females can no longer be distinguished from the adults, but the young males can until they are about three.

The flight is typical of harriers, but even lighter than that of the other species, being almost tern-like, very buoyant, with slow, wavering glides interspersed with series of 5–6 wingbeats executed with such power that the bird appears noticeably to lift. In soaring and gliding the wings are held in a distinctive shallow V.

Breeding

The mostly monogamous pair-bond is generally formed for the first time at 2–3 years old, though year-old females are sometimes seen on the nest. There is no

The single clutch of 4–5 (range 2–10) eggs is generally laid from mid- to late May in Britain; replacements are laid after early egg loss. Average egg size is 42 × 33mm (1.6 × 1.3in) and the laying interval is 1½–3 days.

proof that the same mates sometimes pair again in successive years, but as there is a strong attachment to former breeding sites, coupled with scarcity of suitable sites in some regions, it is likely that some do. Polygyny is occasional, being mainly simultaneous or successive bigamy.

Pairing takes place on the territory. Courtship involves mutual high circling and flight-play and solo high circling, mostly by the male. High circling usually involves gentle soaring up to about 500–600m. Food passes are common. Sky-dances are typical of harriers, with varied aerobatics including diving, rolling and talon presentation.

Nesting may be solitary or in loose colonies with nests less than 100m apart. Recently, British birds have taken to nesting in standing crops, especially cereals, but other sites — always on the ground — are in natural tall vegetation such as grass and reedbeds, in young forestry plantations, and on moorland; exceptionally on open sites such as sand-dunes. Building takes about 4–5 days and is primarily by the female using material brought to the nest in the bill and feet. Any available vegetation such as twigs, reeds, heather and coarse grass is used to form a flattened mound with a height of 5–10cm (2–4in) and diameter of 20–30cm (8–12in), exceptionally to 80cm (30in), lined with finer vegetation.

Incubation, which begins with the first egg but may not be continuous until more are laid, is by the female alone, takes 27–40 days per clutch, 27–30 days per egg, and hatching is asynchronous; on one occasion a male was recorded sitting. Generally though, during incubation and while the chicks are very young, the male is restricted to delivering food for the female in characteristic harrier mode, mostly just dropping prey from the air.

The female broods the chicks continuously while they are small, sheltering them from the sun and rain till they are at least 25 days old, but from 21 days they may sometimes crouch in surrounding vegetation, perhaps creating paths or tunnels. Later, in the 32–42-day fledging period, the female helps to provision the young, which feed themselves from prey brought. Despite the marked size differences between the chicks, they are rarely aggressive towards each other; death of the smaller ones is usually due to food shortage. Independence is achieved about 10–14 days after fledging.

Production is often very low. During 1978–88 in Britain, the average number of young fledged from known nests was 2.2. In earlier studies 45 (67 per cent) of 67 eggs hatched in 13 nests, and 28 (53 per cent) of 53 young in 13 nests fledged.

Diet and Feeding Behaviour

Hunting is in typical harrier fashion, in low flight over open country with low or sparse vegetation, sometimes following natural features such as reedbeds or hedgerows. Foraging is carried out at a constant low speed, but when prey is sighted the bird can stop rapidly and change direction with great ease. Most prey is caught in a stoop, but fast-running animals are pursued, and the Montagu's catches more birds in flight than the other British harriers do. Sometimes hunting is from a perch, or even from on the ground.

Prey is mainly small, especially rodents. Mammals taken include voles, young rabbits and hares, shrews, and mice. Birds are mostly passerines from open country, including larks, pipits and buntings, but the young and eggs of a greater variety of ground-nesting birds, including partridges, are taken. Prey also includes lizards, snakes, frogs and toads, and large beetles and insects, especially dragonflies. Like the other harriers, the Montagu's uses its keen hearing to detect prey which would otherwise be very hard to locate in dense vegetation. The species has catholic tastes and the proportions of food taken vary with local abundance.

MONTAGU'S HARRIER

Migration, Movements and Roosting

This long-distance migrant is almost entirely a summer visitor to the west Palearctic, wintering in Africa south of the Sahara, with few winter records in Europe, as far north as England. British breeders arrive in April and depart September–October, travelling over a broad front; young birds start to move at the beginning of August. The small number of ring recoveries (mostly shot birds) indicates that British birds move through France and Iberia, south-west in autumn, north-east in spring. Passage migrants are mostly seen on the south and east coasts. Although it hunts mostly alone, it may congregate temporarily where prey is abundant, and two birds sometimes migrate together.

The night roost is on the ground, the male and female separate in the breeding season even before the eggs are laid. The female roosts with the young until they are about three weeks old, after which she roosts elsewhere in the territory, but the male may go up to 8km (5 miles) away throughout. Males and non-breeders sometimes roost communally, in long grass, standing corn, reeds or suchlike; each bird makes its own form, which is probably re-used on successive nights. Birds arrive about 30–60 minutes before dark from up to about 16km (10 miles) away, often alighting first on a nearby patch of open ground. Daytime loafing points may be on bare, open ground, fence-posts, mounds of earth, stumps and bushes, and in young trees.

COMMON BUZZARD
(Buteo buteo)

COMMON BUZZARD
Once known as puttock, puddock, bascud, barcutan, shreak, gled, buzzard hawk, goshawk, kite and bald kite

For centuries one of the most enduring and adaptable of European raptors, the 'scavenging' buzzard has not been a great favourite of man. In the 17th century Dr Johnson scathingly defined it as 'a degenerate or mean species of hawk', and in 1799 Bewick described it as 'cowardly, inactive and slothful'. But these supposedly educated men knew little of this marvellously adaptable bird of prey.

History and Conservation

Buzzards appear to have been widespread for a very long time, going back to the Pastonian Interglacial of the Early Pleistocene, some 1½ million years ago. However, it is almost impossible to separate the bones of this species from those of the roughlegged buzzard. But we can be certain that it was widespread and quite common in post-glacial times, extending its range considerably with the early, partial forest clearances because it evolved as a forest species and is most abundant in habitat where there are both trees and open space. A further boost came with the introduction of the rabbit, a major prey.

By the mid-15th century it was listed as vermin alongside many other raptors, as

COMMON BUZZARD

There are surprisingly few old local names for such a widespread and conspicuous raptor, but this is partly explained by its common confusion with other birds of prey. The current name comes to us via the French *busard*, known since the 12th century, itself deriving from *buson*, previously *buison*, going back to the Late Latin *buteonem*, the onomatopoeic syllable *but* being indicative of the call. When 'busard' or 'basard' entered Middle English (first record 1300), it ousted the Old English *tysca*. The spelling 'buzzard' dates from 1616.

a predator on poultry and the then-protected rabbit. With a price on its head throughout the land, it was the favourite target of bounty hunters who had the benefit of increasingly efficient guns — so much so that by the 18th century it was already uncommon in southern and eastern England. Its dramatic decline is well documented in old churchwardens' accounts, as these officials paid the bounties which peaked in the late 17th and 18th centuries.

Bounty payments ceased with the near disappearance of buzzards and kites in many areas, and with the enclosure of land for agriculture vermin control passed largely into the hands of gamekeepers, who in the 19th century set about systematic destruction armed with traps and poison as well as guns. Thus by 1850 the buzzard had disappeared from central and south-eastern England, where game preservation had become intensive. The species had become primarily a bird of western Britain, with outposts in the wilder parts of southern counties from Sussex to Somerset, inland Suffolk, Lincolnshire, north-east England, east and central Scotland and the extreme north of Ireland. Morris (1850) said that:

> In England, Scotland, Wales and Ireland it is sufficiently abundant, affecting both the wildest and the most cultivated districts, but in both taking a more than ordinary care to choose such situations as will either exempt it from intrusion, or enable it to have timely notice of the approach of an enemy.

But he also noted that it was 'gradually becoming more rare' due to 'The advancement of agriculture upon grounds heretofore wild and uncultivated, the natural consequence of an increase of population within a fixed circumference...' And in 1886 Atkinson wrote:

> I well remember as a schoolboy in Essex, some 30 years ago, that the nests of the puttock, as the buzzard was invariably called in that district, were more frequently found by us than those of any other wood-building hawk; and many a hatch of young puttocks it fell to my lot to see brought within the old school-gates.

But it was the skin- and egg-collectors rather than the child nest-pillagers who drove the bird from many isolated haunts, following the bloody trail blazed by keepers. By the 1880s it was gone from all Ireland, apart from a single pair which hung on in Antrim from 1905 to 1914. By then it was largely restricted to the New Forest, Devon, Cornwall, Wales, Lakeland, the south-west Scottish uplands, the west central Highlands and some islands.

Fortunately, the species was able to recover when keepering was mostly suspended during the 1914–18 war, and when peace returned, the changed economy fortuitously forced a reduction in the numbers of gamekeepers. World War II provided further respite, and steady gains were made in many areas except the intensively shot eastern counties of England and Scotland.

The 1950s brought very mixed fortunes. In 1954 there were about 12,000 breeding pairs, the Protection of Birds Act was introduced, and finally, much of the buzzard's former range was recolonised, including the extreme north of Ireland. Indeed, the population was thought to be the highest for several centuries. But then myxomatosis struck, and by 1956 had killed 99 per cent of the rabbits, the buzzard's main prey in Britain. Geographically the effects on the buzzard were uneven, but numbers subsequently fell in most areas because recovery in the 1960s and 70s was hampered by widespread accumulations of toxic pesticides as

OPPOSITE
The soaring common buzzard is distinguished by broad, rounded wings

buzzards turned to carrion instead of rabbits. By 1970, before the worst chemicals had been withdrawn, buzzard numbers had dropped to 8,000–10,000 pairs.

In 1983 it was estimated that there were 12,000–15,000 territorial pairs (ie breeding pairs plus territory-holding immatures) — very close to the 1954 peak. However, much of the expansion was mainly through infilling rather than pioneering into new districts, and recolonising much of the former range appears to have been severely hampered by persecution. Nevertheless, periodic outbreaks of myxomatosis have been of decreasing importance as the buzzard has learnt to exploit alternative prey — though it will be interesting to see if the dramatic increase in rabbit numbers during 1988–91 has any significant effect on the buzzard population over the next few years.

Afforestation of the uplands has brought mixed blessings for the buzzard. There is no doubt that the spread of conifer blocks has hampered recolonisation because former hunting grounds have been smothered, but mature trees can be valuable in providing colonists with new breeding opportunities where food is abundant but nest-sites scarce. The trees can also be valuable in reducing persecution by concealing previously exposed crag nest-sites. It is very much a question of getting the balance right in each area.

Throughout much of its international range, this robust predator has already responded well to reduced pressure from shooting, becoming less shy and faring well in the vicinity of man. This is especially important because the bolder and the more enterprising have access to more food sources, such as game and other wildlife killed by traffic, and therefore have a greater chance of survival in winter.

Distribution, Habitat and Population

The buzzard has an extensive Old World range, breeding in boreal to temperate zones, from the Azores and Cape Verde Islands, through Europe and central Asia to the Soviet Far East and Japan; and wintering in western temperate to warm temperate zones, some into Africa and southern Asia. Heavy persecution has caused extensive range reduction throughout the west Palearctic, but there has been recent local recovery, Britain providing one of the bright spots. The population of the British Isles remains largely confined to south-west England, Wales, the Lake District, central and western Scotland and some islands, places where the habitat is diverse. Recent advance eastwards out of Wales, Somerset and Hampshire has been surprisingly slow. British distribution changes little the year round, though there is gravitation to lower ground, related to food supply, in winter. Irish birds, too, are sedentary, being largely confined to the far north. Few birds breed in central and eastern England, where the number of winter sightings is also small.

The preferred habitat is a mixture of open countryside with rich foraging alongside copses, larger woods and crags for nesting, such as that found in the valleys of Wales and the farmland of south-west England and Lakeland. Extensive tracts of forest, moorland and mountain support few birds. Unusual among lowland birds of prey, it does not appear to be significantly restricted by areas of high rainfall, but there is a preference for areas which generate thermals and airstreams suitable for soaring, such as in valleys. Forestry plantations provide useful foraging only when young. In winter the buzzard ranges more freely into treeless areas.

Ringing recoveries indicate that the greatest mortality occurs in January–May.

This is the second most common raptor in the west Palearctic, and Britain now holds an important part of the European population – probably at least 15,000 territorial pairs in the United Kingdom, including over 100 pairs in Northern Ireland, but only some 1–10 pairs each year in the Irish Republic since the 1950s.

Field Characters and Anatomy

Soaring and wheeling majestically and effortlessly in circles over hills and valleys, on broad, rounded wings raised in a shallow V, the common buzzard is easily recognised, especially as it frequently utters a loud, plaintive mewing. It is a very compact bird, with relatively short tail, large head and short neck on a thick-set body. The sexes are similar but the plumage is very variable, ranging from almost uniform dark-brown to almost white, but most commonly with warm- or dark-brown upperparts, sometimes with slightly paler wing-coverts, rump and base of tail in various combinations; the head, body and underparts also mostly dark but mottled and streaked with grey to tawny-brown, especially on the throat and upper breast, with dark rear edges to the underwings and tail and contrasting pale area on the outermost primaries. Young birds are generally paler, lack the sharply defined band at the edge of the tail, and the underparts are often clearly striped longitudinally, particularly under the wings. The head appears larger than that of the honey buzzard, which has a longer tail and wings with more rounded hand. Pale birds may be confused with the roughlegged buzzard, which has a distinguishing white tail with a broad, dark end-band.

When soaring, the wings are pressed distinctly forward and the tail well spread. In gliding, the wings are almost flat, but with the inner wing pressed forward and the primaries back, sometimes with the hand drooping and the 'fingers' clearly seen. Glides are interspersed with series of stiff, rather fast and shallow wingbeats. Sometimes it hovers when hunting. It is often very conspicuous because it frequently perches in prominent positions, such as on telegraph poles.

Breeding

First breeding is usually at 2–3 years old, though some yearling females breed. The pair-bond is almost always monogamous and is sustained over the winter by some sedentary pairs in well-defined territories held throughout the year. In such cases the pairing is long-lasting and probably for life. Lost mates are usually replaced in the following autumn or winter.

Territorial display flights are mostly at the start of the breeding season and are often spectacular, with much soaring and screeching. The birds often follow each other in level, flapping flight, the second bird copying the actions of the leader. High circling can involve one or both birds and sky-dancing includes repeated stooping and rising almost vertically; sometimes the higher bird dives at the other, which turns and parries with its talons — these are rarely interlocked, however, contact generally being confined to touching wings. Most displays take place in fine weather and are accompanied by frequent calling.

Being strongly territorial birds, buzzards usually nest well apart: 1.3–1.9km in a New Forest study of fifty-four nests, but where breeding density is high — such as in parts of south-west England and Wales — they may be as close as 100m. Each defended territory usually contains several nest-sites (up to fifteen recorded) and the same territories are often occupied for many years by one or successive pairs. Territory size seems to vary little with habitat despite varying population density, but is generally relatively small; for established pairs, it may average 50–250ha (123–617acres), the distribution depending on the availability of suitable nest-sites. In Britain, the mean density in ideal habitat is one pair per 1.6km^2 (0.6 square miles).

Length 51–7cm (20.0–22.4in), wingspan 113–128cm (44.5–50.4in), wing 36.8–41.9cm (14.5–16.5in), tail 16–18cm (6.3–7.0in), weight 0.4–1.4kg (0.94–3.0lb), both sexes being heavy in winter and losing about 20 per cent of their weight during the breeding season. The female is 5–10 per cent larger than the male.

The most common call, the *mee-ooo*, is far-carrying and often draws attention to the bird in flight. The vocabulary is quite small but is used freely throughout the year, especially during the breeding season. Variations of the prolonged mewing are similar in both sexes, but with considerable individual variation, sometimes quite husky.

COMMON BUZZARD

The single clutch (replaced on loss but with fewer eggs) shows great variation in number and egg size throughout the range. In Britain the average is 2–4 (range 1–6) laid at 2/3-day intervals and measuring 55 × 44mm (2.2 × 1.7in), but studies have given a mean clutch size ranging from 2.7–2.96 for northern Scotland to 1.9 in southern England.

In 1886 Atkinson said: 'The buzzard seems to think there is a deal of sound sense in the saying "Foolish birds build fine nests for wise hawks to live in them", and acts accordingly.' However, the species does not seem to use the nest of another species, such as a crow, very often. Nest-sites are probably changed according to success, continuous use in up to fourteen successive seasons having been recorded. Tree sites are most common, usually at a height of 5–25m (16–82ft.) and close to the main trunk, supported by one or more branches. Where trees are scarce or absent the nest may be on a rocky crag or ledge, or exceptionally on steeply sloping ground. In most years a new nest is built, but sometimes an old one is renovated. Both sexes build the substantial structure of sticks, heather and other vegetation, whose shallow cup is lined with finer vegetation, roots, twigs with green leaves and even wool. The average size of a new nest is 1m (39in) across and 60cm (24in) deep, but a re-used nest may have a diameter in excess of 1.5m (60in).

Incubation is by both parents when the male will sit for part of the day only, or by the female alone, and takes 36–38 days per egg in Britain, 33–35 days in Europe. It begins with the first or second egg and hatching is asynchronous.

The chicks remain in the nest for 50–55 days, being cared for mainly by the female, who broods them almost continuously for the first week, and they are not left alone until they are about two weeks old. At first, the female feeds them bill-to-bill with food brought by the male, but by 25 days both hunt and provision the young, which can feed themselves at about 30 days. With this considerable variation in their size, the smaller chicks will die when food is very short. Inter-sibling aggression is recorded and cannibalism is said to be frequent, but fratricide is thought to be rare. Independence is achieved about 40–55 days after fledging, but in some areas, including the New Forest, families may stay together for up to 4½ months after fledging. Some dispersed juveniles are subsequently fostered in response to food-begging flights.

Production various considerably according to food supply and human interference. In a study of 645 British nests, 83 per cent of 146 failures were probably due to human interference; and of 187 eggs laid in 63 Scottish nests, 94 per cent hatched and 89 per cent resulted in fledglings.

Month-old buzzards at nest with remains of prey, including a lamb's leg, jackdaw and cuckoo feathers

Diet and Feeding Behaviour

In 1799, Bewick wrote: 'This well-known bird is of a sedentary and indolent disposition; it continues for many hours perched upon a tree or eminence, whence it darts upon the game that comes within its reach'. Today little has changed, and the buzzard — the most familiar of Welsh raptors — differs from our other diurnal birds of prey in that it hunts mostly from a perch, gliding down swiftly to seize prey in its talons. Sometimes it glides, flaps slowly, or hovers over its favoured open habitat, or it may walk about awkwardly on the ground in search of invertebrates; but it is enterprising, too, and groups of ten or more may gather to exploit a food source, such as the worms or beetles exposed in a newly ploughed field.

The buzzard takes a wide range of prey, but it is not a fast bird and must concentrate on relatively slow-moving birds, reptiles, amphibians and larger insects as well as small rodents. However, despite its slothful reputation, most food is taken by active predation and scavenging is of lesser importance. Carrion appears to be more important in winter.

Mammals taken include rabbits, young hares, moles, rats, voles, mice, shrews, squirrels, and weasels. Before myxomatosis the rabbit was probably the most important prey in Britain, but since the disease took hold the buzzard has learnt to exploit other prey, notably voles, and there is always considerable local and seasonal variation. For example, in severe winters with prolonged snow cover when voles are hard to locate, more birds are taken. In summer these are mainly the young of songbirds such as larks, buntings, finches, tits, woodpeckers, thrushes and starlings, and to a lesser extent those of larger species such as crows, partridges, pheasant, doves and woodpigeon. Stoops on adult birds such as the woodpigeon and grouse are known, but are unusual.

The importance of reptiles and amphibians varies greatly with local abundance. Snakes, lizards and slow-worms are common prey, as are frogs and toads, which for some individuals can form a substantial part of the diet. Indeed, one of the buzzard's old names — 'puttock' or 'puddock' — derived from local dependence on amphibians, the Middle English word for toad being *padde*. Any fish taken are mostly those incapacitated through disease or injury or as carrion; a buzzard's carrion intake includes sheep and deer carcases.

Occasionally the buzzard is an air pirate, robbing smaller birds such as the merlin and sparrowhawk of their prey. Slaughter-house offal still attracts a gathering of buzzards in some areas, and the increase in wildlife fatalities on roads has provided further variety in many places.

Migration, Movements and Roosting

Although it is migratory in the colder, more northerly and eastern parts of its range, the common buzzard is resident in Britain. Indeed, it is very sedentary, studies having shown that only 26 per cent of British-ringed birds had moved more than 50km (31 miles), movements of 100km (62 miles) being exceptional. Small numbers have been recorded on North Sea oil installations. One Hampshire bird was recovered in France, but there have been no records of foreign-ringed birds in Britain. It is assumed that some Continental birds visit our east coast in response to cold-weather movements, but there is certainly no significant winter influx. Indeed, migrating buzzards rely on thermals and are reluctant to undertake sea crossings, so it is more likely that winter records in eastern Britain

are predominantly of British stock. However, there are substantial local cold-weather movements as small prey birds leave the bleak uplands and buzzards follow them into the more sheltered valleys and lowlands. Thus in winter the species is most common on land below 300m.

Roosting is usually solitary, but a pair or a family may roost close together after the young have fledged. Territorial birds tend to roost at 'home' even in winter when they are foraging far away. However, there are communal winter roosts, usually within or at the edge of a wood. Where there are no trees, crags or cliffs may be used. Usually at least one of a breeding pair roosts near the nest, but rarely actually on it after the female has stopped brooding the young. Birds go to roost late, in winter within about half-an-hour either side of sunset, and they may leave as early as one hour before sunrise to visit distant feeding grounds. Much of the day is spent loafing as well as looking out for prey, with the head hunched and underparts fluffed up, hiding the legs and feet, often on a favourite perch such as a rock, post or tree.

HONEY BUZZARD
**Once known as bee hawk
and honey kite**

It is unlikely that such a rare species ever acquired a widespread folk name, but among some ornithologists of the 18th and 19th centuries it was known as – perhaps more accurately – the bee hawk. The current name was coined by Willughby when he discovered wasp combs in the bird's nest, and it appeared in Ray's translation of his work in 1678. When Pennant adopted it in 1768 it became standard.

HONEY BUZZARD
(*Pernis apivorus*)

CONTRARY to popular belief this species does not have a 'sweet tooth', but for a large raptor it does have a remarkably specialised diet, concentrating on wasps and bees. Such specialisation increases its vulnerability so it is perhaps not surprising that this century it became temporarily extinct in Britain, in a climate where insects have varying fortunes.

History and Conservation

There are no British records of this species before the 17th century, and we can only assume that it has always been rare in this country, its range largely restricted to southern counties. But no doubt during exceptionally warm phases it was encouraged to spread northwards.

Hampshire appears to have been its favourite county for as far back as we can trace. The New Forest has probably been its greatest stronghold, and we know that it bred at Selborne in the 18th century because Gilbert White referred to it in his famous book on that village. He recorded its nest in 'a tall, slender birch-tree', but sadly the one egg was taken by a boy. We also know that in the same century it was common in France, because Buffon noted that it was 'frequently caught in the winter, when it is fat and delicious eating'.

Along with all other 'hook-beaks', the species featured on gamekeepers' grisly gibbets from time to time, but more significantly, because it was such a rare bird it was keenly sought by skin- and egg-collectors. As early as 1860 a clutch of honey buzzard eggs fetched £5, and a pair with their chicks made almost £40 — a huge sum in those days. Ten years before that Morris had observed that 'In this country many more specimens have been noticed and procured of late years than formerly, doubtless from more attention having been directed to the study of ornithology'. But presumably it was not that rare because he added, rather oddly, 'It is easily tamed'.

Nevertheless, persecution by collectors drove the bird to temporary extinction in the New Forest by 1870; though there were breeding records from Herefordshire in 1895 and County Durham in 1897 (possibly also 1898–9). Also, it was said to breed as far north as Aberdeen and Ross-shire in the 19th century.

This century it appears to have been extinct as a British breeder at various times, including the period 1911–23, though we cannot say for sure. However, it did nest near the Welsh border 1928–32 and in southern England in 1923 and 1932, several pairs having nested in the New Forest and elsewhere in most years since then. There was also a Scottish nest in north-east Fife in 1949.

In recent years there has been a small but encouraging increase in the number of honey buzzard sightings and nest records, all in England, perhaps encouraged by a succession of exceptionally mild years. Understandably their locations have been kept secret — except for one. A pair started to breed at Haldon Forest near Exeter in 1979, and when they were discovered by 'twitchers' in 1987 it became necessary for the Forestry Commission to protect them. However, the authority had the foresight to provide a wardened viewpoint, and in the first three years over 3,000 people visited this facility — as many as eleven other raptor species on migration have been recorded here, too. Fortunately, the Haldon honey buzzards do not appear to have been stressed by this attention, and raised twelve young between 1979 and 1989.

Sadly, the rare honey buzzard is in relatively safe countries such as Britain for only a short time each year. Much of its huge international population decline is due to hunting, and it is still shot in considerable numbers when on migration through countries such as Spain, Italy, Malta and Lebanon. Even protection has made little difference in some areas. Fortunately it does not appear to have been greatly affected by environmental poisoning because its main insect prey does not accumulate toxins to any significant extent. How much the widespread loss of favoured deciduous trees to blanket conifers has affected its numbers is not known, but mature softwoods seem to be acceptable for breeding. Honey buzzards show great fidelity to nest-sites, so it is essential that woods they use regularly are managed to maintain tall, mature trees. There should be no forestry operations within 200m of an occupied nest — artificial nest platforms may attract breeding pairs to new or safer areas of woodland.

Distribution, Habitat and Population

The honey buzzard breeds successfully right across Eurasia, in boreal to temperate zones, from Spain to Japan, wintering in southern Asia and Africa south of the Sahara. Its range has altered considerably in modern times, but how much this is due to climatic change rather than persecution is not known.

It is a woodland bird, concentrating in areas where its specialist food is plentiful, preferably deciduous forest, but also in more mature pine and spruce woods in the northern part of its range. It breeds in both large forests broken by glades and meadows, and in smaller woods where it forages along the margins.

Because it favours such dense habitat and is a secretive bird, it has almost certainly been under-recorded, especially as it arrives after the leaves appear. Numbers appear to fluctuate significantly with the weather, as wet, cold springs seem to suppress the reproductive drive. It is estimated that there are some 35,000 pairs in the European part of the USSR and 40,000 pairs or 153,000 birds in the rest of Europe. Densities are highest in dry areas where prey is more abundant.

In Britain in 1988 honey buzzards were reported from twelve localities, with a maximum of ten pairs but only one confirmed. However, information was witheld in order to preserve security in two important areas, and it was thought that the true population could be over thirty breeding pairs.

The British breeding range is concentrated in southern England, where sufficient insect food is available. Apparently it has never bred in Ireland.

Field Characters and Anatomy

Slightly larger than the common buzzard, the honey buzzard is sometimes reminiscent of a kite, to which it is more closely related. Its distinguishing features are the fine bill, small head, slender neck and long, often half-closed tail. Compared with the common buzzard, mature birds have narrower wings, more rounded 'hands' and a slightly greater wingspan. Unfortunately, the plumage, especially that of the head and underparts, is so variable it is often of little use in aiding identification. Perhaps the most useful pointers on typical individuals are the bold barring of the body, and the three dark bands across the flight feathers and tail – the species is unique in having two bands close together at the bases of the primaries and another across their tips. Pale birds resemble the rough-legged buzzard, but lack the latter's bold tail pattern. The sexes are similar, but the male usually has a slate-grey head whereas the female's is usually dark brown. The juvenile has less striking plumage and is often reminiscent of the common buzzard, in proportions as well as plumage. Young birds have a yellow cere like that of the common buzzard, whereas the adult's is blue-grey. Full plumage is acquired at about two years.

This species has particular adaptations to suit its specialised insect diet. On the forehead and lores it has small, dense, scale-like feathers which apparently reduce the possibility of stings, while the slit-like nostrils minimise soil blockage when digging. The bird may also have some internal immunity to venom. The small head is convenient for investigating confined spaces containing insect nests, and the slender bill has a gently curved upper mandible ending in a long point, which is ideal for securing insect prey. The feet are powerful and have thick scales and slightly curved, rather blunt claws of near-equal size and are therefore suited to walking about a lot and digging out nests.

The wingbeats are deeper and more elastic than those of the common buzzard, emphasising the longer wings. The honey buzzard cannot hover properly but is agile in woodland, using its long tail to steer between trees — this is reminiscent of the kite, which will also droop the primaries and twist the tail simultaneously. Whereas the common buzzard soars with wings held forward and upward, the honey buzzard holds its wings straight out and flat, and its tail is fanned. Its gliding is very characteristic, the wings more arched and often sharply angled back, and the hands depressed; when an old bird is gliding slowly, the rear edge of its wing is almost straight, whereas that of the common buzzard is curved. On the ground it walks about with horizontal posture, the head extended like a gamebird, its easy gait resembling that of a crow. It can also run.

Breeding

Relatively little is known about the pairing of this species, and it is not known how old they are when they first breed; however, the monogamous pair-bond is of at least seasonal duration, and some pairs use the same nest-site in successive years, returning to the former site together. Courtship display is most common during the birds' first 2–3 weeks here, including solo or mutual high-circling and sky-dancing. The male is especially active, flying steeply upward, pausing to beat his

HONEY BUZZARD

Length 52–60cm (20.5–23.6in), wingspan 135–150cm (53.1–59.0in), wing 38.6–43.9cm (15.2–17.3in), tail 21–26cm (8.3–10.2in), weight 0.4–1.0kg (0.96–2.3lb). With considerable seasonal variation, the female is up to 5 per cent larger than the male.

The honey buzzard is a very quiet bird at all times, with little – if any – noticeable difference in voice between the sexes. More musical than the common buzzard, it has an attractive, jingling flight-call which varies greatly according to the bird's emotions but is usually di- or trisyllabic, variously rendered as *glee-yee, whi-whee-uo,* and so on. A more unusual call is one which sounds like a piece of card held against the spokes of a bicycle wheel – it is uttered mainly by the male at the nest in response to danger or, more often, when relieving its mate or bringing food. One of the calls heard from the ground is like the *kuick* of a tawny owl.

OPPOSITE
The rare honey buzzard preys on wasps and bees and appears to be immune to stings

HONEY BUZZARD

The 2 (sometimes 1–3) eggs – average size 52 × 41mm (2.0 × 1.6in) – are laid at intervals of 3–5 days, and the single clutch is rarely replaced because the season is so short.

near-vertical wings rapidly several times, clapping them together over his back, then ascending further, as if climbing a succession of steps. There is also a descending version of the sky-dance in which height is lost through a series of plunges, the downward momentum providing the energy for periodic upward swoops with wing-quivering. The 'butterfly' display flight is often the first indication of this secretive bird's presence.

Breeding density is said to be related to the abundance of the main food — wasps, and British studies reveal well-spaced nests, never less than 3–5km (2–3 miles) apart. But this is hardly surprising in a country where the species is so rare. With only a short season at their disposal, the birds usually start nesting as soon as they arrive, in late May, and sometimes start laying within about eleven days. Both sexes build the nest, which is of variable size and usually 10–20m (33–66ft) up in a large tree — many species are used — in a fork or on a large side branch. Although the nest is mainly of twigs, it is easily distinguished from that of other raptors because the upper part, and occasionally the entire nest, consists of leafy twigs so that the structure appears as a mass of greenery. Even after completion, further greenery is broken off nearby trees and added to it. A new nest is completed in about 10–15 days and measures about 65–80cm (26–31in) across, by 25cm (10in) high, with a shallow cup; it can be much bigger when an old nest — sometimes that of a crow or common buzzard — is used as a base.

Incubation is mostly by the female (who probably sits all night), and takes 30–35 days per egg, a clutch of two typically taking 37 days. The particularly beautiful eggs were once a great prize for collectors.

For the first 7–10 days the young are brooded almost continuously, being fed bill-to-bill by the female with food brought by the male, who sometimes feeds direct. They are fed the combs of wasps and bees carried in the parents' crops and regurgitated. After about 18 days they learn to feed themselves, picking the larvae out of combs and tearing up other prey. At 35–40 days they hop around neighbouring branches, returning to the nest for food; by the time they fledge at 40–44 days the nest is littered with empty combs. They may return to the nest for a further two weeks or so to be fed, and independence is achieved at 75–100 days, by which time it is late August or September and time to migrate.

Productivity figures for Britain are too sparse to be reliable.

Diet and Feeding Behaviour

There is no doubting this bird's liking for wasps and bees. Morris recorded an instance of one forcing its way into a hole after wasps, getting stuck and being caught by a countryman before it could extricate itself; and Lilford said a woodman in Salcey Forest pulled one out of a wasps' nest when he saw its tail protruding. In fact the honey buzzard often digs to some depth — 40cm (16in) or so — until most of its body is underground, excavating with its feet and sometimes with the bill, too. Wasps are most frequently taken, then bumblebees, including the larvae and pupae as well as the adults. Some observers say that wasps are caught with the bill and their stings nipped off before eating; others maintain that adult wasps are rarely eaten, and are only killed to remove them. Pieces of honeycomb are eaten too, and cell walls found around nests are almost always chewed down, presumably providing the roughage that is not otherwise available from a high-protein, predominantly wasp-larva diet.

Wasps' and bees' nests are located by the bird when it is soaring or hovering, or watching from a perch. Generally the insects are spotted going in and out of the nest itself, although some are apparently followed over long distances. Free-flying insects are sometimes taken, while at other times the bird ranges widely on the ground. In Africa at least, suspended wasps' nests are sometimes snapped off in flight.

The proportion of insects taken varies with the season and location. At the start of the breeding season in Britain it is necessary to supplement the diet with other foods such as birds (mainly nestlings and eggs), small mammals, earthworms, beetles, spiders, frogs, snakes and slow-worms. Later, fruits and berries are also taken. The young are fed mainly on wasps and their larvae. In rainy weather, the adults turn more to frogs and birds.

HONEY BUZZARD

Migration, Movements and Roosting

A summer visitor to northern and central Europe, the honey buzzard winters in Africa, south of the Sahara, mainly in wooded equatorial regions. European birds arrive from mid-April to late May and depart from mid-August to the end of September, later birds generally being juveniles. It is a soaring species which depends on thermals over land to conserve energy, so on migration it concentrates where sea passages are narrowest; however, the tiny British population is unlikely to be concentrated much by the narrow English Channel, and in any case, the honey buzzard is more capable of sustained flapping flight than other large raptors. Birds moving north in June and July are likely to be non-breeders. Passage birds do not turn up anywhere in Britain with regularity, but a number have been seen on the East Anglian coast.

Mostly solitary, or sometimes in pairs when feeding, the species roosts in trees at night on passage, sometimes communally, and mostly in large woods. Breeding birds do not roost near the nest until building is complete.

ROUGHLEGGED BUZZARD
(Buteo lagopus)

O NE of only two diurnal raptors which regularly visit Britain in winter from more northern climes, the roughlegged buzzard tends to avoid man in its breeding haunts. However, birds from such wild places tend to be relatively naive (especially the juveniles) when in their more densely populated wintering grounds, and this has made them an easy target for gunners. Thus despite their scarcity, they very often turn up in old collections of stuffed birds. However, such specimens were often incorrectly labelled because the bird's feathered legs, which gave rise to its name, led to some early writers classifying it as an eagle. Indeed, the scattering of records from the late 18th and early 19th centuries is further confused because when the roughleg turned up in any unusual quarters it was generally reported in the press as an eagle.

ROUGHLEGGED
BUZZARD
**Once known as rough-
legged falcon**

History and Conservation

Britain is well to the west of the main migration route of this most northerly of Eurasian buzzards, but it is a regular autumn and winter visitor to eastern Britain,

where occasional invasions are related to the cyclical availability of food in the Arctic tundra. For example, there were notable influxes in 1839–40, 1858–9, 1875–6, 1880–1,1891–2, 1903–4 and 1915–16; then there were no more until 1966–7, when at least sixty-seven birds arrived between October and April. The last, in 1974–5, was the largest on record, with some 250 recorded on passage in eastern England in October 1974, and a subsequent wintering population of up to 100. However, it must be remembered that the number of observers has grown rapidly in recent decades.

Such cyclical movements related to food supply are in turn governed by weather, and as the incidence of irruptions seems to have diminished with climatic amelioration over the first half of this century, it is tempting to suggest that the species was much more abundant here in earlier, colder times. However, roughlegged buzzard bones cannot be separated with certainty from those of the common buzzard, so there are no definite Pleistocene records for it. There is no reason to suppose that it was ever common in Britain in post-glacial times, though it is likely that it was generally much more numerous during the 'little ice age' of 1550–1850, when not only was the incidence of severe winters much greater, but also the environment generally was less hostile to birds of prey. We do not know if the species has ever bred in Britain, but there may well be a niche for it in the far north, where the smaller common buzzard is scarce or even absent, especially in Shetland. Indeed, individuals are occasionally present in Scotland in June, and in 1980 one was seen displaying near Inverness.

Fortunately, much of the bird's northerly breeding range has been well outside the main zones of environmental pollution and persecution, but shooting and poisoning remain significant hazards in parts of its winter quarters, where it is more likely to encounter an agricultural environment.

Distribution, Habitat and Population

Except in irruption years, the British winter population is usually less than about twenty birds, and the danger of duplicated records is considerable because individuals cover a large hunting range. The Fennoscandian population, from which most British birds come, is generally over 5,000 breeding pairs.

This migrant breeds in the arctic to subarctic zones and arctic/alpine areas of Eurasia and North America, and winters in the temperate zone, which includes eastern Britain and especially south-east England. Some of the very few central and western British records may have confused the roughleg with pale-phase common buzzards. It is an accidental in Ireland.

The preferred breeding habitat is low-lying tundra or in the transition area between forest and tundra. In years with an abundance of prey it also breeds in woodland far south of its normal breeding range, but always near large, open areas with good visibility and low, rough vegetation rich in prey. In winter it moves into lower areas, cultivated as well as uncultivated, especially where there are plenty of vantage points when at rest. British haunts are mostly moorlands, coastal wetlands, dunes and open farmland. Forestry plantations, some quite small, have become important winter roost sites.

Field Characters and Anatomy

OPPOSITE
In most years the roughlegged buzzard is a rare winter visitor to Britain

At close range the species is readily identified by the legs, which are feathered down to the toes, and the eye, which is conspicuously larger than that of *B. buteo*. At longer range it may be distinguished from the slightly smaller common buzzard by several features: the white-based tail with black distal band, its greater bulk and generally paler head, usually a brown breast band, longer tail and wings, and

ROUGHLEGGED BUZZARD

Length 50–60cm (19.7–23.6in), wingspan 120–150cm (47.2–59.0in), wing 40.3–45.4cm (15.8–17.8in), tail 18–23cm (7.0–9.0in), weight 0.7–1.6kg (1.5–3.6lb), varying with the season and the part of its range. The female is only marginally larger than the male.

The main call of this generally quiet bird is a clear, ringing *mee-oo*, usually longer, louder and higher-pitched than that of the common buzzard, and once described as 'like the screaming of a cat'.

The single clutch has an average of 3–4 eggs, average size 55 × 44mm (2.2 × 1.7in); this falls to 2–3 in a year with little food (in particular, lemmings and voles), but rises to 5–7 in good years. Laying is from late-May to mid-June.

slow, more elastic wingbeats. The sexes are similar, but the male has 3–5 bands on the underside of the tail (4–5 upper) whereas the female mostly has only the broad distal band, sometimes with one other narrow band. The male's lesser wing-coverts are much darker and his secondaries have numerous cross-bands. The female's belly marking is darker. The juvenile resembles the female but has less contrast, much paler secondaries without the dark trailing edge, pale throat and front of breast, and a weak tail-band. Full plumage is acquired at two years.

In elegant and easy flight, the roughlegged buzzard makes full use of wind currents. The slow, loose wingbeats, its habit of hovering in search of prey, and the way it glides low on slightly raised wings, all give the impression of a harrier. In soaring, the wings are more raised than those of the common buzzard and pressed slightly forward.

Breeding

First breeding is probably at 2–3 years old and the monogamous pair-bond is of at least seasonal duration. Birds often arrive at their breeding sites together so it is assumed that they have paired in their winter quarters. When the food supply is exceptionally poor some pairs do not even attempt to breed. Courtship display begins soon after arrival, up to 3–4 weeks before laying, and is similar to that of the common buzzard, including soaring in high circles with wings and tail fully spread, soaring together with frequent calling, and sky-dancing involving repeated stoops and steep climbs ending in stalls with the body vertical. The roughleg is a vigorous defender of territory.

Breeding density varies greatly with the food supply, nests being as little as 1km apart in most favoured areas. Nests are often re-used in successive years, or several may be used in turn, situated in a tree where available, but more often on a cliff or mountain ledge or on the ground, usually with an overhang. A nest consists of a relatively small pile of twigs and any other available material, and has an average diameter of 60–90cm (24–36in) and height of 50–60cm (20–24 in), its deep cup being lined with moss and green vegetation. Both sexes build.

Incubation is almost entirely by the female for 28–31 days per egg, starting with the first so that hatching is asynchronous. Lost clutches are probably replaced.

The young are tended by both parents, but mainly by the female at first as the male does the provisioning of the whole family. At 15–20 days the chicks can tear their own food and are provisioned by both parents. Little is known about inter-sibling rivalry, but some fratricide is suspected in lean years. Fledging is at 39–43 days, but it is a further 20–35 days before independence is achieved.

Diet and Feeding Behaviour

Small mammals are the main food, often comprising 80–95 per cent of the diet, the chief species taken being lemmings and voles, secondarily leverets, stoats, shrews, squirrels and rabbits. In poor rodent years, birds become the most important part of the diet — sometimes over 90 per cent; they include a wide range of species, from buntings and young grouse, to gulls, geese and capercaillie, though the larger species are generally taken only as carrion. Less important foods include insects, fish, amphibians and carrion of larger mammals such as caribou.

In foraging, the species hovers at a height of about 10–15m, quarters the ground systematically, or stoops from a low perch with talons extended. It hunts with the flying skills of a harrier and is both quicker and stronger than the common buzzard, enabling it to exploit abundances of larger prey in its winter quarters, such as might be found at undisturbed rabbit warrens. Indeed, rabbits can be especially important in Britain, and during the influx of 1966–7 roughlegged buzzards took full advantage of the outbreaks of myxomatosis.

ROUGHLEGGED
BUZZARD

Migration, Movements and Roosting

As Britain is well to the west of the main migration route, only small numbers of roughlegged buzzards turn up regularly on our east coast on passage. However, in years of cyclical rodent prey abundance in the bird's Fennoscandian breeding range, many large broods are raised. Then, as prey numbers subside, there is exceptional dispersal as birds move out in search of sufficient food; as a result, relatively large numbers arrive in Britain, many staying at coastal localities throughout the winter. Such influxes are usually concentrated in late October and are over by late November; many of these visitors are immatures and are unusually tame. In poor prey years birds may turn up as early as August. A few midwinter arrivals have been recorded; the spring passage brings relatively few birds to Britain.

Generally the species is solitary or lives in a pair, but it is often gregarious on migration, gathering to exploit food sources, and roosting communally. Breeding birds roost on or near the nest. Some couples have been seen feeding and roosting together in Britain, using sites such as plantations and quarries. A Suffolk-based 'pair' regularly used the window-ledge of a large empty house. More crepuscular than the common buzzard, the roughleg often hunts in the deep dusk and goes to roost late. Daytime loafing places include rocks, dead trees and poles, but posts, bushes and small, sparse trees seem to be favoured in winter quarters.

PEREGRINE FALCON
(Falco peregrinus)

SINCE time immemorial man has been in awe of the peregrine. It is the Ferrari of falconry, the essence of poetry and the embodiment of wildness. Possibly the fastest moving creature on Earth, it is also one of the most widespread and successful of all birds.

PEREGRINE FALCON
Once known as blue hawk, blue-backed falcon, great blue hawk, spotted falcon, passenger falcon, duck hawk, sharp-winged hawk, great hawk of Benhulben, hawk of Cadia, gull-hawk, puffin-hawk, game hawk, hunting hawk, stock hawk, faakin hawk, goshawk, perry hawk, and tiercel gentle (male)

History and Conservation

The peregrine is well represented in our fossil record, but there is no reason to suppose that it was ever much more common. British records go back to the middle of the last glaciation, in Derbyshire, and to a Cheddar cave towards the end of the same period. It was also present on the South Wales coast during the early Holocene, when it was killed by man in Scotland, as it was in the Dark Ages. But when falconry was introduced to Britain between the 6th and 8th centuries the peregrine became so highly prized that it was afforded legal protection. Indeed, its nest-site was regarded as a valuable asset until shooting became the main sport of hunters, from the 17th century. Under the terms of their tenure, occupiers of land were often made responsible for the well-being of nest-sites,

PEREGRINE FALCON

Albertus Magnus of Cologne (1206–80) named this bird *Falco peregrinus* (foreign falcon) in about 1250, applying it to a young one which had been trapped after making a long journey from unknown parts. (The Latin adjective *peregrinatory* remains in our language, meaning wandering.) But before Ray anglicised the name to 'peregrine falcon' in 1678, many scribes simply referred to it as 'falcon', though there had also been earlier English interpretations, starting with *ffaucon peregryn* in 1386, the order of the parts denoting French origin. In falconry the male became known as the 'tiercel' ('tassel' or 'tercel') gentle' because it was about a third (a *tierce*) smaller than the female, known simply as falcon. The term 'gentle' could have been based on the bird's good temperament in training, but is more likely to have originated in the 'gentillesse' of the Middle Ages, a concept embracing noble character, an apt description for a bird sported only by the highest nobility – 'gentil' men.

OPPOSITE
The powerful peregrine falcon has a prominent moustache

many traditional eyries being commemorated in place-names which survive to this day, including Killing-Nab Scar, Falcon-Scar and Hawk-Scar.

From the 18th century it suffered along with other raptors through increasing disturbance as mankind invaded wild places in larger numbers, and in the 19th century many were shot for skin collections or had their eggs stolen. Habitat loss or degradation was less of a problem than with other birds of prey, owing to the largely inaccessible nature of its preferred haunts, but the theft of chicks for falconry continued unabated. At the same time, increasing interest in gameshooting led to many being shot, trapped or poisoned, especially on grouse moors. In 1850, A.E. Knox summarised the bird's changed fortunes: 'In the reign of James I a sum equivalent to a thousand pounds was once given for a well-trained "cast" or pair — yet in these degenerate days he attracts but little notice, except when he brings down the vengeance of the keeper.' But the bird was obviously still common because he also wrote: 'There are few sportsmen who have shot much on the maritime moors of Scotland or Ireland who could not recall to memory having seen one of their wounded birds struck and appropriated by the peregrine.'

In his *Tour of Sutherlandshire* St John described how the young of peregrines and other birds of prey were caught for falconers: 'A cap or bonnet is lowered over the border of the cliff, down upon the nest; the young birds strike at, and stick their claws into it, and are incontinently hauled up in triumph.'

Despite all these pressures, it has been suggested that by the end of the 19th century the decline in population from mediaeval times was as little as 9–16 per cent. In the early 1900s numbers seemed fairly steady, with about 700 pairs in the British Isles, despite continued shooting and burning of nests by farmers. Peregrines still nested on virtually every headland around our extensive coastline; in the 1930s there were about 850 known territories, and 41 out of 49 sites recorded in the 16th to 19th centuries were still occupied.

When the 1914–18 war came along, the Government became concerned about peregrines taking pigeons carrying urgent messages from the front, and put a bounty on their heads. Ridiculous as this notion was, the same preposterous procedure was adopted during the 1939–45 war, with the result that virtually the entire peregrine population of southern England was eliminated, amounting to some 600 birds, and the English population overall was reduced to about half its pre-war level, yet once peace returned it showed amazing resilience and, no doubt helped by a decline in keepering, increased again to 65 per cent by 1948–9 and 76 per cent by 1955. Birds in more isolated northern regions had already gained through the lapse in keepering during the war.

From 1956 a decline was noticed — even though selfish pigeon enthusiasts claimed that an increasing peregrine population was ruining their sport. As a result, the Home Office asked the Nature Conservancy Council to assess the situation and a survey was carried out by the British Trust for Ornithology in 1961–2. It proved that not only was the decline real, but also that it had spread northwards. By 1962 the pre-war population had been halved; only about 360 pairs remained, and many of these were failing to breed. Persistent organochlorine pesticides were responsible: these accumulated in the birds and caused thin eggshells which were easily broken in the nest, infertile eggs, and even the inability to lay.

When the worst of the chemicals were withdrawn there was a slow recovery. In 1971 the population was 54 per cent of the 1939 figure, with 25 per cent rearing young, and by 1981 there were some 700–750 pairs in Britain. Ireland had suffered similarly, with about 190 pairs in 1950 falling to 70 in the mid-1960s, with 70

per cent of known sites occupied in 1971. However, the recovery has been patchy; there is continued absence from many former coastal-cliff territories in southern England — yet the highest-ever densities have been recorded in North Wales, northern England and the Scottish southern uplands.

A number of serious problems remain. Between 1971 and 1987 the RSPB recorded 74 peregrines shot, 6 trapped and 7 poisoned, 54 of these 87 deaths occurring over the short period 1982–7. No doubt many more such illegal killings go unrecorded.

Egg-collecting as a hobby is now a relatively minor problem for this species, but the taking of eggs and chicks to supply falconers is very serious. Although Britain's peregrine population recovered in the 1970s, overseas populations remained extremely low, so jealous eyes focussed on our shores in the search for young birds. Newly oil-rich Arabs in particular finance the illegal trade, and with one brood worth thousands of pounds it is no wonder that thieves will go to incredible lengths to raid eyries. Because peregrines use the same sites for many years in succession, their nests are relatively easy to find, and even with today's great public interest in birds there is no way in which all of them can be guarded. Sadly, as the eggs are harder to get, the thieves become bolder as their rewards increase. But now the law is at last cracking down on the worst offenders, and imposing severe penalties: in 1990 two West Germans were fined £6,000 each after Scottish police found two peregrine eggs in an incubator hidden in their car. Later that year, two other West Germans were sentenced to 2½ years and 15 months imprisonment respectively after attempting to smuggle peregrine eggs through Dover. Acting on a tip-off, customs officers found twelve eggs behind the dashboard of the Germans' car, along with an incubator, climbing equipment and a two-way radio. The eggs had been taken from two nests in Scotland and two in Wales, but fortunately eight of them were subsequently hatched and seven chicks survived to be taken back to nests in Scotland. The men were thought to be part of a large, well-organised, illegal trade in birds of prey, based in West Germany and with strong Middle Eastern and North American connections. Those twelve eggs were said to be worth a total of £120,000.

With a wild female falcon worth up to £10,000, it is thought that the above activities represent only the tip of the iceberg. It has even been alleged that Arab embassy staff have smuggled out live peregrines in their diplomatic bags. Falconry is a national pastime in the Middle East and some owners may get through as many as fifty birds in one year, many of the imported birds dying in the unaccustomed heat. Although there is a legal trade in captive-bred falcons, Arabs prefer birds taken from the wild. It is unfortunate that licensed breeding aviaries, most of which are reputable establishments, are available to 'launder' wild eggs and young to make it seem as if they are wild-bred.

But the theft of eggs is by no means confined to overseas visitors. British falconers, too, have been tempted by wild stock, which is more highly prized than the far cheaper, captive-bred birds. Even more incredible is the continuing selfishness of some pigeon-fanciers who have gone to extremes of cruelty to protect their birds. The Hawk and Owl Trust has commented:

> We must not tolerate the law being frustrated by the raising of a fund — Defence Against Peregrines — to pay the fines of pigeon-fanciers in North Wales prosecuted for persecuting peregrines. The latest method of persecution is said to be the nauseating practice of releasing pigeons baited with glued-on pellets of paraquat poison.

An established pair with a nesting territory may stay together outside the breeding season, but the association is often only tenuous, as permitted by food supply. Otherwise, the species is markedly solitary; even migrating birds rarely gather.

As prime breeding stock, the most successful racing pigeons are worth up to £150,000 each and their owners maintain that many of their valuable progeny are being taken by a peregrine population which they claim is ten times as high as estimates by recognised authorities such as the RSPB and BTO. Whatever the true situation — and there is no doubt that the number of pigeon kills is widely exaggerated — there can be no justification for culling even one magnificent peregrine for the sake of mere sport, whether it is pigeon racing or shooting. Many of the peregrine's former strongholds are yet to be recolonised.

One of the more interesting concepts recently put forward is 'buffer' feeding of raptors such as peregrines in order to reduce their predation on gamebirds, especially grouse. In 1990 experiments by gameshooters were underway to establish the value of providing a dovecote with free-flying feral pigeons within two kilometres of a peregrine eyrie, in the hope that this preferred food would ease pressure on grouse at critical times of the year, especially outside the pigeon-racing season. Exponents point to the 'honourable history' of buffering, including the recent provision of food for reintroduced sea eagles and red kites. Nonetheless, there is a great deal of difference between supplying carrion for reintroduced or critically endangered species,and providing 'sitting ducks' for those well able to look after themselves. The proposal is based on minority human interest, has no conservation value, and smacks of unnecessary interference with the food chain.

Since the 1939–45 war the Services and aviation authorities have put the peregrine's skills to good use in helping to clear birds from airfields in order to reduce the risk of airstrikes, which can be enormously expensive both financially and in terms of human lives.

Distribution, Habitat and Population

The peregrine falcon is remarkable in that it has a worldwide breeding distribution virtually as extensive as that of the entire genus — *Falco*, itself the most widespread genus in the most widespread landbird family in the world, with seventeen races, only absent from the high Arctic and Antarctic. However, the distribution has become increasingly fragmented through man's interference. More northerly birds are migratory.

As cliffs and crags are favoured for nest-sites, the resident British population is concentrated around the coasts and in the rugged hills of the north and west. As well as a safe nesting-place, an important requirement is a good food supply and so colonies of seabirds are a major attraction. Extensive forests are avoided, open country being preferred for hunting. Grouse moors often meet all needs. But the peregrine is a very adaptable species, and while it generally avoids scenes of intense human activity, it will nest on man-made structures; also, where food is particularly abundant it is less fussy in its choice of nest-site.

British winter distribution is similar to that of the breeding season but with a more easterly spread, especially in northern England and Scotland, and greater numbers venturing into lowlands in pursuit of food. In winter the peregrine uses a great variety of habitats and can turn up almost anywhere, even in city centres. Some pairs continue to occupy breeding territories in winter, but there is a general exodus from the most inhospitable places where there is seasonal food shortage. In Ireland, the distribution is more general throughout the year, especially around the coast, as the milder climate results in less seasonal variation in the food supply.

The peregrine population of the British Isles is now one of the most important in Europe with probably at least 1,000 pairs, about a quarter of which are in Ireland, and over 4,000 birds at the onset of winter. Expansion continues slowly as the law clamps down on persecution, and former haunts await to be resettled.

Length 36–48cm (14.2–18.9in), wingspan 95–110cm (37.4–43.3in), wing 29.1–36.7cm (11.4–14.4in), tail 10–13cm (3.9–5.1in), weight 0.58–1.3kg (1.28–2.86lb).

The peregrine is rarely heard away from the nesting area, but it can be very noisy, especially when disturbed, with a persistent, harsh, screeching chatter. Although their vocabulary is similar, the sexes are easily distinguished by their calls, the female's a fierce and more powerful cacking, sometimes rendered as *hek, hek, ek-ek-ek*, which is coarser than the male's higher-pitched but slower *hak, hak, hak*.

The single clutch of 3–4 (range 1–6) eggs, average size 52 × 41mm (2.0 × 1.6in), is laid at 2 to 3-day intervals in late March or April (the later clutches being further north) and may be replaced after loss.

Field Characters and Anatomy

This powerful, compact, bull-headed falcon is easily distinguished from most other raptors. With long, pointed wings and a tail shorter than that of other falcons, at a distance it looks like a black arc or rapidly moving crescent, varying with the speed and angle of dive. Closer, it sometimes looks rufous from below and blue-grey from above. Its wing has a relatively short, broad arm and a long, narrow hand, but it is proportionately shorter than in many falcons. The head is always dark, with a prominent moustache, dark crown and white cheeks; the adults have barred underparts whereas those of the young are streaked. The male is about 15 per cent smaller than the female, and often has a larger unmarked area on the breast. Differing proportions distinguish it from the generally much larger gyrfalcon. The smaller hobby also has a pronounced moustache, but its wings are relatively longer and its underparts have conspicuous longitudinal stripes. Young birds usually retain some juvenile feathers in their second summer.

Active flight always gives the impression of power, but on long journeys the wingbeats are relatively stiff and shallow whereas those of a hunting bird are faster and deeper. In soaring, the wings are slightly upturned, but fully extended and with a noticeably straight trailing edge. It can also hover and float on upcurrents, hunting at a greater height than other falcons, stooping spectacularly on prey, with wings held close to the body and tail. In so doing it may be the world's fastest moving bird with speeds up to 180kmph (112mph), although there is still considerable uncertainty and difficulty in measuring bird speeds. There are many variables to be considered, including the speed of the bird before entering the dive and the speed of any head-, tail- or cross-wind. It has been claimed that the male (which is the better flier) has reached 360kmph (224mph) in the display dive, and mathematical theory suggests that even greater speeds are possible, but even at the lower figures it is baffling how the peregrine can pull out of such a dive and avoid blacking out. Baffles in the nostrils are thought to slow down wind intake and avoid bursting the lungs. Recent use of sophisticated laser measuring devices should soon produce statistics more reliable than those from air speedometers attached to trained birds, which are necessarily slowed down.

Breeding

There are only a few records of peregrine bigamy. Most birds breed for the first time in their second or third years, though some one-year-old females have been known to breed with older males. Pairing is apparently for life, though a new mate is obtained if one dies. Evidently pairs are formed in the nest territory early in the year, when the complex courtship displays begin. These include spectacular sky-dancing with solo or mutual high-circling and stooping at each other, sometimes passing food in the air, and frequent screaming. Many flights are complex, with figures-of-eight and ascending spirals and soaring with the tail fanned. Some of the undulating flights and flight-rolls at speed are spectacular, especially against the backdrop of coastal cliffs on an early spring day with the bright sun breaking out of dramatic cloudscapes. There are also more gentle moments when the birds deftly turn in flight to touch talons and breast feathers, or 'kiss' with their beaks.

In Britain the minimum distance between eyries is usually about 4–5km (2–3 miles), but this varies considerably with the food supply, the greatest density recorded being four pairs within a linear distance of about 1.6km (1 mile) on the

Peregrine falcon with chicks: a prime target for the black market

Sussex coast, contrasting with an average of 9.6km (6 miles) apart in barren areas of the western Highlands and islands.

Most nests are on bare cliff ledges, either coastal or inland, but overseas other sites commonly include the old nests of other birds such as raven, buzzard, heron or crow — these might be high in a tree or on a ledge, as well as occasionally on a ledge of a tall building (once on Salisbury Cathedral), chimney or ruin. Most rock-face ledges used are usually at least 45cm (18in) deep and virtually inaccessible without climbing equipment; but some inland eyries are easily reached. Some sites are used many years in succession, but some pairs have several alternatives up to about 6.4km (4 miles) apart. No nest material is used, the female merely forming a depression by turning and pressing with her chest and legs.

The female does most of the incubating, which takes 29–32 days per egg. Incubation begins with the last or penultimate egg so that hatching is virtually synchronous; this is unusual for a raptor.

The chicks are mostly cared for by the female, provisioning of the family being the main role of the male. At first the female tears up food to give the chicks, but when they can feed themselves after about thirty days she joins the hunt and the male may take his turn at sheltering the chicks from the rain. Both male and female have been known to raise a brood successfully when a mate has been killed. Because they hardly vary in size, there is little aggression between the young, but the parents defend the nest vigorously, attacking intruders with much raucous screaming. Fledging is at 35–42 days, but independence is not achieved before a further two months have passed, the whole family sometimes being in the air together.

Before the environmental poisoning of the 1950s and 60s, British studies revealed productivity of 2.53 young per successful pair, compared with 2.09 in 1971. It is calculated that with breeding success averaging about 1.25 young per territorial pair, over 1,000 peregrines fledge annually in Britain nowadays.

Diet and Feeding Behaviour

The peregrine is a specialist bird feeder, taking nearly all its victims in flight. Once the prey is spotted (from a perch or on the wing), the falcon gains height as necessary to stoop down at its quarry with half-closed wings. It descends with such speed that just one glancing blow with the powerful hind claw is often sufficient to kill in mid-air, the hapless victim tumbling in a flurry of feathers and is soon collected from the ground. A bird not killed immediately is finished off with a bite to the neck or head. Sometimes predator and prey bind together and tumble earthwards. A strike lasts only one tenth of a second or less, the feet being lowered and thrown forward at the last moment to maximise impact. Simultaneously, the tail may be fanned and the wings thrown up to increase braking. The bird is such a skilful flier that its path may be altered even just a few milliseconds before impact. Usually there is a characteristic trail of feathers leading to the remains of the prey with the breastbone picked clean of meat. Despite the great speed, many stoops fail and the hunt often continues as a direct chase. Sometimes, in a desperate

Prey remains found at a peregrine eyrie, including curlew, starling, oystercatcher, teal, golden plover, grouse, pigeon (with leg ring) and jackdaw

attempt to save itself, the hunted bird may fold its wings and fall to the ground, as the falcon usually gives up if it cannot pursue prey in flight. Really severe strikes can dismember a wing or sever the head. Fast fliers such as pigeons and waders try to escape in horizontal flight, but slower species such as herons and gulls make a spiral ascent to keep above the falcon.

Prey varies considerably according to location, and ranges in size from passerines of 10g (0.35oz) to geese and herons weighing over 2kg (4lb), the heavier female peregrines generally taking the larger prey. Sometimes other raptors such as kestrels and owls are taken. Over 132 prey species have been recorded in the diet of British peregrines, including mammals, reptiles, amphibians, and even fish. The most favoured birds are pigeons (homing, feral and wild) and gamebirds, notably grouse on the uplands, with local concentrations on seabird colonies and crows. With a normal cruising speed in the region of 65kph (40mph), the peregrine can catch most fast-flying species in level flight under its own muscle power, but with a maximum level flight speed of 110kph (68mph) in only short bursts, it can seldom catch up with a good homing pigeon. Sometimes the prey is on the ground when spotted and flies up on becoming aware of the stoop, only to be struck down almost immediately. Prey is often taken to a special station for plucking, which takes several minutes. A meal usually starts with the brain and breast, occasionally followed by the entrails. Carrion may be eaten during extreme cold.

Migration, Movements and Roosting

Although more northerly populations are wholly migratory, British and Irish peregrines are entirely sedentary, only one ringed bird having been recovered overseas (Northern Ireland to Portugal). Birds of passage and winter visitors are not uncommon in Britain, especially on the east coast, but their incidence has greatly diminished as the Scandinavian breeding population has declined. In autumn young British birds disperse, many drifting east in northern England and Scotland, along with adults which move with prey species to lowlands and coasts as winter sets in. Most British peregrines winter below 400m. Ringed, first-winter British birds are usually recovered within 150km (93 miles) of their birthplace. There are two records of the highly migratory Greenland or North American races, *F.p. anatum* and *tundrius*, in England.

A sheltered spot on a bare cliff face, sometimes at or near an eyrie, usually suffices as a night roost – some are so narrow that the occupant is forced to face inwards or sideways. Sometimes trees or high buildings are used, especially in winter quarters, the sites being made obvious by the white streaks of droppings. Both the roost and hunting area are selected for their proximity to suitable bathing places, where the birds generally go on leaving the roost. Before the eggs are laid, a pair often loafs and roosts together at or near the selected breeding site, but during incubation the male roosts away from the eyrie. After the young have fledged, the whole family usually roosts together, mostly at or near the eyrie. Outside the breeding season birds usually arrive at a roost within half-an-hour after sunset and leave within the half-hour before sunrise. The hunting day can be surprisingly long, with birds travelling considerable distances to feed when food is scarce, and exceptionally they will forage in artificial light, especially when feeding young. Loafing birds (usually alone) on trees, posts and rocks may be distinguished from those watching for prey by their sitting posture.

HOBBY
(Falco subbuteo)

THIS spirited falcon not only gives the impression of a large swift, it eats swifts, too. Britain's only long-distance migratory falcon, it has long been esteemed for its flying skills.

History and Conservation

The earliest hobby records in the British Isles are from cave deposits, the bird apparently having been taken by an eagle owl when roosting. Remains are from the Ipswichian Interglacial in South Wales and Late Devensian to Early Holocene at Cheddar. Being a migrant, it could easily have expanded or contracted its range with climatic fluctuations. At first the early forests were only partially cleared for settlement, and the species would undoubtedly have made considerable gains; but later, wholesale destruction of woodland and other habitat would bring decline.

The hobby was associated with falconry from early times, but only in a minor capacity. The *Boke of St Albans* (1486) stated: 'Ther is an Hoby. And that hauke is for a yong man'. In sport the hobby was more of a toy or decoration, suitable only for taking small birds, perhaps partridges, and teaching a boy the basics. It was sometimes used in taking larks, which were a popular delicacy: when the falcon was cast off the larks were supposedly fixed to the ground through fear, so they became easy prey for the fowler, who drew a net over them.

In the 19th century the hobby was shot and trapped extensively along with other raptors. In 1850, Knox wrote:

> It prefers the wooded districts of the Weald to the downs or the open country near the coast, being there a summer visitor. Yet, even in these his favourite haunts, he must be considered scarce, and you will rarely discover his decaying form among the rows of defunct hawks which garnish the gable of the keeper's cottage — a sort of ornithological register, which would appear to indicate, with tolerable accuracy, the prevalence or scarcity of any species of raptorial bird.

Equally serious in both the 19th and 20th centuries has been the close attention of the egg-collector, right up to the present day. As the weather varied, and with it the hobby's important insect food, its distribution was erratic, so any opportunity to steal its attractive eggs was taken, especially as widespread habitat loss and degradation brought general decline at the end of the 1800s.

There is a considerable amount of confusion over its past distribution, and it now seems that the species has been more widespread than was previously thought. It is not only a bird of southern lowland heaths and has certainly bred as far north as Perthshire in 1887 and west to Wales and Cornwall, making greater use of farmland than had previously been suspected. Recently there appears to have been considerable range expansion in Britain, into more varied habitat.

Fortunately the population did not crash in the 1950s and 60s through environmental poisons. This may have been because the hobby's diet consists largely of insects and insect-eating birds but only a few of the seed-eaters which are exposed to persistent, toxic agrochemicals. Nonetheless, there have been marked declines in some countries — including France, Denmark, Finland and Hungary — in

HOBBY

Between 1978 and 1988 the number of confirmed pairs rose from 70 to 101 and there is no doubt that it is becoming more firmly established in counties where it was formerly an irregular breeder. In 1988 it was thought that there were as many as 361 pairs breeding in England and Wales. The latest estimate suggests an English population of between 500 and 1,000 pairs, with greater use of farmland than was previously supposed.

Length 30–36cm (11.8–14.2in), wingspan 82–92cm (32.3–36.2in), wing 23.7–28.2cm (9.3–11.1in), tail 8.0–10.0cm (3.1–3.9in), weight 0.13–0.34kg (0.28–0.75lb).

A highly vocal bird when not incubating, with a variable vocabulary, the commonest call being a high-pitched, wryneck-like *kew-kew-kew*.

recent decades, no doubt partly due to continuing extensive shooting as the bird migrates through southern Europe.

Distribution, Habitat and Population

This migrant breeds in the boreal and warm temperate zones of Eurasia, and winters in the subtropical zone, in Africa, India and south-east Asia. Southern Britain is at the edge of its range, where its distribution fluctuates considerably with climatic change, which governs the important insect element of its diet. It is mainly a lowland species, its traditional British stronghold being on the dry heaths and downlands of southern England, where there is suitable open country for hunting alongside woods and tall hedgerow trees for nesting.

In 1981 it was thought that over three-quarters of some 100 pairs were found in Berkshire, Dorset, Hampshire, Surrey, Sussex and Wiltshire. The New Forest and Ministry of Defence training grounds in Dorset, Wiltshire and Surrey, where there is relatively little disturbance, were particularly important. Only a few pairs nested north of a line from the Wash to the Severn, though there had been sporadic breeding in Wales and northern England, and at one time in Scotland. But this elusive bird was always difficult to monitor and it now seems that, even allowing for a better network of observers, it is considerably more abundant than recently supposed. The range has expanded east into Essex, Suffolk, Norfolk, Cambridgeshire and Lincolnshire, west into south-east Wales – notably Gwent – and Cornwall, and north to Yorkshire and Derbyshire. The only probable decline is on southern downland through habitat change.

Only a small number of passage birds have been recorded in Ireland, in the south-east.

Field Characters and Anatomy

With a flight silhouette like that of a large swift, the hobby is one of the most elegant and beautiful of all falcons. Flying extremely fast, with rapid, shallow wingbeats interspersed with short glides, its grace and skill on the wing are unsurpassed. Powerfully built, it has very long, slender and pointed wings and a shortish tail. Although it is about the size of a kestrel and will occasionally hover over a bush, its swift gliding flight and bold plumage will easily distinguish it from that species. It can be recognised from the smaller merlin by its rust-red thighs, prominent moustachial streak and longer wings. The redfooted falcon, which is increasingly seen in May and June, has a slightly longer tail but shorter wings. The hobby is quite easy to approach – when perched it is very upright, and its long red shank feathers are usually noticeable. A rather dark bird, its underparts are heavily streaked and the throat and cheeks pale. The juvenile is very similar to the adult but has cream rather than rufous flanks, and there is a good contrast between the primaries and the paler upper wing-coverts. The sexes are almost alike, but the female is up to 10 per cent larger than the male and has broader wings.

The flight is very variable, and adapted according to the prey being hunted; when not hunting, the wingbeats are relatively slow and shallow. In soaring, the wings are outstretched and flat, and the tail well spread. Before each floating glide the wings winnow quickly, in the manner of the peregrine.

Breeding

The monogamous pair-bond lasts for at least one season, birds usually breeding for the first time at two years, a few females at one year. Some birds arrive at the breeding grounds already paired. Courtship display is extremely varied with spectacular aerobatics mostly by the male. There is also mutual soaring in which the male dives rapidly down to the female, and an occasional food-pass, when the male dives towards the female who turns on her back to receive the prey in flight. Other activities include fast aerial pursuits, looping the loop, and dives in which the male's wings make a sound reminiscent of the drumming of a snipe.

Breeding density on mixed farmland is apparently related to the availability of prey, especially house martins; spacing of 3–5km (2–3 miles) between nests is the average where such prey is abundant. Many sites are very well established and may be used for several years in succession, or a pair may use alternative eyries; some sites have been used intermittently for over forty years. Most have a commanding view so that the female can see the male over a long distance in at least one direction.

In one study, over 90 per cent of 208 English nests were in old crows nests, the remainder in those of rook, magpie, jay, sparrowhawk, heron and red squirrel. Sometimes the old lining is removed, but there is no building. Until recently, many sites had gone unrecorded because few people appreciated the extent to which this elusive bird had begun to make use of farmland and woodland habitats. In particular a wider variety of trees is used, as Dutch elm disease has forced the host crows to find new accommodation. In two areas of mixed and

Hobby and 21-day-old young. Fledging takes 28-34 days

The hobby, from egg to adult: top left hatching; centre left at 7 days; below left at 14 days; top centre at 21 days; top right at 28 days; left full-grown bird

The single clutch (often replaced on loss early in the cycle) of three (occasionally two, exceptionally four) eggs, average size 42 × 33mm (1.6 × 1.3in), is usually laid in June in England, at 2 to 3-day intervals.

arable farmland in the south Midlands, between the Cotswold and Chiltern Hills, the minimum densities were 3.8 and 4.8 pairs per 10km², with sites at 2.0–9.6km (average 4.6km) apart. The closest distance recorded between nests is less than 140m. Nest height is extremely variable, from a few metres to over thirty.

The 28/31-day incubation is almost exclusively by the female and begins with the second egg so that hatching is slightly asynchronous.

Typical of the genus, the male provides most of the food for the family. The female broods the chicks for the first ten days, feeding them bill-to-bill, but after they can feed themselves at 15–18 days she usually joins the hunting, though some males continue to supply all the food. Inter-sibling rivalry is apparently insignificant. Fledging is at 28–34 days, after which the young begin to take food from the male in flight, as in the courtship food-pass between male and female. At first the young are clumsy at this, but later both parents often drop prey for their offspring to catch in mid air. Independence is achieved about 30–40 days after fledging.

In a study of forty-seven successful English nests, 138 eggs were laid, 122 hatched (88.4 per cent), and 109 (78.9 per cent) young fledged, a mean of 2.3 per pair. In recent years it is likely that breeding failure through shooting and egg-collecting has diminished, while nest-robbing by corvids has become more significant.

Diet and Feeding Behaviour

The hobby has to be a skilled hunter because it specialises in aerial prey, taking birds and insects in proportions varying with local abundance. It is often very active at dusk to take advantage of birds gathering to roost, swarming insects, and (less frequently) bats. Exceptionally it hunts insects and bats by moonlight. Before the eggs hatch, insects seem to be more important, but thereafter the hobby concentrates on birds both for itself and its young; once the chicks have fledged, the emphasis often returns to insects. However, in Britain's fickle climate there is always considerable flexibility.

The insects taken are generally large, and include beetles, butterflies, moths, craneflies, mayflies, damsel-flies and dragonflies, skilfully snatched with the feet and transferred to the bill. Dragonflies are seized in a stoop from above, the hobby rising at once to eat its victim as it flies. When insect-hunting its flight is relatively slow, with flatter wingbeats, occasionally hovering. Insects are mostly taken in low-level quartering and in brief sorties from a perch, but sometimes also on the ground.

At least seventy bird species are taken, the majority being open-sky species — especially swifts, swallows and martins — and passerines of open countryside such as finches, buntings, sparrows, starlings, larks, pipits and wagtails; these are often taken in their song-flights. Even escaped budgerigars are regular victims, though larger birds such as woodcock, cuckoos, waders and partridges are taken only occasionally. The hobby's late breeding is thought to take advantage of the large number of naive passerines and swifts which fledge from July onwards.

Birds are caught in a variety of ways, including straightforward stoops and chases high in the air, but also low-level dashes in which good use is made of cover in surprise attacks; this is especially effective in taking fast species such as swifts and swallows. An equally productive method is swooping upwards to confuse the prey, especially at a flock. A hobby may return frequently to exploit concentrations of small birds at roosts or nesting colonies, such as those of martins. Some birds are eaten in flight, but most are plucked and consumed at a perch.

Mammals taken include small rodents (often taken from kestrels), including voles, shrews and mice, young rabbits, moles, and bats up to the size of a noctule. Reptiles are rarely eaten.

HOBBY

Migration, Movements and Roosting

This long-distance migrant spends a relatively short time in Britain and northern Europe, arriving at its breeding grounds between late April and late May and leaving for Africa as early as late August. There are few winter records as far north as central Europe. Most hobbys winter in savannah, scrub and cultivated areas south of the Equator where there is an abundance of insect life, but there is recent evidence that some go to West Africa. Because it is such a strong flier it does not need to focus on easy sea crossings so most passage takes place over a broad front. In Britain it is particularly conspicuous in late August and September when birds released from the constraints of breeding join Fennoscandian passage birds to exploit large swallow and martin roosts shortly before their departure.

Although it is mainly solitary, it may feed and roost communally on passage and in winter. In Britain during the breeding season there are many records of apparently unmated birds wandering around, sometimes visiting the territory of a pair, and it is believed that these are yearlings. Sometimes these strays respond to food-begging calls of fledglings.

Night roosts are always in trees, the male and female often well apart but near the chosen nest-site at the start of the breeding season. With young in the nest, the female — and sometimes the male — roosts in or near the nest-site. Newly-fledged young roost in the nest-tree, but gradually move away. Daytime loafing places are also in trees, usually well hidden. These are unusually important because the species hunts intensively at specific times of day – notably dusk, rather less at dawn – and can therefore afford to spend much of the day sitting quietly.

GYRFALCON
(Falco rusticolus)

T HIS magnificent bird is Britain's rarest non-breeding annual visitor, and is just about regular in occurrence. For many centuries it has been the greatest prize of falconers around the world, rivalling even the peregrine.

The gyr's plumage is extremely variable and traditionally three races have been recognised, leading to confusion among some 19th- and early 20th-century naturalists who persisted in describing the Greenland falcon and Iceland falcon as separate species.

History and Conservation

We know very little of the early history of this most northerly of all falcons, but there is no doubt that periodic range expansion southwards has been linked to occasional cooling of the climate. While there is no record of breeding in Britain, there has been an increasing incidence of visitors during the coldest spells

GYRFALCON
Once known as jer-falcon, gerfalcon, Greenland falcon, Iceland falcon and gyr falcon

GYRFALCON

The English name 'gyrfalcon' is known from 1768, when Pennant drew on the Latin *Gyrfalco* of Aldrovandi in 1603, based on the mediaeval Latin *gyrofalco.* But English use is also traced back to *girfaucones* in a Latin document of about 1209. From circa 1300–30 we have *gerfauk* and *girfauk,* from 1382 *jerfacoun,* and from circa 1440 *Gerfaucun.* Other sources are the Old French *girfaucon* or *gerfaucon,* and the Old Norse *geirfalki,* the ephithet *geir,* meaning spear, denoting excellence and being a native Germanic word. Viking settlers in the northern isles perplexingly used the name *geirfugl* for both the gyrfalcon and the now extinct great auk. The spelling 'gerfalcon' seems to have become popular in the 1860s, but this century 'gyrfalcon' (sometimes 'gyr falcon') has been more popular.

of the 19th and 20th centuries. But overall decline in the southern part of the range during the last 100 years has probably been as much to do with persecution as climatic change. For example, the gyrfalcon became extinct in southern and central Sweden in the 19th century, in Norway there was a steady retreat northwards, and in Iceland skin- and egg-collectors caused a marked decline in the late 19th century.

In 1799 Bewick noted that 'It is found, but rarely, in Scotland and the Orkneys'. Sadly, he also recorded the keen interest by falconers which led to its decline before that of other falcons:

> Next to the eagle it is the most formidable, the most active, and the most intrepid of all voracious birds, and is the dearest and most esteemed for falconry. It is transported from Iceland and Russia into France, Italy, and even into Persia and Turkey; nor does the heat of these climates appear to diminish its strength, or blunt its vivacity.

In 1850 Morris, too, stated that it occurred in the Shetland and Orkney Islands, but 'has been rarely killed in this country; a few in Scotland, and still fewer in England, Wales and Ireland. In Ireland but three have occurred'. He also pointed to the long association with falconry:

> This noble bird may well be regarded as the personification of the 'beau ideal' of the true falcons, at the head of which it pre-eminently stands. Its courageous spirit, together with its rarity, even in its native countries, and the difficulty of procuring it, made it highly estimated in the days of falconry, as it was qualified and disposed to fly at the larger kinds of game of those days, such as herons and cranes.

The supremacy of the gyrfalcon was clearly recognised in the well-known *Boke of St Albans* (1486): 'Ther is a Gerfawken. A Tercell of a gerfauken. And theys belong to a Kyng'. Regrettably, that interest established so long ago led to exploitation that continues to this day. Although the gyr is harder to train than the peregrine and generally stoops less spectacularly at prey, it has a regal air and exceptional beauty which make it highly desirable as a status symbol. The remoteness of its breeding places and improved international law enforcement have helped to reduce the number of nest robberies, but the wicked trade goes on. For example, in 1990 a West German was sentenced to 18 months imprisonment after trying to smuggle young gyrfalcons through Dover. Customs officers had found four chicks beneath the rear seat of his car; he claimed to be a courier, paid £600 to carry the birds, but refused to identify his employers. Two of the birds survived and were released in arctic North America, where they probably came from. The main market for these birds is the Middle East, where thousands of pounds are paid for a single falcon.

Fortunately, the remoteness of gyrfalcon breeding grounds, well away from agriculture and farm stock, has meant that the species has suffered very little from environmental poisoning. However, there is some evidence that birds *are* being affected by toxic chemicals. For example, a female wintering on Islay in 1978–9 died of alphachlorate poisoning, and there were very high levels of toxins in a first-winter female which died on Fetlar in May 1979. But perhaps the greatest threat now comes from proposals for future development and exploitation of the Arctic wilderness.

Most visitors to Britain are from Greenland and Canada; in most years only a few occur – in 1989 there were five, a good year, bringing the total to ninety-three since 1958. As with other rarities, it is likely that some individuals were counted more than once, but this is a shy species and it is probably under-recorded in parts of its range. The biggest influx recorded in the British Isles was twenty-seven, all in Ireland and west Scotland, betwen 20 November 1909 and 17 March 1910.

Distribution, Habitat and Population

The gyrfalcon is an Arctic species of the Old and New Worlds, distributed around the North Pole in the high latitudes of Europe, Asia and North America. It is mainly resident, breeding north of the tree-line, though some are partially migratory. Occasional visitors to Britain occur mainly in Shetland, Orkney, northern Scotland, Cornwall, Devon and the Isles of Scilly. In the extreme Arctic it occurs mainly on coasts, where suitable nest-sites are near substantial food sources, especially large seabird colonies. It also inhabits tundra, interspersed with rivers and rocky outcrops or cliffs, mountains with steep cliffs (especially where ledges have overhangs), and in light woodland on the southern edge of its range. Away from seabird colonies it hunts over wide areas of open terrain with sparse or short vegetation, and migrant or dispersing birds seek similar conditions, such as those found on the moors and islands of northern Britain. In winter there is a general movement to lower ground and coasts.

In many areas the distribution fluctuates considerably with the prey population. At peak times Iceland has about 200 pairs, but Norway now has only about 30 pairs, and Sweden 30–50 pairs.

Field Characters and Anatomy

In the past, the widely varying plumage of the gyrfalcon led to several races being described, but now some authorities simply regard it as a highly variable species, paler forms being more abundant in the north and darker birds in the south. They range from mainly grey or brown to mainly white with a few black spots, those which visit Britain originating mainly from Canada and Greenland and of the formerly *G.r. candicans*, almost pure-white variety. There are many intermediate phases, which are also affected by age. All morphs are larger than the peregrine,

This stylised gyrfalcon painting by Stubbs reflects early falconry interest in the species

birds from the Greenland and Iceland populations being the largest, with a wingspan as great as that of the buzzard. The sexes are similar in plumage. The long wings are particularly broad-based and the hand very rounded for a falcon. It is a stocky bird with large head, strong beak and long, broad tail. Young birds are generally darker.

Overall, this bulky bird gives an impression of great power, but for a falcon it has very slow wingbeats, which are quite shallow, the hand alone appearing to move. When soaring the wings are level, but slightly upturned at the tips, and the tail is well fanned. In gliding the wings are level or slightly depressed. When hunting it can accelerate rapidly, the wingbeats increasing dramatically. Perched birds adopt a very upright, thickset posture. The greater size, much longer arm, more rounded wing, longer tail and generally less contrasting plumage should distinguish it from the peregrine on the rare occasions they are seen together.

Breeding

The monogamous pair-bond is probably of long duration, and first breeding is likely at two years. Selection of territory depends on snow cover at the start of the breeding season, and the distance between eyries varies with food abundance, densities being greatest on coasts near seabird colonies. The male's active defence of territory starts as early as January, the female sometimes arriving later, in February or March, if she has not overwintered there. Display flights begin immediately and involve the scintillating variety typical of large falcons, with steep dives, loud screeching, sky-dancing, talon grappling, high circling, figures-of-eight, and nest-site fly-pasts at speed or with slower undulations.

The nest is usually on a cliff ledge with a sheltering overhang (very important in the northern climate), but it can sometimes be in the old nest of another species, such as a raven or roughlegged buzzard, either in a tree or on a ledge. Some nests are re-used in successive years but others are mysteriously ignored while new ones are used nearby. There is no actual building, only a slight scrape or depression in whatever material happens to be there.

Incubation takes 34–36 days per egg and is mostly undertaken by the female; it only really gets underway with the third egg, so in larger clutches hatching is partly asynchronous.

The young are cared for by both parents, the female feeding them bill-to-bill at first; later she joins the hunt, and chicks can feed themselves at about 30 days. The fledging period of 46–49 days is the longest of the genus *Falco*, but independence may be achieved within a further 30 days, often only half the time taken by young peregrines. Despite their greater size, the parents are less aggressive towards intruders than peregrines are, probably because of their relative isolation, which generally leads to naivety.

Productivity varies considerably with the food supply, both during the preceding winter and the breeding season itself; and it is the availability of bird prey such as ptarmigans which is important, not the cyclical abundance of mammals which other Arctic predators rely on. The average number of young per successful pair is about 2.5.

Diet and Feeding Behaviour

Like the peregrine, this is primarily a bird-eater; inland the main prey comprises up to 92 per cent grouse and ptarmigan by weight, but there is considerable local

GYRFALCON

Length 50–60cm (19.7–23.6 in), wingspan 130–160cm (51.2–63.0in), wing 35.2–41.5cm (13.8–16.3in), tail 17–19cm (6.7–7.5in); weight: male – 0.8–1.3kg (1.77–2.86lb); female – 1.4–2.1kg (3.08–4.62lb).

The gyr has a deeper, gruffer voice than the peregrine, its main calls being a hoarse, rhythmically repeated *krery-krery-krery* and a guttural *kack-kack-kack*.

The single clutch (sometimes replaced after loss) is of 3–4 (range 2–7) eggs, average size 59 × 46mm (2.2 × 1.8in); these are laid at 2 to 3-day intervals, mainly within a relatively short period during late April to early May, exactly when being dictated by the shortness of the Arctic summer.

GYRFALCON

variation. Some birds concentrate on prey from large seabird colonies, especially in winter. Mainly medium-sized birds are taken, species including auks, kittiwakes, diving ducks, waders, passerines, black grouse, capercaillie and geese. More unusual victims include owls, ravens and roughlegged buzzard.

The gyrfalcon's wingbeats are deceptively slow, but unlike the peregrine it routinely overtakes and catches fast birds in level flight, in which it is probably the fastest of all falcons. Some species, such as owls, skuas and gulls, try to rise above the falcon, but when the prey is sufficiently tired the gyr takes it spectacularly through rapid ascent.

Most hunting is from a good vantage point on a rock or other prominence, but the falcon also quarters low over its territory, using every scrap of cover well in surprise attack. Some victims are struck to the ground but others are seized in flight. Sometimes two gyrs hunt co-operatively, hovering over scrub to flush birds out. Unlike the peregrine, the gyr rarely gives up after an unsuccessful first strike.

Prey may be plucked on the spot or carried off in the talons. That taken to the nest is usually decapitated and has the main flight feathers removed.

Although mammals are not particularly important in the diet, cyclical abundance of rodents such as lemmings can contribute to breeding success. Hares, shrews and weasels are sometimes taken, along with occasional fish, frogs and insects.

Migration, Movements and Roosting

The few gyrfalcons which come to Britain occur mostly in the far north and west, especially in Shetland, the Outer and Inner Hebrides and Orkney. They are much less frequent elsewhere, but occasionally turn up in Ireland, Cornwall, Devon and the Isles of Scilly. A few have been caught on oil rigs, trawlers and weather ships and released ashore. Peak arrival times are November/December and March/April, but a few have occurred in September, October, January, February and May.

The bulk of the Western Palearctic population is sedentary, though considerable wandering occurs in relation to varying food supply. Formerly, the origin of British visitors was related to their colour phases, dark birds being classed as Iceland falcons and white ones as Greenland falcons, the two being treated as separate races. But it is now known that plumage is not a foolproof indicator of origin. Icelandic and Scandinavian birds are mostly non-migratory, dispersing coastwards in the winter, but high-Arctic Greenland birds are markedly migratory. It is these predominantly white birds which travel via Iceland to produce most British records. Some have been recorded as far south as Portugal, Spain and northern Italy. Icelandic birds are indistinguishable from grey Greenland falcons and there is still no proof that they visit the Faeroes, Britain and Ireland, though the grey-plumaged birds from lower altitudes which do occur in the British Isles could be from either source.

The gyrfalcon is usually a solitary bird, though small groups have been seen on autumn passage. Birds wintering south of their breeding range are always solitary. Little information is available on roosting, but it is likely that most nest-ledges double up as roosts because they inevitably provide good shelter. During the summer, the adults are active well into the dusk, exceptional twilight vision apparently a major factor in enabling them to winter so far north.

MERLIN
(Falco columbarius)

ALTHOUGH the smallest of Britain's diurnal birds of prey, the merlin is by no means lacking in spirit and style. Just as the hobby entrances birdwatchers on southern heaths, so the merlin casts its spell on visitors to northern moors. Sadly, this is the only British breeding raptor which is probably currently declining overall.

History and Conservation

In the British Isles the merlin is known from Devonshire and Derbyshire caves towards the end of the last glaciation. Being a bird of open country, it is assumed that its population decreased along with forest spread as the climate warmed, but gained as trees were felled. When sheep farmers moved into the uplands it probably made further advance, but with the arrival of large numbers of grouse-keepers it was persecuted along with all raptors. Before that, some were taken for

Merlin with part of a ring ouzel, which had been hidden in the heather earlier in the day

MERLIN

The origin of the name 'merlin' is confused, but may be traced back to the Anglo-Norman *merillon* and Old French *emerillon*, deriving from the Franco-German *smeril*, paralleled in the Old Norse *smyrill*, denoting a term of Germanic age. Another possible route is through the Latin *merula* for blackbird, which was once called 'merle', but that species is an unusual prey for the merlin. The merlin's specific, *columbarius*, may also allude to prey, in that gentle doves or pigeons were fitting quarry for a lady, for whom the merlin was considered to be the most suitable hunter. But whatever the derivation, we first find 'merlyon' in about 1325, 'merlyn' in the 15th century and 'merlin' frequently used from 1616.

falconry, but the species seems to have been of only minor interest in that sport: *The Boke of St Albans* (1486) stated: 'Ther is a merlyon. And that hawke is for a lady'. It was used principally for taking small quarry such as larks and quails, but occasionally may have been flown at partridges.

In the mid-19th century it bred much more extensively throughout the British Isles, but was steadily eliminated from those few parts of central and south-eastern England where pockets of suitable habitat remained. By 1900, apart from Wales and Devon, it was rarely found nesting south of Derbyshire.

Over the next fifty years there was a slow and steady decline, probably due to persecution, habitat loss and increasing disturbance, and from the 1950s this suddenly accelerated. The crash was thought to be due to accumulations of poisons such as DDT, because even though merlins generally bred well away from the worst affected areas, in winter they regularly move to lowlands where they feed largely on flocks of small birds, and these were exposed to toxic agrochemicals. However, unlike other raptors, the merlin failed to recover after the worst chemicals were banned in the 1960s, and it was found that the predominantly ground-nesting British merlins have a lower breeding success than do more northerly populations which often nest in trees. Even small reductions in productivity could tip the balance, and these are easily brought about because of greatly increased disturbance by hill walkers, sportsmen and birdwatchers, habitat loss and even low pesticide levels.

Currently a great deal of research is underway to determine and remedy the reasons for this long-term decline. Organochlorine pesticides and mercury residues in eggs certainly affect breeding success, yet much of the blame can also be put on the loss of heather moorland to agriculture and forestry. Moreover it has been shown that the best places for merlins coincide very closely with the best places for grouse, and that the pairs with a greater abundance of heather moorland breed more successfully than those in areas with more grassy sheep-walks.

However, very recently British merlins have followed the example of overseas birds, in that increasingly they nest in trees at the edges of conifer plantations, effecting a revival in places such as parts of Wales and Northumberland. To encourage this, the Hawk and Owl Trust recently issued guidelines to forest managers to help conserve the merlin population.

Much as this local improvement is welcome, some 75 per cent of British merlins still nest on the ground — only on grouse moors. Why they took to this artificially maintained habitat with such success remains a mystery. But whatever the reason, we do know that the variety of heather stages generated by systematic muirburn is important to the merlin in providing both suitable nest-sites and food. Furthermore, the correlation with good moor management is shown by the fact that where keepering has declined and the fox population has been allowed to increase (especially in mixed forestry and sheep landscapes) the merlin population has generally continued to decline. Hopefully, renewed interest in grouse shooting will improve the viability of moors, and the resultant improved management, such as the recent pilot heather-regeneration schemes, will help both merlins and grouse in the long-term. It is ironic that the grouse shooter is now the merlin's greatest hope for a secure future, whereas the sheep farmer has become the falcon's arch enemy: his new husbandry techniques have led to the heather and other native plants being grazed right out, letting in coarse grasses with negligible conservation value. The answer seems to lie in compensating hill farmers for lower stocking rates.

Although conifer plantations are of some benefit in harbouring prey birds when the trees are young, and provide a small number of nest-sites when mature, their uncontrolled planting may well sound the death knell for the merlin in Britain. Already vast acreages of forests planted earlier this century have matured, denying the merlin extensive hunting grounds — the small number of prey species which frequent mature forests offer only minimal compensation. Forest planners must therefore pay more than lip service to the needs of conservation.

Similarly, the alarming spread of bracken must be arrested. With a growth rate of 2.8 per cent per annum, bracken is even outstripping afforestation — estimated at 2.75 per cent. Bracken is rarely used by merlins for nesting, nor is it of much use to their prey: only 15 species of bird generally breed in it, compared with 33 species in heather and 25 on acidic grasslands. Some species, such as the hen harrier and greenshank, avoid it entirely.

In assessing the merlin's decline perhaps we should also look more closely at the interrelationships between all birds of prey, most of which have had widely fluctuating fortunes this century. For example, the recent boom in peregrine numbers may have robbed merlins of a considerable number of crag nest-sites in some areas, while on a lesser scale the merlin itself is sometimes preyed upon by the recently increasing goshawk population.

Finally, we must not overlook the accidents which frequently claim the lives of merlins: an unusually high number have been known to kill themselves by crashing into overhead wires, houses, fences, cars and other obstacles while in hot pursuit of prey. In one study of 122 ringing recoveries, no less than 32 merlins were killed in such ways. Since then the number of man-made hazards has increased dramatically, posing yet more problems for a bird on the brink.

Distribution, Habitat and Population

The merlin has an extensive northern holarctic range, breeding in arctic/alpine to boreal zones across North America, Europe and Asia, and wintering in temperate to warm temperate zones. Although mainly migrant, it is resident in a few marginal and western areas, including the British Isles, where it nests mainly in the north and west. It breeds in the most suitable tracts of upland countryside over much of Scotland (including most larger islands), northern England south to Derbyshire and Staffordshire, Wales and Ireland, with lower numbers in Shropshire and on Exmoor. It has been suggested that marked gravitation towards coasts in winter is partly an illusion created by concentration of birdwatchers in those areas. However, there is no doubt that in winter the highest ground is vacated as the merlins follow the flocks of their prey species into the lowlands, especially in the north. In Ireland, the widespread but patchy distribution changes little the year round because the climate is generally milder and the terrain less rugged. During winter, merlins are found in almost any stretch of open country, including much of central and southern England. Heavily wooded areas are avoided throughout the year, but recently some British merlins have taken to nesting in forest edges. Hilly districts are preferred for their abundance of vantage points.

In 1976 the population of the British Isles was put at 600–800 pairs with possibly 100 pairs in Ireland. In 1990 the RSPB estimate was only about 650 pairs, with Wales holding some 40 pairs and the UK 95 per cent of the European Community population.

Field Characters and Anatomy

Perhaps it is the little merlin's size which gives the impression that it is always flying at breakneck speed. It has been likened to a miniature peregrine and indeed

it has much in common, with a very short, broad arm and a long, pointed hand, powerful body and a broad breast. At long distance it appears uniformly dark at all ages, but at close range the male's blue-grey upperparts and often rusty, streaked underparts distinguish it from the female, which has mainly brown upperparts and a paler ground colour below, making the streaks more conspicuous. The face is less boldly marked than that of other falcons. The juvenile is like the female, but darker below and lacks the grey sheen on the rump. Sometimes the species is confused with a sparrowhawk which is hunting low, when the hand is folded so that is appears pointed and falcon-like; but it may be distinguished by its narrower wings and much shorter tail. In silhouette, when there is nothing against which to assess size, it can be very hard to distinguish from a peregrine.

The wingbeat is clipped and extremely rapid, more so than in all other British falcons, giving an impression of purpose to every flight; every now and then there is a short glide in which the wings are held close to the body. The overall effect is of jerkiness, especially as the bird accelerates before each glide. But it is a most skilled aeronaut, banking to follow the contours on the hill, climbing steeply and turning sharply in pursuit of its quarry, its small size allowing it to hover and hang in the upland breeze with the greatest of ease. It rarely soars, however.

Breeding

First-year breeding is more common in the female than the male. The monogamous pair-bond lasts at least one breeding season. Little is known about the courtship display; generally it is concentrated at the start of the breeding cycle in fine, warm weather, both sexes circling high over the nest-site with wings shivering, the male sometimes flying with very slow wingbeats, while both birds call. Other activities include the male fluttering from perch to perch and making low, direct flights which appear to entice the female towards the nest; also flight chases, fast parallel flights and steep dives.

Some territories may be used for many years, though the nest-site itself may change with the food supply or because of disturbance from year to year. Yet one patch of heather was used by one pair for nineteen consecutive seasons, and another for twelve, despite repeated destruction of the birds and their nests. Some sites recorded by egg-collectors in the 1890s were still in use in the 1970s. The importance of deep heather for nesting has long been established, and although burning of heather may end a long series of nesting attempts, traditional — cyclical — heather-burning by an experienced gamekeeper should ensure that suitable cover continues; a variety of heather lengths in small patches benefits both grouse and merlins. Nonetheless, the disturbance factor inevitably limits success, and there is the correlation between productivity and the frequency of burning: because heather grows at widely varying altitudes and in very different climates around the country, its rate of growth varies too, and the burning cycle must be altered accordingly. Whereas many English moors get by on a 10/15-year rotation (ie between a tenth and a fifteenth of the moor is burnt each year), a 30/50-year cycle may suffice in northern Scotland. Because of this, in areas such as north-east Scotland the great majority of merlins still nest in deep heather, whereas pairs in places with more frequent burning and greater disturbance have shown an increasing tendency to nest in trees. Some of these have been in old crows' nests in isolated Scots pines on the moor, and some along the edges of forestry plantations,

MERLIN

Length 25–30cm (9.8–11.8in), wingspan 50–62cm (19.7–24.4in), wing 19.1–22.2cm (7.5–8.7in), tail 8–10cm (3.1–3.9in), weight 0.12–0.30kg (0.27–0.66lb). The female is 10 per cent larger than the male.

The merlin generally gives voice only around the nest, when its call of anger or alarm resembles that of the kestrel: a hurried, high-pitched *kik, kik, ik-ik-ik-ik* or *kee-yee-yee*. Other calls are reminiscent of the peregrine, but are higher-pitched.

OPPOSITE
Although our smallest diurnal raptor, the merlin (male above) is among the most accomplished hunters

115

Female merlin feeding newly hatched chicks. Undisturbed nest sites may be used for many years

where they have been encouraged by artificial nests.

Nests within heather or bracken are usually within a few metres of a path or clearing. Some nests are on crags or boulders well hidden by the heather. Where suitable habitat abounds, nests are regularly spaced, about 3–4.5km apart; they are often within a few metres of last year's site, and consist of no more than a shallow scrape lined with small twigs, heather and other material. Those on steep slopes have the outer edges raised like a parapet, and those in the old tree nests of other species may have a lining added. The female forms the scrape.

The female undertakes about two-thirds of the 28/32-day incubation (about 26 days per egg). Most unusually for a bird of prey, the male sometimes sits all night.

With hatching being only partly synchronous, there can be significant size differences between the chicks, but there appears to be little inter-sibling aggression. The male usually provisions the whole family from before egg-laying till after fledging, though once the chicks no longer need brooding, after some ten days, the female may start to hunt. After about eighteen days the chicks can feed themselves with prey brought to the nest. When the male approaches with food he calls, whereupon the female flies to meet him and the prey is usually passed bill-to-bill or talon-to-talon on a nearby perch, aerial talon passes being rare. At about 18–20 days the young crouch in surrounding cover, gradually becoming more adventurous and fledging at 25–27 days. Independence is achieved after a further month or so.

Breeding success is very much governed by human activity. Where there is good moorland management not only is a reasonable spread of suitable habitat maintained, but also predators are kept under control — crows take a significant number of eggs, and foxes take eggs, chicks and adults. Therefore it is not surprising that tree nesting has become more common where there is afforestation, conifer blocks acting as great reservoirs for the fox population. One British study of

The single clutch (replaced after early loss) of 3–5 (range 1–7) eggs, average size 40 × 31mm (1.6 × 1.2in), is laid mostly during mid-May in southern England, but late May and early June in northern England and Scotland. However, exceptional weather may advance laying to late April. The usual laying interval is two days, but the last egg is sometimes laid after 3–7 days.

116

84 clutches revealed average offspring production of 3.21 per successful pair. In a northern England study, 126 of 176 clutches hatched at least one egg and 119 fledged at least one young. Tree nests showed the greatest productivity.

Diet and Feeding Behaviour

This bold bird hunter sometimes take species larger than itself. The emphasis is on open-country passerines — pipits, larks, finches, chats, wheatears, starlings etc — and waders, including snipe, dunlin, redshank, lapwing and golden plover, varying with local abundance. The size ranges from the diminutive goldcrest to a young capercaillie, young woodcock and green woodpecker; red grouse are usually taken only as very small chicks. In some areas meadow pipits have comprised 90 per cent of the prey. Small mammals, lizards, snakes and insects — especially dragonflies and moths — are also taken, but far less frequently.

The merlin rarely stoops on prey in the manner of peregrine or hobby, but flies down a victim with great persistence and agility, twisting this way and that in low, erratic flight before rising above it to strike it down with its talons. Very often it is so intent on its quarry it passes close by humans, as many grouse shooters will testify. Small birds are often grasped in the air. Most prey is spotted from an elevated perch and is quickly taken in surprise attack, or after a long pursuit following an initial miss. A pair often hunts together. Most birds are taken in the air just above the ground or actually on the ground, with a few snatched from perches. The merlin is a fastidious feeder, and usually plucks the bird's head and peels back the skin and feathers before eating – almost everything except the wing feathers is devoured. Plucking stations usually command a good view.

Migration, Movements and Roosting

The merlin is mainly migratory throughout its range in northern Europe, but birds born in the British Isles rarely cross the Channel. Indeed, most British birds stay within 50km (30 miles) of their birthplaces. However, a few have been recovered in France and Spain, one being found dead in south-east Spain — over 2,000km (1,250 miles) away. British birds gravitate towards lowlands and coasts in winter, in search of sufficient bird prey, and the most inhospitable uplands of the north are always vacated. Young northern birds are the most mobile, generally drifting south-east, but Irish birds move little since the climate is so much milder. Most Icelandic birds winter in north-west Britain and Ireland, some passing through to the Continent. An Orkney-reared bird was recovered in Germany, but it is not clear where most birds of extreme northern Britain spend the winter. It is thought that some of the birds wintering in south-east England are from Scandinavian stock, but Britain is probably only a minor wintering ground for these birds.

Although mostly solitary, the merlin may roost communally outside the breeding season, on the ground among rank vegetation, or on low branches in conifer plantations or sallow thickets. One used the outbuildings of a cottage during a winter. Some sites are traditional — one attracted up to eight birds for over fifty years. During the breeding season a pair roosts separately on rocks or in tall heather within their territory. Roosting birds arrive and depart close to sunset and sunrise, sometimes performing spectacular aerial chases, or hunting small birds roosting in the same area before settling down.

male

KESTREL
(*Falco tinnunculus*)

KESTREL

Once known as windhover, windcheater, windsucker, wind bivver, windbibber, wind fanner, wind cuffer, hover hawk, vanner hawk, creshawk, cristel hawk, stannel, stanchel, stannel hawk, stand hawk, stanniel, stonegall, steingale, stand-gale, red hawk, wind hawk, kite, keelie, maalin, sparrow hawk, blood hawk, mouse hawk, mouse falcon, and field hawk

Because the kestrel has long been a common bird it has acquired many folk names. In Shakespeare's *Twelfth Night*, Sir Toby Belch (Act II, Sc 5) referred to the bird as 'stanniel', which is thought to be the earliest native English name for the species. Not surprisingly, some later writers thought the word derived from 'stand gale', alluding to the kestrel's ability to hang in the wind. However, stanniel is said to originate from the 15th century 'stanyel', going back to the Old English *stangella*, meaning 'stone yeller', alluding to the bird's habit of calling from rocks and walls in northern areas.

THE way in which the kestrel has accepted the rush and tear of mankind and learnt to hunt along roadside verges has made it one of the most familiar of British birds. Indeed, in the British Isles it far outnumbers all the other diurnal raptors together. Thus it is not surprising that this is one of the most intensively studied of all birds of prey, especially as it takes to nestboxes and artificial nest-sites so easily.

History and Conservation

Kestrel records go back a long way in Britain, to cave-sites from the Wolstonian Glaciation, although when the forests closed in again the species must have declined enormously. Then when the woods were opened up for settlement and agriculture, it once again made steady gains. In falconry it was of only lowly status, but nonetheless many peasant folk took it for catching small birds. More serious was the sport of shooting, when 19th-century gamekeepers virtually blasted the bird out of existence in many areas. It was also a popular cagebird in Europe. Bechstein wrote: 'Lime twigs placed over the nest will easily secure the old ones when they come to feed their young; or a bird of prey's basket, with a lark or mouse put in it, as a lure, may be placed where these birds are most frequently seen.' As late as 1886, Atkinson wrote: 'And have not more than one or two of us taken the young, and reared them to be our pets.'

There was some respite from persecution when keepering lapsed during the 1914–18 war; and in the 1930s the kestrel started to colonise many urban and suburban areas. Thus when keepering largely fell into abeyance again during World War II, it was in a much stronger position to recolonise lost territory, reaching the Scilly Isles in 1956. However, its recovery was severely hampered by loss of ideal habitat through intensification of agriculture and drainage, as well as fluctuations in vole numbers.

During the height of the organochlorine pesticide era, 1959–63, it suffered a serious decline on cereal farmland in eastern England; but overall the trend was upward as the species adapted so successfully to the environs of mankind. Even the loss of so many tree nest-sites to Dutch elm disease in the early 1970s did not halt the ascendancy.

In the late 1970s the population levelled off and was followed by a patchy decline in the early to middle 1980s. Since then there has been general stability, at a level only slightly higher than that when the Common Birds Census started to monitor the bird in 1965, thus indicating that all the suitable habitats available may have reached their maximum carrying capacity. Much of the recent national decline has been due to decreases in western England and Wales — as in Europe, there may be correlation with cyclical rodent–prey abundance in the long-term. However, in Britain it is difficult to equate fluctuations with severe weather, especially when there was an exceptionally mild and dry spell spanning the latest decline. Nationally, there has been insignificant snow cover to deny kestrels access to rodent food, and in any case, the kestrel is very good at exploiting other foods when voles are scarce. Clearly we have a lot to learn about the population dynamics of our commonest bird of prey.

OPPOSITE
In Britain, the kestrel outnumbers all other diurnal raptors together. The male is hovering in the background

Shakespeare also used the name 'coystril' in *Twelfth Night* (Act I Sc 3) and 'coistrel' in *Pericles* (Act IV Sc 6). Some say that kestrel derived from coystril, meaning a knave or peasant, from being the 'hawk' formerly used by persons of inferior rank. Whatever, there is no doubt that today's standard came to us from the Normans, from the Old French *crecele*, the modern version of which – *crecerelle*, meaning rattle – is said to be imitative of the bird's *kee-kee-kee* cry. The spelling 'kestrel' goes back to Turner in 1544, yet 'castrel' survived locally well into the 19th century. The Orkney name 'mouse falcon' died out long before this but has great ancestry, going back to the Old English *mushafoc*.

In Britain it is both the most widespread and most numerous raptor at all times of year, with some 70,000 pairs – this is slightly down on recent years, but apparently stable in many areas. Locally it may be outnumbered by the sparrowhawk, which is probably the most numerous raptor in Ireland.

There is no doubt that much of the kestrel's success this century has been due to its readiness to use nestboxes and artificial nest-sites, enabling it to exploit much habitat which is suitable but lacking in breeding sites. Hardly a year goes by without some attracting wide media coverage through nesting on man-made structures such as high-rise flats. But not all publicity is welcome. For example, when the film *Kes* featured the close relationship between a boy and his kestrel, many birds were illegally taken from the wild.

Distribution, Habitat and Population

The kestrel is both resident and migrant in boreal to tropical zones. Widespread throughout Europe, Asia and Africa, it has close relatives with similar habits in every other continent except Antarctica. Northern birds winter south to central Africa and India. Since it will use a wide variety of natural and artificial nest-sites, it is able to exploit an extremely wide range of habitats, so there are few parts of the British Isles without any kestrels. The only real gaps in the breeding distribution are in Shetland, where it last bred in 1905, and much of the Outer Hebrides; there are no recent records for some of the islands, including Coll and Tiree, and there has been steady decline in Orkney. Nests are scarce in the fen country of eastern England and at low density in the mountains and moorlands of north-west Scotland.

As the kestrel is a partial migrant, its winter distribution in the British Isles differs quite markedly from that in summer, with a distinct shift to the south-east, the greatest concentration being in eastern England. But in Scotland the greatest winter concentration is in the south-west, where snow cover is generally the lowest. In Ireland, where breeding numbers are equally widespread but below those of Britain, there is little seasonal change, presumably related to the milder climate. The autumn and winter concentration in south-east England is enhanced by visitors from the Continent. Although kestrels take most of their food (by weight) from uncultivated land, it has been shown that tilled land is important, particularly in eastern England, where it provides an autumn and winter food source — especially for young birds — in the form of invertebrates. Winter roosts, too, are common on farmland.

Because we know little about the volume of emigration and immigration, it is difficult to estimate the wintering population, but a midwinter figure of 100,000 birds was suggested for the whole of the British Isles in 1986. The species is also the most common European raptor, with some 250,000 pairs excluding the Soviet Union. However, it is likely that the numbers of Continental birds fluctuate much more widely than those in Britain because of the more extreme climate, mortality being great in severe winters.

Field Characters and Anatomy

With its long, narrow, pointed wings and very long tail, the kestrel is easily distinguished from the only other widespread and common diurnal British raptor, the sparrowhawk, which has short, rounded wings and a shorter tail. In addition, the kestrel is much more tolerant of man and may easily be approached when hovering along roadsides, so that its colourful plumage may be appreciated. The male is a warm red-brown above, with a grey tail and grey back with dark spots; the female's colour is more subdued, with a brown, barred back and tail. The juvenile resembles the adult but is duller and paler above and more heavily streaked below. At all ages the legs and feet are yellow and the bill blue-grey with a dark tip.

The rapid, whirring wingbeats and fanned tail easily distinguish a hovering kestrel. In open flight, too, there is no difficulty in recognising it from the other raptors because it has a relatively weak flight for a falcon, with fast, but rather stiff and shallow wingbeats which do not seem to generate a great deal of power. Sometimes the bird seems to flutter from side to side, though on longer flights it can be quite elegant, employing frequent long glides. But there is no denying its total mastery of the air in its ability to hold its position to hunt, effortlessly using every nuance of wind to advantage. The long tail seems to enhance a perched bird's very upright stance.

Breeding

Kestrels can breed at one year old. The pair-bond is generally monogamous, bigamy being rare in more than 1–2 per cent of pairings. The bond is usually sustained long after the breeding season and may last for several years, though migratory birds are less likely to keep the same mate. Birds are quite likely to mate with others of the same age, usually a consequence of the different arrival times of adults and yearlings. Courtship display may start very early in the spring, both male and female chasing and circling each other, sometimes soaring to great height. The male often dives at his mate in mock attack, and if she is airborne she

KESTREL

Length 32–35cm (12.6–13.8in), wingspan 71–80cm (27.9–31.5in), wing 22.9–27.2cm (9.0–10.7in), tail 12–15cm (4.7–5.9in), weight 0.14–0.31kg (0.3–0.7lb). The female is slightly larger than the male.

Kestrel with young: a good hunter can rear a large family

KESTREL

Although quiet for much of the year, the kestrel can be a noisy bird, especially during the breeding season; indeed the Latin name *tinnunculus* derives from its ringing call. The female's voice is a little deeper than the male's and the main alarm call is variously described as *kee-kee-kee, kik-kik-kik* or *vite-vite-vite*, and is mostly heard when adults with young are disturbed at the nest. Signal calls vary greatly, the most common being a series of high-pitched trills – *vrii-vrii-vrii, heerre-heerre-heerre,* or *quirr-rr quirr-rr.*

The single clutch (sometimes replaced after failure or loss) of 4–6 (range 1–7) eggs, average size 39 × 31mm (1.5 × 1.2in), is usually laid at 2-day (very occasionally 1-, 3-, 4- or 5-day) intervals. The laying date is very variable according to location and weather, though generally earlier in more favourable habitats, being from late March to early June (majority April or May in Britain). Contrary to earlier supposition, northern birds do not necessarily lay later than those in the south. Indeed, the reverse may apply, food supply being the governing factor as hatching is timed to coincide with peak food abundance.

Like other falcons, kestrels do not build their own nests

may roll over and present her talons. High, level flight often involves flicking wingbeats interspersed with short glides, with occasional rocking from side to side and sometimes accompanied by the *tsick* call. This rocking flight often ends with a spectacular dive to the nest from 100m or more, the bird dropping at great speed with the wings held backward in a V. The V-flight is mainly a male display, but both sexes often perform a slow, winnowing flight, in which the wingbeats are rapid but shallow, sometimes only the wingtips appearing to move. As the bond strengthens, the male feeds his mate more frequently and she spends less time hunting in order to lay down reserves for egg-laying and incubation.

Like other falcons, kestrels do not build nests. In many areas the most common site is a hole or a fork in a tree, but a hole or ledge on a cliff is frequently used, the female forming a scrape with chest and leg movements. Other favoured locations are in the old tree nests of other birds, or the tops of squirrel dreys, and ledges on buildings and other structures such as bridges and pylons. Nestboxes are readily accepted. Less common sites are on the ground or a low bank, and even down a rabbit burrow (notably on Orkney, where foxes are absent). Window-boxes are commonly used in towns. A few groups of close-nesting kestrels have been reported in Britain, but there is no marked colonial nesting of the type found in Germany. Nesting is usually solitary, but a pair often has several alternative sites within its territory. Small clumps of nests within 50m of each other may occur where suitable sites are scarce, and in most areas regular spacing is unusual. Some sites may be used for many years, but kestrels are not strongly territorial. They defend against other kestrels only within a radius of about 30m of their nest, and their hunting ranges often overlap.

Incubation usually starts about four days before the last egg is laid, takes 26–34 days, and is almost entirely by the female, the male merely covering the eggs for short periods while the female feeds, preens and bathes.

The first three eggs usually hatch together and the rest over the next few days, which results in some difference in chick size. However, although nestlings have been seen to kill and eat brood-mates, most chick deaths are probably due to failure to compete for food. The chicks grow remarkably quickly, but taking such large amounts of energy for growth makes them especially vulnerable to cold, so the female must brood them carefully for the first 10–14 days. During this time the female feeds the young with food brought by the male, and in the first week she eats very little — generally only the skin and entrails of prey — so that her young may grow quickly. After about twenty days the chicks can feed themselves on prey brought by both parents. Fledging is at 27–32 days, but the young remain very dependent on their parents and take a long time to learn to hover and hunt efficiently; they must be fed for a further 3–4 weeks. Some young remain in the breeding territory throughout the first winter.

Pairs which lay early generally have larger clutches and the chicks are more likely to fledge young than those which hatch late. Moreover, chicks which fledge earlier in the year gain hunting skills more quickly and are more likely to survive their first winter. Productivity is related to a pair's age and experience, especially that of the male in provisioning his mate — a good hunter can rear a large family even in a year when many young die because of a crash in the small-mammal population. However, it is interesting to note that although kestrels generally have slightly larger clutches in good vole years, nestling survival is in fact scarcely affected and second broods are unknown. This inability to exploit good vole years may be the penalty for living in widely varying habitats, and therefore breeding

KESTREL

where prey is scarce. An average of 30–40 per cent of ringed kestrels survive their first year.

Diet and Feeding Behaviour

Unlike the other British falcons, the kestrel concentrates on terrestrial prey, especially small mammals. Many of these are spotted from a perch, but it can also locate them while hovering, a skill which has enabled it to exploit open areas without natural vantage-points. Kestrels are also better than most vole-feeding raptors at changing to alternative foods when necessary, which is why they can occupy poor vole habitats and maintain reasonable numbers during cyclical slumps in the vole population. The main alternative foods are birds, lizards, insects and earthworms, varying in proportions according to local and seasonal abundance and east of capture.

In Britain the most important prey is the short-tailed vole, which inhabits rough grassland and makes runs in the surface vegetation. Other prey mammals include bank voles, mice and all three species of British shrew. The young of larger mammals such as rabbit, hare, squirrel and rat, and those that are difficult to catch or find such as mole, weasel and bats, are taken only rarely.

A wide range of birds is eaten, but chiefly the nestlings and fledglings of open-country species such as meadow pipits, skylarks, starlings, sparrows, buntings and finches. Chicks of larger birds such as waders, gamebirds and moorhens are taken, and also adult birds as large as the woodpigeon, but it is likely that most of these are either already dead or dying. However, kestrels have been seen carrying birds as large as a turtle dove, though with great difficulty and only in short stages.

Most invertebrates are hard to identify in pellets, so relative importance is difficult to establish. However, the concentration seems to be on the larger, slower, surface-living species which the kestrel can find and catch most easily; these include beetles, grasshoppers and crickets. Flying insects are also taken, though faster species such as dragonflies are less usual. Softer invertebrates such as earthworms, snails, spiders and slugs are much harder to detect but probably have occasional importance.

Among reptiles and amphibians, lizards are most important, though only in summer. Only a few snakes and slow-worms are recorded in the diet, and the few frogs and toads eaten are generally taken when they are most vulnerable, during the spawning period. More unusual items include larger mammals as carrion, fish, crabs and even apples during a severe winter.

As there are no voles in Ireland, the main summer prey there is young birds (chiefly starlings) and woodmice, with a few other small mammals. In winter the emphasis switches to woodmice, birds, beetles and frogs, and then the species' ability to hunt in very bad light is especially important since the woodmouse is chiefly nocturnal; the kestrel becomes not only extensively crepuscular, but also it has been seen hunting by moonlight. In early spring it concentrates on lizards and birds.

The kestrel obtains most of its food through quickness of eye, not wing; nonetheless it drops smartly out of the air with its wings raised almost vertically above its back to seize prey in the grass. It is too slow to catch flying birds in a straight chase, but it is expert in energy conservation, choosing the most economic method of hunting for every season. In summer the breeding male is forced to employ the energy-expensive hovering technique to catch sufficient small mammals to feed his family, but in winter he concentrates on perched hunting because it requires relatively little energy expenditure.

This adaptable bird even protects itself against temporary food shortages by storing prey in a cache, and in fact does this on most days. Most caches are of larger prey, such as voles and birds, and are on the ground in or against some prominence such as a tussock or post. Although they are rarely covered or buried, few seem to be stolen and most are retrieved in a day or two. This practice enables kestrels to take advantage of a food concentration such as a brood of birds or a nest of young rats. In winter cacheing is especially important, in that it ensures an evening meal which produces sufficient heat energy to survive the night.

Strictly speaking, the kestrel does not hover in an aerodynamic sense, holding station in still air as a hummingbird can: it flies with a force which exactly matches the lift of the airstream. Thus in a strong wind it hardly needs to flap its wings, and appears almost to hang in the air. But whatever the physics, the kestrel's extraordinary co-ordination in holding station while being buffeted is to be marvelled at; and while its body moulds to the airflow, its head hardly moves at all, enabling it to spot prey and judge the strike distance accurately. Hovering is less frequent on calm days, when the increased amount of flapping needed takes much more energy. Soaring is rarely used in hunting because it depends on thermals and is an ineffective way of spotting small prey far below. Its greatest use may be in hunting bird flocks over flat, open areas. Even the wariest birds may be taken by surprise in a strike from above.

Kestrels will also take food from each other, and will even force other predators — including short-eared owls, barn owls and sparrowhawks — to give up their prey.

Migration, Movements and Roosting

In the cooler, more northerly and eastern regions of its range, with continuous winter snow cover, the kestrel is strongly migratory, but in most of Europe, including the British Isles, it is resident, dispersive and partially migratory. Only a few British birds winter abroad, though some have been recovered as far south as North Africa. Generally, juveniles move further than adults, and northern British birds further than those in the south, though most Continental recoveries are from England, due to geographical proximity. Post-fledging dispersal in July/August is mostly over short distances and in random directions; late-fledged young tend to move the most. Greatest movement occurs when a good breeding season is followed by prey shortage in autumn and early winter. Passage migrants and winter visitors come to Britain from much of north-west Europe, mainly from Fennoscandia and the Low Countries, but sometimes from as far east as Poland and Czechoslovakia. Most come into eastern England and Scotland from August to December, many dispersing throughout the country.

A pair may remain on the breeding site throughout the year. During the breeding season they roost on or very near the nest, but in autumn and winter the attachment is looser and the birds are more likely to roost separately. Sometimes several roost together. Most common sites are in trees, old buildings or crevices in rocks, usually with a sheltering overhang. Birds roosting in towns can be surprisingly indifferent to light and noise. During the early autumn, farmland birds may use several roosts, often in trees, but when the leaves fall in October and November they tend to move into more permanent winter roosts, especially in buildings or straw stacks.

GOSHAWK

Once known as goosehawk, goss-hawk, go-hawk, gooseahawk, great hawk and tiercel

GOSHAWK
(*Accipiter gentilis*)

THIS is the largest and most powerful of Britain's two species of true hawk, and has been both loved and hated by mankind for hundreds of years. It has been revered by falconers since the Middle Ages, and when gamekeepers exterminated it in these islands during the 19th century it was falconers who brought it back. Indeed, even in the days when goshawks were still common in Britain, there is evidence that falconers deliberately released goshawks in order that they might breed in the wild and obtain the requisite degree of ferocity and skill.

History and Conservation

The earliest British goshawk remains are from caves in Devon and Derbyshire, dating back to the end of the last glaciation. It is a true woodland species and as the forest cover increased it became very common; however, as the forests were cleared for settlement, agriculture and shipbuilding, it started to decline. Indeed, the goshawk suffered more than most woodland birds because it needs relatively large tracts of suitable habitat for successful breeding. However, it was afforded some protection in early times because it was a popular falconer's bird, being large enough to secure useful 'pot' quarry such as partridge, hare and rabbit. The *Boke of St Albans* (1486) stated: 'Ther is a goshawke, and that hawke is for a yeman'. It was flown from the fist by an austringer and was regarded as relatively difficult to train. In falconry it was rather on the level of modern roughshooting — the large, dashing falcons were more on a par with today's more élitist driven gameshooting.

When forest cover was at a low point in the 19th century, the very sedentary goshawk was fully exposed to the wrath of an army of gamekeepers who most unfairly exaggerated the species' depredations on game. And the rarer it became, the more it attracted the interest of skin- and egg-collectors. Breeding in Ireland and most of England ceased in the mid-19th century, late records being from Lincolnshire (1864), Perthshire (1880s) and Yorkshire (1893).

During the early part of this century it was described as a 'rare vagrant'. Several pairs nested in Sussex from the 1920s, but it is thought that these could have been the first of a steady stream of falconers' escapes and releases which have allowed a viable feral population to be slowly established. Helped by the maturation of extensive conifer plantations, the breeding population soared from 10–30 pairs in 1976 to at least a hundred in the early 1980s. Yet amazingly, the old prejudices of a minority of gamekeepers have continued; pigeon-fanciers and poultry-owners, too, have expressed their hostility through gun, trap and poison. Moreover, the goshawk is still subject to intensive illegal shooting in many countries, and it is often exempted from protection; under certain conditions it may still be killed in parts of Scandinavia and eastern and western Europe. Fortunately, there has been a good reservoir of birds in places where man's influence is minimal. Sadly, much of the hatred is based on ignorance: research has shown that many of the goshawk's victims are sick or severely weakened, and would not have survived for long anyway. There is no doubt that individual goshawks, especially young birds, *can* make their mark on concentrations of reared pheasants, but there is a great deal more that most gamekeepers can do to protect their charges. It is equally certain that as the goshawk population continues to build, the problem will increase;

Falconers used to call only the female 'goshawk'; the male was known as a tiercel, and because of this there is a great deal of confusion with the peregrine. The name 'goshawk' derives from the Old English *goshafoc*, literally 'goose hawk'. However, that is an unlikely quarry for the goshawk and it seems that the name 'goshawk' was originally used for a peregrine, a species more likely to attack wild geese. In this context it is interesting to note the Old High German *ganshabuh*, denoting a species of falcon (*gansa* in modern German means 'goose'), and the Old Norse *gashaukr* (species undetermined). The first record of the spelling goshawk is from Aelfric's *Glossary* of 998 AD. The Latin *gentilis* means noble, alluding to the bird's tremendous 'presence' and hunting prowess.

For the large and fearless goshawk, a grey squirrel is easy prey

GOSHAWK

we can only hope that the relatively new compassionate outlook among all interests will increase in proportion. As it stands, the law is feeble in deterrence. Falconers still sometimes take eggs and chicks, too.

The goshawk population now has the potential to expand dramatically. The Forestry Commission is already helping considerably by recommending that no forest operations or other activities take place within a 400m circle surrounding an occupied nest. Even better, it plans for the retention of known goshawk nesting areas, rather than risk the accidental destruction of unknown nests. The Commission made its first retentions in 1979 and goshawks have bred in these in every subsequent year. It is most important that forest planners ensure that these retained areas of mature forest are free from human disturbance, ideally well away from footpaths.

In recolonising lost territory, or indeed gaining new ground which was formerly unsuitable, the goshawk should benefit from the increase in population of various prime quarry species. In particular, the woodpigeon is now far more common than it was when the goshawk population was still widespread in Britain. Although it now feeds mostly on farmland, the woodpigeon still depends on woodland for roosting and breeding. An increase in the magpie population and the recovery of the rabbit from myxomatosis should be significant, too.

Distribution, Habitat and Population

Both resident and partly migrant, the goshawk is distributed right around the northern hemisphere, in both the Old and New Worlds, in subarctic to warm temperate zones. Across this huge range it has nine geographical forms. It is primarily a woodland species, preferring areas of at least 100ha for breeding, ideally alternating with open areas for hunting. However, smaller woods sometimes suffice and it hunts mainly within a few kilometres of the nest. In winter it makes more use of open areas where prey species flock. Fortunately, it seems equally at home in both deciduous and coniferous woodland, so for once the concentration on coniferous plantings in Britain this century has not been a disadvantage. Indeed, its new success in Britain has been significantly aided by the recent maturation of conifers, especially spruce, but also pine and larch. Broadleaves such as oak and beech obviously provide good habitat, too, because when the species was at its commonest there were relatively few conifers in Britain. This hawk particularly likes the regimentation of planned forests, such as those of the Forestry Commission, making good use of the rides and firebreaks which provide relatively easy hunting and easy access to nests in tree-tops. Human habitation is avoided.

Because goshawks are so sedentary in Britain, their distribution is much the same the year round, though quite rightly precise locations are kept secret to protect the birds from undue persecution. There are four main centres of breeding: in the Home Counties, central Wales, central northern England and southern Scotland, but the bird is on the brink of expanding in many directions. No breeding is disclosed in Ireland.

Field Characters and Anatomy

Being almost as big as a buzzard, the female is unlikely to be confused with any other British bird; the male, however, is up to 20 per cent smaller and may be mis-

In 1988 the number of confirmed pairs in Britain was 108, with a further 68 possible pairs. In England and Wales birds were found at 141 localities in 26 counties, and 89 pairs attempted breeding, hatching at least 135 young. In Scotland there were 27 localities in five regions, 19 pairs breeding and hatching at least 39 young. These figures were regarded as minima, informed opinion being that the true population is already at least 200–250 pairs.

The powerful goshawk has always been a falconer's favourite

taken for the similar-sized female sparrowhawk. However, there are significant differences in proportions, the male goshawk having greater bulk (especially across the chest) than the sparrowhawk, a larger, more protruding and more angular head, a bulging trailing edge to the secondaries, and a broader tail. The rounded corners of the spread tail also distinguish from the sparrowhawk, whose tail has sharper angles. The wing is relatively longer than that of the sparrowhawk, especially the more pointed hand. The general impression is of a typical hawk, with broad, short, rounded wings and a long tail. The sexes have similar plumage, but the brown upperparts have more of a blue-grey sheen in the male, while the superciliary stripe and white under-tail are more noticeable in the female. Many of the birds which have been released in Britain are thought to be of Scandinavian stock, which is larger and paler than more southerly birds. First-plumage birds have yellowish underparts with longitudinal markings, and the flight feathers have more prominent transverse bands. In its second year the bird is still developing the dark head-pattern, and full plumage is acquired at about two years. The piercing iris is bright yellow for about four years then changes to orange-yellow in the female and orange-red in the male.

Like the sparrowhawk, the gos is expert at weaving through woodland in pursuit of prey, but although its wingbeats are rapid they are slower and deeper, with longer glides in which the wings are held flat. In soaring, the tail is more fully spread and the wings raised, especially in the female.

Breeding

The monogamous pair-bond is of at least seasonal duration and may be lifelong in sedentary populations. However, pair-formation must be re-established each season as mates associate little, if at all, when sharing a winter range. Scandinavian studies have shown that most birds are 2–3 years old when they first pair, but the few recent British observations confirm that first-year birds, especially females, do breed successfully, usually in a pairing with an older bird.

Aerial displays often start as early as January and continue till April. Not sur-

Length 48–62cm (18.9–24.4in), wingspan 135–165cm (53.1–65.0in), wing 30.6–36.6cm (12.0–14.4in), tail 18.0–22.0cm (7.0–8.6in), weight (of Scandinavian stock) 0.62–2.05kg (1.36–4.52lb).

The voice is mostly heard during nest-building and early incubation, the two main calls being a rapid, rhythmical, chattering *gek-gek-gek* and the female's protracted *hcc-aa*, reminiscent of the buzzard but more of a scream than a mew. Unlike most birds of prey, which are silent during the early morning, a pair of goshawks invariably calls on waking during the early part of the breeding cycle.

GOSHAWK

Goshawk eggs are large, averaging 59 × 45mm (2.3 × 1.8in), and unusual among diurnal raptors in being completely unmarked. Why they should not have camouflage markings like those of the sparrowhawk is a mystery. It has been suggested that hiding the eggs is unnecesary because the birds are such excellent guards, but small numbers are still eaten. The clutch size, too, is large for a bird of this size, a study of 47 in lowland Britain 1980–87 yielding a mean of 3.96 within a range of 2–5. Lost eggs may be replaced after 15–30 days. They are laid at 2 to 3-day intervals (captive birds apparently lay at alternate 2- and 3-day intervals) from mid-March to early May, but mostly late March to early April.

prisingly, the larger female plays the dominant role in courtship, at first screaming persistently to attract a mate in the dense woodland habitat. She may also display to advertise her tenancy of a territory. Once united, the pair engage in solo or mutual high circling – they soar on extended wings and show the underwing pattern, or beat the wings slowly, occasionally raising them high like a pigeon, spreading the tail and exposing the white under-tail coverts. There are also various diving and swooping manoeuvres with a great deal of mutual calling. Activity is greatest on warm, sunny days.

Nests are usually widely separated (rarely closer than 3km) and often re-used in successive years, though most pairs have several alternative sites. The female establishes and maintains the territory and generally starts nest refurbishment in February, continuing calling and nest-building through March. She is vigorous in defence of her territory, even against human intruders. Well before the eggs are laid, the male starts providing the female with food, often leaving it for her at a disused nest nearby and always announcing his arrival. This continues until after the young have hatched and may well serve to draw the attention of predators away from the nest in use. Refurbished nests are usually in broadleaved trees, whereas in conifers new ones are generally built. The untidy structure of twigs and branches is usually lined with greenery, and sometimes bark. A new one has an average diameter of 75–90cm (30–36in) and height of 25cm (10in), with a cup about 25cm (10in) wide and 10cm (4in) deep. Re-used nests may be much bigger. Apparently new nests are built mostly by the male but the female does most of the upgrading of an old one. The birds may start on the nest more than forty days before laying, and continue adding material, especially greenery, until the young have fledged. Most nests are in a tree fork or on a main side branch at a height of 10–20m (30–65ft).

The 35/38-day incubation is mainly by the female and starts with the first or second egg. However, the whole clutch usually hatches within two or three days because during the early stages of incubation the female does not sit tightly enough to generate temperatures sufficient to start embryonic development.

The female broods the young for the first 8–10 days and always stays close to the nest for at least 16 days. At first the male provisions the entire family, the female feeding the young bill-to-bill. If he is a good hunter she may remain at the nest for the entire nestling period, but in the event of shortage she may join the hunt earlier, in particular taking prey which has been spotted from the nest. After about 28 days the young can feed themselves with food brought to the nest, though apparently the male is incapable of rearing the brood if the female is lost. The chicks are not particularly aggressive to one another, but during periods of severe food shortage the larger ones will repeatedly attack, and even kill and eat their siblings. They fledge at 35–42 days, moving to nearby branches, and become independent at about 70 days, quickly dispersing.

For 45 British broods 1980–87 the mean brood size at fledging was 2.76, equivalent to 2.30 chicks per pair for the 54 pairs which attempted breeding. Larger broods saw the highest success rate, but were produced during the early stages of colonisation, when it is assumed that prime sites were selected and there was less competition. Fledged young were produced by 48 (84.2 per cent) of the 57 breeding attempts in which eggs were known to have been laid. Three of the nine failures were due to deliberate persecution, three to accidental disturbance by forest workers and three to natural causes — the eggs fell through one poorly renovated nest, another nest collapsed, and the eggs in the third failed to hatch.

Chick losses during the same period included three which were kicked out of the nest by a departing female, one falling during a gale, four dying of infection at two nests, and one probably preyed on by a tawny owl. Failure at the egg stage was mainly due to desertion (mainly through disturbance), infertility or cracking, but a few either fell from nests or were preyed on. An analysis of eleven of the sixteen eggs which failed to hatch showed low organochlorine levels in six, and nine had thin shells.

GOSHAWK

Diet and Feeding Behaviour

This fearless and utterly determined hunter takes a wide variety of prey, varying in proportions with local abundance but always concentrating on birds and mammals, up to the size of capercaillie and hare. Birds taken are mainly those which live in woodland or which frequent open country adjacent to forests, including jay, carrion crow, rook, magpie, woodpigeon, doves, feral pigeons, coot, moorhen, woodpeckers, thrushes, starling, owls and diurnal raptors, pheasant, grouse, duck, and a wide variety of songbirds, including nestlings. Mammals include rabbit, red squirrel, voles, mole and shrews. Few cold-blooded animals are recorded in the diet, and carrion is rarely taken. The larger female tends to take bigger animals.

Most prey is taken through surprise, in an attack showing astonishing bursts of speed which may be maintained for up to about 500m. In woodland this is usually far enough to overhaul any quarry, but in the open the hunt is generally abandoned after a relatively short distance. This is a supremely versatile hunter, swooping around tight bends to take prey in mid-air, snatching it from nests and branches and on the ground, stooping from height like a peregrine and even scrambling along branches or through thick undergrowth to make a kill. More unusually, it has been seen wading in shallow water after ducklings. In a vice-like grip, the prey is killed by the claws and may be plucked and eaten on the spot or taken to a favourite station, which may be an old nest. With larger mammals the stomach is usually rejected, but the other internal organs are eaten. Where a kill is too big for one meal, the left-overs may be stored for later consumption.

Migration, Movements and Roosting

Only the northernmost populations of goshawks must withdraw south for the winter, below the Arctic Circle in Fennoscandia and below the taiga zone in the USSR, movement being most marked when prey numbers slump. In Britain the diet is wide-ranging and generally there is plenty of food in winter so that the bird has no need to move. Indeed, the current feral population shows very little sign of seasonal movement. A great deal of suitable habitat remains to be exploited and there is minimal pressure on young to disperse. It is assumed that small numbers of birds which turn up in eastern England during August–November and March–May are of Continental origin, such vagrants becoming more likely as the western European population has recently increased.

This is a particularly solitary species for much of the year, mostly roosting alone in thick tree-tops (mostly evergreen) within woodland. Usually each bird has several alternative sites, although it may use one on several successive nights. A breeding pair usually roosts within the nest territory about 50–100m apart until the eggs are laid, after which the female roosts on or near the nest, with the male close by, if not in the nest-tree itself. Daytime loafing points are also in trees.

SPARROWHAWK
(Accipiter nisus)

Take it for all in all, there is perhaps no bird of the hawk kind more daring and spirited . . . The organ of combativeness, according to phrenologists, would appear to be largely developed in this bird: it seems to have universal letters of marque, and to act the part of a privateer against every thing that sails in its way.

Thus wrote Morris in 1850, and today the sparrowhawk has lost none of its zest. For example, in the week before I wrote this chapter, when I was slowly driving through a queue of traffic in town, a sparrowhawk seized a sparrow between my car and the next and nonchalantly killed it on the pavement while the traffic rolled by just three feet away.

The sparrowhawk has impressed man for many centuries. Shakespeare was but one of Britain's literary giants to have drawn on the raptor's qualities for illustration. For example, in his *Merry Wives of Windsor*, Mrs Ford addressed Falstaff: 'How now, my eyas-musket?' 'Eyas' or 'eyess' was an old term for a nestling or young bird from an eyrie or nest. The male sparrowhawk was then known as a 'spar', a separate name for the male being particularly important in the then common sport of falconry because the female is so much larger — about double the weight of the male; her requirements and lifestyle are therefore in some ways as different as those of a distinct species.

History and Conservation

The earliest British sparrowhawk records are from the end of the last glaciation — the Holocene — in Devon and South Wales, when the warming climate encouraged afforestation. It is therefore assumed that when most of Britain was forested some 2,000 years ago the population increased steadily and was large. However, the sparrowhawk prefers more open and young forest, leaving larger stretches of more mature forest to the larger goshawk. Thus the sparrowhawk population may well have continued to increase even as some of the forest was cleared for settlement and agriculture; but then it would have decreased steadily as deforestation increased and removed its breeding habitat, reaching a low point at the end of the 19th century when less than 5 per cent of Britain remained wooded.

It is thought that in the Middle Ages two of the sparrowhawk's few natural predators — the goshawk and pine marten — were much more common and would have had a significantly limiting effect. Human impact was still negligible, the sparrowhawk being of relatively little interest to the falconer. Naturally the larger female was preferred, a good one being capable of taking partridges, woodcock and young pheasants, though species such as blackbird and lark were more regular quarry. However, aristocratic ladies liked to carry them on picnic hunts, and they were given as prizes at tournaments with a frequency disproportionate to their usefulness. In the 13th century the sparrowhawk was said to be worth about one-sixth of the goshawk's value.

However, when gameshooting became popular and the shotgun was perfected, in the mid-19th century, persecution of the sparrowhawk began with a vengeance. The species was extensively shot and trapped by an army of gamekeepers which grew until it numbered about 22,000 by 1911, although it declined thereafter. The

extent of this slaughter was only too obvious when keepering was almost entirely suspended during the two world wars and the sparrowhawk made dramatic, if temporary recoveries.

The species was put on the protected list in 1961, but although sparrowhawk carcases were no longer displayed on keepers' gibbets, the shooting, trapping and poisoning continued behind the scenes. That said, it must be admitted that only a minority of the more selfish keepers continue the killing, and that the sport of pheasant shooting has in fact been of enormous help to the sparrowhawk, preserving huge areas of woodland. Indeed, the particular mix of wood and open country now recommended for game provides the ideal habitat for sparrowhawks.

Obviously the effect of this killing has been greatest in those areas where keepering has been most intense, notably in eastern England, where sparrowhawk numbers were kept well below the natural level for very long periods. Unfortunately these areas are also those hardest hit by the uncontrolled use of agrochemicals in the 1950s and 60s. East Anglia in particular is a long-established cereal-growing area where organochlorine pesticides were used extensively before their ill-effects were identified. Even now, long after the worst chemicals to cause eggshell-thinning and infertility have been withdrawn, sparrowhawks remain absent from parts of the south-east; this is probably because lowland farmland supports far fewer small prey-birds and nest-sites than it did before the last war.

However, not all habitat changes have been for the worse. The national reafforestation programme has provided many new breeding areas, especially in the uplands, allowing sparrowhawks to recolonise former territory — as the conifer plantations are managed on a rotational basis, cropped and re-planted regularly, there is always a high proportion of forest at a suitable stage for the sparrowhawk. Although these softwood forests harbour far fewer prey-birds than indigenous hardwoods do, they do at least make some provision in places where there had been no trees at all in modern times.

The sparrowhawk population has always shown a remarkable ability to respond rapidly to environmental change. Just as its numbers crashed alarmingly during the organochlorine era, so they have rocketed during these more sympathetic times. With the last few persecutors being rooted out, and every aspect of land use being scrutinised by caring conservationists, it is almost certain that the sparrowhawk population will continue to grow apace. With de-intensification of farming, more hedgerows will be planted and saved, more hardwoods grown and, hopefully, prey-bird populations will recover. Sadly, many sparrowhawks die on the roads or because they unwittingly dash themselves against buildings when in hot pursuit of prey; but this is an adaptable species, and its ability to thrive near man (providing it is not molested) should secure its future.

Distribution, Habitat and Population

The sparrowhawk has a wide distribution throughout Eurasia and North Africa, breeding in warm temperate to subtropical zones, from steppe to tropical broadleaf forest, from Ireland to Japan and south to the Mediterranean. Only the northernmost populations are migratory, the winter range extending south into the desert scrub of Africa, India, the Middle East and south-east Asia. For breeding the sparrowhawk prefers mature, fairly open stands of coniferous or deciduous or mixed trees down to about 10ha in size. Continuous stands of purely deciduous

Sparrowhawk numbers appear to be reaching maximum carrying capacity in many areas, though the population will continue to increase as further suitable habitat is made available, notably in upland plantations. For Britain (excluding Ireland) the maximum has been estimated at 32,000 pairs and currently there are thought to be at least 25,000 pairs plus 9,000 pairs in Ireland. In addition there are at least 40,000–45,000 non-breeders and about 66,000 young, giving a total British Isles resident population of about 170,000 at the end of summer, falling to about 105,000 by spring. Females are reported more than males because they tend to hunt in more open country in search of larger prey.

trees are used less often because they leave less scope for flight-paths. The ideal habitat includes glades, clearings and rides interspersed with copses, hedgerows, extensive woodland edge and other cover which facilitates surprise attack on small birds. Thus the species has moved readily into suburbia where orchards, parks and large gardens are used extensively, especially in winter.

There are not many places in the British Isles which are unsuitable for the species, and the current gaps in its range are mainly the legacy of persecution rather than unsuitability of habitat. Thus the most patchy distribution is in eastern England, where keepering has been most intense and compounded the depressive effects of intensive cereal farming, which has demanded an excessive use of toxic chemicals and the removal of trees and hedges. The only other gaps are in mountainous regions of the north and west, where there is no woodland and no small-bird prey to support the species. However, the recolonisation of eastern England continues, and in recent years the sparrowhawk has even moved into parts of some inner cities, including Bristol and Edinburgh.

Sparrowhawks are resident in the British Isles; newly independent young disperse from their natal areas, but there is no evidence of extensive winter movements. However, some Scandinavian birds overwinter in Britain, chiefly in eastern England where autumn- and spring-passage birds have been increasing in number as northern populations have recovered following the banning of organochlorine pesticides.

Field Characters and Anatomy

The female is up to 25 per cent larger than the male. Length 28–38cm (11.0–15.0in), wingspan 55–70cm (21.7–27.6in), wing: male 19.6–21.2cm (7.7–8.3in), female 23.1–25.6cm (9.0–10.0in), tail: male 14.3–15.6cm (5.6–6.1in), female 16. 9–18.4cm (6.7–7.2in), weight: male 0.11–0.19kg (0.24–0.43lb), female 0.18–0.34kg (0.40–0.75lb).

With the typical hawk characters of long tail and short, broad, rounded wings, the sparrowhawk is fairly easy to identify. However, the male is only a little larger than the merlin and about the size of a kestrel, with which it is sometimes confused in poor light and a strong wind, when it bends its wings backwards and appears sharp-winged like a falcon. The much larger female may be mistaken for a small goshawk, but is slimmer (especially across the breast), with a square-ended (not rounded) tail, proportionately shorter wings and faster wingbeats. The underparts have the typical hawk stripes, which in the female are brown on the belly. She also has a distinct pale stripe over the eye, which is usually lacking in the male. The male's upperparts are grey whereas the female's are brown. The juvenile also has brown upperparts, but with a rufous tinge in good light. Its underparts are spotted and blotched brownish in ragged bars. Although the full plumage is not acquired until about two years old, the young cannot usually be distinguished from the adults after the first moult.

Usually silent in winter, the sparrowhawk has several common breeding calls, including the fairly loud and rapid *kek-kek-kek-kek*, and a wailing, plaintive *whee-oo*, reminiscent of the goshawk. The male's calls are usually higher-pitched and more anxious than those of the female.

Most commonly seen dashing and swerving in low flight in pursuit of prey, the sparrowhawk beats its wings rapidly in short bursts interspersed with short glides, using its noticeably long tail to steer around obstacles. In soaring, the tail is usually fully closed or only slightly fanned, the wings held flat and slightly forward. A perched bird stands very upright and looks more leggy than the kestrel. Sometimes single birds are seen wheeling lazily high in the sky, as if through sheer enjoyment.

Breeding

Some birds are still in their juvenile plumage when they first breed at 1–2 years old. The pair-bond is mostly monogamous, and most break up after each breed-

ing season. Those that remain together stay in the same territory. Pairs form early in the year in Britain, often up to three months before laying.

Like the goshawk, and typical of woodland species, the sparrowhawk displays above the nesting territory, where it can be seen easily. The female appears to take the dominant role, though this impression is perhaps exaggerated by her tendency to frequent more open areas while the male is habitually more secretive. Both birds soar and swoop over the nest-site, with steep dives and shallow undulations, and they make good use of tail-flagging — exposing the white under-tail coverts in both aerial and perched displays. High-circling peaks during nest-building and egg-laying, birds ascending in tight spirals, occasionally beating the wings rapidly. In an exaggerated, slow display flight, the wingbeats are deep and deliberate. There are also high-speed chases, when the birds cartwheel and roll over to present talons.

Territories are usually at least 400m apart, but may be as close as 200m, regular spacing occurring only in well-wooded landscapes, but varying with tree mix and age. The larger female usually establishes the territory. The spacing of nests varies according to altitude and land fertility, which in turn govern the availability of prey. Woods are unacceptable when they are too thick to permit easy flight, such as young plantations which have yet to be thinned; or too open, when nests are extremely vulnerable. In most years a new nest is built, usually near the old ones, sometimes on the old nest of another species such as woodpigeon, but rarely on another sparrowhawk's. Most nests are in a fork or where several side-branches

Most sparrowhawk nests are in a fork, or where several side branches meet the trunk, conifers being preferred

The single clutch (replaced up to three times, on loss, but with fewer eggs) of 4–6 (range 3–7) eggs, average size 40 × 32mm (1.8 × 1.3in), is laid at 2 to 3-day intervals, mostly starting in May, but sometimes in late April or early June.

meet the trunk, conifers being preferred for their convenient platforms. Height is very variable, up to about 25m, but mostly 6–12m, and the position is usually close to a ride or clearing for easy access. The loose structure of twigs — average diameter 60cm (24in) — has a cup about 15cm (6in) across and 6cm (2.4in) deep. The lining is of fine twigs and bark chips, rarely of green foliage. In most pairs the female does most of the building, usually over about thirty days.

Incubation is by the female alone and takes 33–35 days per egg, 39–42 days per clutch, starting with any egg after the second. Generally, the larger the clutch the greater the spread of hatching dates, with increased initial size variation among chicks. During incubation the male brings food to the female, normally plucking each item beforehand so that the female may eat it quickly near the nest and get back to the eggs as soon as possible. It is thought that the male does not take over incubation at all because he is too small to cover the eggs properly.

Like other raptors, sparrowhawks hatch with a complete covering of down and their eyes open, and they are able to take food from their mother's bill immediately, turning to defecate towards the nest edge. Females gain weight faster than males and are heavier on fledging, but plumage and behavioural development is faster in males, helping them to survive alongside bigger sisters. Fledging is at 24–30 days, the males before the females. The female joins in the hunting during the last week of fledging and the young can tear up prey for themselves at about three weeks. If the female is killed the young will die because the male is unable to feed the well-grown young alone. Independence is achieved about 3–4 weeks after leaving the nest, when the young will have acquired the necessary survival skills and will disperse.

Post-fledging survival is generally greater in lowland habitats, and at a higher percentage from adult rather than yearling mothers. Early layings generally produce most young and achieve greater productivity, the later the laying the fewer the number of young fledged. This is contrary to the seasonal trend in food supply, and appears to be related to the lack of experience in hunting skills of late layers. Also, productivity has been greatly affected by toxic chemicals and persecution. In studies before 1947, 92 per cent of hatchlings fledged; all the young in 78 per cent of broods survived; and of 80 clutches, all produced at least one young. But in the period 1947–55 only 66 per cent of 19 clutches produced at least one fledgling; and in the period 1956–70, 55 per cent of 48 clutches produced at least one fledgling, the mean brood size for all pairs being 1.6. The brood size declined from 4.0 in a sample of 117 before 1947 to 3.2 in a sample of 29 during 1947–55, when BHC and DDT were commonly used; and to 2.9 in a sample of 219 during 1956–70, when aldrin, dieldrin and heptachlor were widely used. Many failures have been due to infertility, egg breakage, desertion and shooting of the female. Productivity increases with the age of the female up to the seventh year, after which it appears to deteriorate, though too few birds studied have attained this age to facilitate accurate analysis of the decline. In Newton's 14-year study in south-west Scotland, 1971–84, for every 100 eggs laid, an average of 60 chicks hatched and 50 fledged, but only about 14 survived to breed and just 12 were successful. Thus only 12 per cent of eggs resulted in productive breeders.

Diet and Feeding Behaviour

As its name implies, the sparrowhawk is a specialist bird feeder, the larger female tending to take larger quarry. Although both sexes take almost any bird available

in an area, the emphasis is on species which are conspicuous or easily caught, and this includes sparrows, finches, tits, thrushes and starlings. Fledglings are commonly taken along with adults, but nestlings and carrion infrequently. Larger prey includes woodpigeon (often the most significant prey species), stock dove, jay, lapwing, partridge, young pheasant, red grouse, young black grouse, kestrel, and even both male and female of its own kind. Both sexes can carry prey as large as themselves.

Small mammals taken are mainly voles and small rabbits, but also include shrews, weasel, young hare, mole, wood mouse, rat, squirrels and bats. Insects and amphibians are rarely taken. Regional and seasonal variation in the diet is pronounced, and some individuals may specialise through ease of capture, but generally birds account for over 90 per cent, and as much as 98 per cent of the diet.

This dashing hawk displays amazing manoeuvrability in high-speed chases, but sometimes it is so intent in the pursuit of its prey that even its great agility cannot prevent it crashing into buildings or smashing through windows. Some birds are even pursued inside buildings, such as barns. In a study of 341 sparrowhawks received by Monks Wood Experimental Station 1964–80, a staggering 48 per cent had died through collision or other accidents, with 11 per cent attributable to shooting, 14 per cent to haemorrhages, 9 per cent to starvation, 4 per cent to disease, and 14 per cent to unknown causes. A small number have also been killed by cats, presumably when on the ground at their own kills. However, although these figures are impressive, they must be balanced against the fact that the bulk of mortality is unseen, and there is no way of knowing what proportion of the total number of deaths is attributable to accidents. While the proportion of sparrowhawks killed by motor traffic and in collision with windows has increased in recent decades, it is pleasing to report that the number shot has declined.

A variety of hunting methods is used, but always the emphasis is on concealment and getting as close as possible before launching a surprise attack. In searching for prey, the hawk mostly moves through woodland, from perch to perch, pausing briefly at each to scan the surroundings. There is also a low, contour-hugging flight, using the cover of hedgerows and woodland edge to approach distant birds or chance upon others, which are seized before they can react. Individual birds in flocks are singled out and pursued with great single-mindedness, despite the cries and mobbing of companions. Small birds are frequently frightened out of cover by the hawk striking at their protecting foliage, or simply by its flying over them.

If prey is not killed outright by the strike, it is stabbed by the talons until it stops wriggling and then eaten on the ground or a favourite plucking post. However, prey is often still alive when eaten. The hawk stands with both feet on its victim, droops its wings so that they form a kind of tent (mantling), spreads it tail as if to give support, and rips off the feathers or fur. Its long legs help it to keep the jabbing bill and thrashing wings of a struggling victim at bay. The hawk's long thin shanks and curved, needle-sharp talons are also ideally suited to grasping quick-moving prey at awkward angles.

Despite the sparrowhawk's hunting skills and the fact that much of the countryside seems to abound with suitable prey, this raptor often goes hungry. Not only are most small birds extremely vigilant in listening for alarm calls, but also many attacks are unsuccessful. The sparrowhawk is not fast enough in level flight to catch many species and is dependent on surprise. Among the more unusual techniques employed is hunting on foot. Sometimes the sparrowhawk hops

Young sparrowhawks: females gain weight faster than males

and runs from branch to branch, especially among conifers, apparently searching for nestlings, and will run across open ground behind low vegetation to approach ground-feeding prey, including small-bird flocks.

Migration, Movements and Roosting

Although the species is migratory in the colder parts of its range, the breeding population of the British Isles is wholly resident, with adults more or less sedentary. Juvenile dispersal is mostly within 100km and in random directions. In winter, individual home ranges are generally centred on breeding sites, but these overlap considerably and birds frequently forage widely in open country.

Passage migrants and winter visitors from Norway, Sweden and Finland occur mostly in eastern districts, their incidence having increased in recent years as overseas populations, too, have recovered from the organochlorine era. Winter visitors also come into southern England from the Low Countries.

Outside the breeding season the sparrowhawk is solitary, though several may roost quite close together within the same wood, generally within thick tree-tops, especially evergreens, and sometimes using the same sites on several successive nights. Blackthorn and large hawthorns are popular alternatives to evergreens. Birds often arrive at and depart from roosts in near darkness to maximise hunting time. During the breeding season the female roosts on or near the nest, the male elsewhere. Even in winter, roosts tend to be near breeding places, but usually in thicker cover than that used for nesting. The male's tendency to use thicker cover than the female may be related to his smaller size, deciduous scrub and thicket-stage conifers being favoured. Adults often use roost sites for loafing during the day. Pre-breeding birds roost more widely, in ranges incorporating smaller woods and more open country.

BARN OWL
(Tyto alba)

FOR many centuries the barn owl was the countryman's constant companion, its distinctive pale form ghosting through the dusk as he toiled homeward. It was the guardian of every village church, and no barn was complete without one. Morris's 'high churchman' was the epitome of old England, a comforting vision of times when the land was in good heart. But sadly, even though it is still one of the world's most widespread landbirds, in this century its British population has crashed and most children now know the bird only from its popular image on greetings cards and posters.

History and Conservation

Although the species is not particularly cold-tolerant and Scotland is the most northerly part of its range, the barn owl was present in Pleistocene Britain, towards the end of the last glaciation, in Derbyshire and Devon. Indeed, it appears to have been widespread in Britain for at least 10,000 years. Little is known about the bird before 1850, but a study of literature reveals that it was a familiar species. During the late 18th and early 19th centuries the widespread creation of boundary hedgerows and ditches through the Enclosure Acts, the creation of water meadows and opening up of woodlands, all greatly increased the amount of 'grassland edge' hunting habitat which is so important for the barn owl. In addition, the spread of non-intensive agriculture, particularly corn production, provided more prey through corn-ricks and straw-bedded cattle yards, and also a wealth of farm buildings suitable for nesting. Thus the species seems to have increased during the early part of the Agricultural Revolution, which is remarkable because there were some very severe winters throughout this period.

Unfortunately, the fortuitous helping hand of man was short-lived, and with the rapid growth in game rearing from about 1850 the barn owl was persecuted relentlessly. Indeed, its conspicuousness and habit of living near man made it particularly easy to shoot and trap, and its great beauty made it a very popular decoration for Victorian living rooms — many thousands were taken by collectors. The species' decline was exacerbated by a succession of fifteen hard winters in the second half of the 19th century, and the increasing efficiency of farming through mechanisation which reduced the prey supply.

During this century the situation has worsened considerably: thousands of miles of hedgerows and ditches have been removed to make bigger fields; marshes and rough grazing rich in prey have been drained and developed; and innumerable nest-sites in trees and buildings have been lost — trees in particular, through Dutch elm disease and freak storms. Amelioration of the climate 1900–1950 provided some respite, and numbers temporarily increased in some areas, such as the north east; and there was also relief during both world wars, when keepering was largely suspended. In the north, the creation of large expanses of rough grassland, through the Forestry Commission's establishment of conifer plantations, brought further temporary aid, but these woods were of little use as they matured. Overall, the nett loss of habitat to agriculture and development has been catastrophic, and the introduction of modern rodenticides has reduced the prey population even further.

BARN OWL
Once known as white owl, white hoolet, yellow owl, silver owl, church owl, dylluan wen, cailleach-oidhche gheal, screech owl, scritch owl, hissing owl, screaming owl, common owl, roarer, Billy wise, Billy wix, Billy whit, Jenny howlet, Jenny owl, Madge howlett, Madge owl, moggy, padge, pudge, pudge owl, oolert, woolert, owlerd, hoolet, hullart, cherubim, hobby owl, gill howter, berthuan, gillihowlett, gil-hooter, ullet, ullat and gilly owlet

The species Latin specific *albus* means white. Its common name is obviously derived from its habit of nesting in barns, and has been in common use since the 17th century, though the term 'white owl' was at least as popular until the end of the 19th century. The bird's many folk names clearly indicate just how familiar it once was to the bulk of the population, especially through its habit of hunting in the late afternoon as well as by night. Indeed, it was even known as the 'common owl' in many districts.

BARN OWL

Periodic climatic extremes, especially prolonged snow cover and drought, are linked with cyclical prey abundance and may bring temporary population crashes, but alone they do not account for the protracted decline of recent decades. Widespread destruction and degradation of habitat, however, is certainly of paramount importance, in that this inhibits the barn owl's reproductive potential through reducing the food supply. Temporarily displaced or dispersing juvenile barn owls suffer a high mortality rate because the bulk of habitat has become so impoverished. And the more fragmented the population becomes, the less viable it is. That is why the establishment of 'conservation corridors' is now deemed so important.

While the barn owl has failed to adapt to the modern farm environment and its population has probably fallen by 75 per cent since the 1920s, the tawny owl has thrived and is now probably about 15–20 times more common than the barn owl. The tawny is much better at switching to alternative prey when voles are scarce, and it is a significant competitor for food and nest-sites. Indeed, it has been reported that tawny owls sometimes kill barn owls in competition for nest-sites, and the latter's increasing tendency towards diurnal hunting this century may be in response to this rivalry.

Among other factors limiting the population, the number of road deaths has been most alarming — 51.9 per cent (387 birds) in a 1982–86 study of 746 deaths where the cause was known. Projected, this suggests that some 5,000 birds die annually on Britain's highways. Even in quieter Ireland, road mortality constituted as much as 49 per cent of reported deaths. The next most significant known cause of mortality was drowning in water butts, cattle troughs, slurry pits, tanks and natural waters, accounting for 6.16 per cent (46) of birds recovered. In the same study, 5.09 per cent (38) of birds were found to have died through collision with overhead wires, 3.08 per cent (23) were trapped in buildings, 2.68 per cent (20) were shot, 3.22 per cent (24) succumbed to chemical poisoning, 2.41 per cent (18) to predation (chiefly by the tawny owl and goshawk), 1.74 per cent (13) to collision with trains, and 0.54 per cent (4) to collision with aircraft. Although the true significance of these figures is unknown in that the vast majority of deaths must go unrecorded, their occurrence is nonetheless serious for such a struggling species.

But the barn owl has many friends in the conservation movement, and there is a great deal going on to improve its status. Much as the panda has symbolised the efforts of the World Wildlife Fund, the barn owl has portrayed the right image for raptor conservation, through its beauty, its human-like face and nostalgic association with pre-war countryside. At the forefront in trying to redress the balance is the Hawk and Owl Trust, which has published several important books and pamphlets which explain what farmers and members of the public can do to help. Although there is nothing we can do about the vagaries of weather, there is much to be done in reinstating the food supply through the maintenance and re-establishment of rough grassland edge to provide valuable links between oases of suitable habitat. But hunting territory cannot be fully exploited without breeding sites, so equal effort is being put into providing homes for barn owls. People renovating or converting farm buildings are urged to consider owls in their plans, and to create owl 'windows' and/or nestboxes. The Hawk and Owl Trust's Barn Owl Conservation Network is also co-ordinating the erection of nestboxes on telegraph poles, which has already been highly successful in helping barn owls to recolonise areas from which they have been absent for many years. The Forestry

Commission, too, is active in this work and has produced a useful bulletin entitled *Barn Owl Conservation in Forests*. In addition, rearing and release schemes have been successful.

At the same time, the control of chemicals in the environment must be improved. Although so-called 'safe' compounds are relatively harmless to birds when used alone, their interaction in the field has been causing problems. In 1990, it was revealed that the insecticide Malathion can produce a lethal cocktail when it comes into contact with fairly non-toxic fungicides such as prochloraz. Such new poisons have been linked with the barn owl's decline.

Distribution, Habitat and Population

In the days when Britain was still mostly covered by forest, it is likely that the barn owl was primarily a cliff-haunting bird; its light coloration may have evolved for camouflage in its original cliff habitat, much of which was composed of chalk and limestone. However, old buildings have now replaced the natural crevices and caves the barn owl once used for nesting, and as the availability of suitable nest-sites increased with the spread of agriculture, the species was able to exploit the wide acreages of open country with thick ground cover which provides a suitable habitat for its small-mammal prey.

The British countryside of modern times, with its patchwork of fields and hedgerows dotted with old buildings and hollow trees, has been ideal for the barn owl, which is quite tolerant of human activity. Where unmolested it will happily live in suburbia, but unlike the tawny owl it shuns towns. The greatest densities are found in low-lying, arable areas near the coast, where prey is abundant and the climate relatively mild. Young forestry plantations below about 300m hold good numbers too, the vole population building in the long grass around the trees. Areas avoided are those with sparse vegetation, especially where winters are severe.

Because the barn owl population is very unstable, governed as it is by weather extremes and cyclical prey supply, its distribution is constantly changing. Overall, however, the cold and wet uplands of the north and west are avoided, and although the distribution is widespread, it is patchy throughout England, Wales, southern Scotland and Ireland. There is little change in winter, but in cold weather the species gravitates towards lower altitudes, arable farmland and coastal marshes. Although Scotland's population is centred on the milder, maritime south-west, and distribution further north is increasingly thin, there are isolated breeding records from the far north. A detailed analysis of distribution is contained in Bunn, Warburton and Wilson's 1982 monograph *The Barn Owl*.

Rather surprisingly, recorders have found the barn owl one of the most difficult birds to locate, so it could be that the species is in fact substantially under-recorded. There is also considerable annual fluctuation in response to vole numbers. For example, the population of south-west Scotland varies between about 140 pairs in poor vole years and some 320 in a good one. The highest densities recorded are 13.4 pairs per 10km square on the Isle of Wight, and 10 per km square in west Cornwall. However, densities are now very low almost everywhere.

Field Characters and Anatomy

At rest and in flight, the 'white owl' should not be confused with any other species in Britain. It is often seen hunting by daylight, especially in cold weather, and its

In 1932 Blaker estimated the population of England and Wales at 12,000 pairs (25,000 birds including non-breeders), but this figure is suspect. In 1982 there were possibly only 4,500–9,000 pairs for the entire British Isles. The latest estimate is from 1987, when Shawyer quoted about 3,750 pairs for England and Wales plus 650 pairs in Scotland – about 10,000 birds altogether, including unpaired individuals. But again the risk of inaccuracy is stressed, especially as it has been shown that within a Scottish region the number of barn owls can more than double across a single vole cycle and prey peaks are not necessarily synchronised between regions. Lack of observers has restricted survey work in Ireland, but projection of sampling 1982–85 suggested 600–900 pairs. In 1986 Glue (for the BTO Atlas) estimated the British Isles winter population at 12,500–25,000 birds.

Length 33–35cm (13.0–13.8in), wingspan 85–93cm (33.5–36.6in), wing 27.9–30.0cm (11.0–11.8in), tail 10.9–12.4cm (4.3–4.9in), weight 0.24–0.36kg (0.53–0.79lb). The sex differences in size are not significant.

BARN OWL

The species' wide range of calls gave rise to some of its folk names, such as 'hissing owl' and 'screech owl'. However, some of the seventeen sound signals described are non-vocal, including tongue-clicking (previously it was thought that this sound was produced by snapping the beak) in excitement, courtship and aggression; and wing-clapping by the male in his courtship 'moth flight'. Most of the calls are very difficult to express on paper, but they include the 'screech' – a penetrating, tremulous, hissing scream about two seconds long and with many variations; a non-tremulous wailing likened to cats fighting; a sustained, defensive hiss; 'snoring' – sustained, wheezy rasping or hissing; a mixture of twitters, squeaks and chirrups; and 'purring' (the female's being higher-pitched.

OPPOSITE
Barn owl on a Norfolk gravestone. Not so long ago no churchyard was complete without one

exceptionally buoyant, wavering flight, often with dangling legs, is most distinctive. Some birds have slightly darker — light grey and buff — underparts, but even with these the heart-shaped facial disc, the lack of streaks or bars on the underparts, and the leg length will always distinguish. Darker birds which occur chiefly in autumn in counties bordering the North Sea are thought to be of the Continental *T.a.guttata* subspecies. The sexes are slightly dissimilar, the female usually having more heavily marked underparts and more grey markings on the upperparts. However, there is considerable individual variation in both sexes, so distinguishing male from female is difficult and generally unsafe with unknown pairs. Once the juvenile has moulted its downy plumage, it resembles the adult, at about three months. Barn owls differ from the *Strigidae* owls in that their tails usually end in a shallow V, their inner and middle toes are of roughly equal length, the claw of the middle toe has a comb-like serrated edge, and the breastbone and wishbone are fused together.

At rest, the leg length is obvious, and the gait is a rolling walk with an occasional lope. The wingbeats are extremely variable, ranging from the slightest flick to deep, elastic strokes, the body and legs sometimes buckling slightly through the muscular effort required in hovering or holding a hunting line.

Breeding

The pair-bond is mostly monogamous (males are occasionally bigamous) and long-term, some pairs remaining at the nest-site throughout the year, presumably defending it through the winter. Other pairs maintain a looser association within a territory, staying at different roosts; this is probably the more common. Individuals, too, sometimes hold territory throughout the year. Both sexes breed for the first time at one year old, though sometimes not until two years when the food supply is poor.

In suitable conditions, true courtship begins in late February, when the male hunts more by daylight to present food to his mate; he screeches as he patrols his territory, to repel rivals and attract the female. There is much chasing as the male persistently follows the female wherever she goes, both birds twisting and weaving intricately, often at high speed. Sometimes the pursuit is more leisurely, the male following at a few metres above and behind the female. Most chases involve frequent screaming, the female's calling being described as wailing. In his 'moth flight', the male hovers before the head of the perched hen, with legs dangling for up to five seconds, occasional wing-clapping probably being involuntary. In further aerial display, the male repeatedly flies in and out of the nest site, trying to entice the hen in. He also calls from inside, but if this fails he will resort to a song-flight. In March and April the male begins to screech more loudly and frequently around the nest site, and when the female is presented with plenty of food she responds by reverting to juvenile behaviour, snoring repeatedly and standing about like an owlet. Bill-fencing, tongue-clicking and cheek-rubbing are common and important features of courtship, and are thought to represent ritualised feeding.

Barn owls show great attachment to traditional nest sites, with successive pairs (most birds live only 3–4 years) often using the same ones for twenty or thirty years, and there are well authenticated cases of sites being in continuous use for over a century — some trees for much longer. In the British Isles the species selects predominantly three distinct types of nest site: the insides of buildings, large tree cavities, and rock fissures, and there is little evidence of change over the last few centuries. In 1932 Blaker found that 44 per cent of 915 nests in England

BARN OWL

Two broods are very uncommon in Britain, yet there are several records of three from years with optimal conditions. The 2–8 (1–9) eggs, average size 40 × 32 (1.57 × 1.26in), can be laid any time from late February to early July, but the majority are laid in April, May and June and there is no regional variation. Clutches laid from July are probably replacements.

and Wales were in hollow trees, 53 per cent in buildings and 2.8 per cent in cliff-like situations. In 1976 Sharrock stated that 39 per cent of nests analysed by the BTO were in trees. In 1982 Bunn gave 32 per cent trees, 65 per cent man-made structures and 3.2 per cent cliffs. Of 2,700 nest sites detailed by Shawyer (1987), 64.68 per cent were in buildings, 34.8 per cent in trees, 9 per cent in caves and cliffs, the rest unknown. With buildings, agricultural were the most popular at 75.78 per cent, with 9.6 per cent in domestic, 5.74 per cent industrial, 3.5 per cent churches, and smaller numbers for castles, mills, dovecotes, bridges, oasthouses and mines. Of the 414 tree nests, 34.3 per cent were in elm, 34.06 per cent in oak, 15.94 per cent in ash, 5.56 per cent in willow, 2.66 per cent in beech and smaller numbers in poplar, walnut, sycamore, pine, chestnut and birch. Choice is not based on opportunism, but primarily climate: in regions of greatest rainfall, the selection is almost exclusively of man-made structures, but where rainfall is light and winds drying, hollow-tree sites predominate. Thus there is a clear east–west divide with, for example, 95 per cent of sites in buildings in wet Devon, and 70 per cent in trees in dry Suffolk. Because the owl's soft, little-oiled plumage is easily waterlogged the bird cannot supply sufficient food for its family during prolonged rain, and fledglings in wet areas are very susceptible to chilling and disease. In coastal regions of Scotland, cliffs, caves and bank cavities are especially important as they are often the only nest sites available. Imprinting also appears to be important in continuing regional nest site specialisation. Recent widespread use of artificial nestboxes has been extremely successful.

No nest is made, and even a scrape is thought to be no more than the fortuitous creation of the male's courtship behaviour. However, because the breeding season is so long there is often a soft bed of pellets plus a few feathers before the eggs are laid. Incubation generally takes 30–31 days, is probably by the hen only, and begins with the first egg. Hatching is asynchronous, at similar intervals to laying — two to three days.

Both parents care for the young, the female brooding them almost continuously for the first ten days and feeding them with prey brought by the male. She is remarkably patient in tearing up and passing morsels to the owlets, which are very ugly at first. Equally exceptional is close attention to nest hygiene, which is essential during the barn owl's unusually long fledging period of some 56 days. At first the female eats the faeces, but when she joins the hunt the young back to the edge of the nest hollow to defecate. Nonetheless, some unfavourably positioned nests become soiled. As with many other birds, the owlets become considerably heavier than the adults before they leave the nest, independence being achieved about 3–5 weeks later. The nestlings are rarely aggressive towards each other. On the contrary, older owlets are known to feed weaker siblings of the same brood, a phenomenon perhaps unique among British birds. The only apparent explanation is that the donor birds are already replete at such times. Cannibalism does occur, but only rarely, and it is thought that in most cases the owlets — not necessarily the youngest — die of starvation before being eaten by their siblings; very young owlets peck at anything to hand when food is short so their fratricide may be fortuitous. However, with older owlets it can be deliberate and cold-blooded, and adults, too, sometimes kill and occasionally eat their young or eggs, but perhaps only after human disturbance.

Breeding success varies according to food supply and the weather. In a study of 214 nests in 1932, Blaker found an average clutch size of 3.8 from which 2.8 young fledged; however, his results were from only one year, and since then conditions

have fluctuated dramatically. A study by Glue of 155 clutches (mainly 1960–80) gave an average of 4.7 eggs produced and 2.2 young fledged. Shawyer's study for the Hawk Trust, 1982–86, gave an average clutch size of 4.86 and a fledging success of 3.00 from 125 nests where at least one young was reared (290 nests started).

The female barn owl is an extremely attentive parent

Diet and Feeding Behaviour

Since it is a nocturnal bird, the barn owl is not easily observed, but numerous studies of its pellets have helped build up a clear picture of its diet. Fortunately, these are easily distinguished from those of other owls, being black, sausage-shaped, about the size of a man's thumb, and usually rounded at both ends. When fresh they are glossy, and even when they are dry they are smooth and dark, being much less friable than those of other owls. Barn owls also cast small, roundish pellets, mostly of fur. Because so many barn owl pellets are deposited in dry, sheltered places they are particularly easy to find.

The barn owl has no distinct preferences in its diet, although it clearly avoids invertebrates. It simply goes for those animals which are found and killed most easily, mainly the small mammals which frequent its preferred open habitat of rough grassland, marsh, farmland and young forestry. In Britain the short-tailed or field vole is the most important prey, followed by the common shrew — proportions vary regionally, more with the habitat and vulnerability than numbers

145

present; these two prey species are the most abundant in the open habitat where the barn owl normally hunts. Although the woodmouse is the most abundant of our rodents, it features less in the diet because it is a woodland and hedgerow species, and thus far less vulnerable. Vole numbers are highest in autumn and winter, while shrews are most common in spring and summer. The numbers of back-up species such as bank vole and pygmy shrew become more important when the short-tailed vole population has one of its cyclical 'crashes'; unless at least one of the secondary prey species is available in compensatory numbers at these times the barn owl will suffer. Ireland and the Isle of Man have no voles or common shrews, so the main prey there are other rodents, especially woodmice and brown rats, backed up by housemice and pygmy shrews. These four species are the only small mammals which are widely distributed in Ireland.

Less important mammal prey are moles, young rabbits, weasels, squirrels (one British record), and bats which roost and breed in hollow trees and buildings (predominantly the four most widely distributed and abundant species). Birds, too, are mostly minor prey, the house sparrow and starling being the most commonly taken, though many other species of similar size and weight are also caught. By day, fast-moving birds are generally too difficult for relatively slow owls, so barn owls concentrate on those at roost, beating their wings against bushes and trees to disturb them. Local exploitation of communal roosts may lead to an above-average number of birds in the diet. Larger and more unusual bird prey recorded includes woodpigeon, common snipe, lapwing, woodcock, young rook, corncrake and dunlin. In Ireland and the Ise of Man, where voles and common shrews are absent, birds are taken in higher numbers than in any other part of Britain. On the British mainland some barn owls occasionally specialise in birds, though this is usually in response to extreme conditions — for example in the deep snow of 1981–2, at least four Cumbrian barn owls hunted flocks of chaffinches and skylarks on barley stubble in the daytime. Prolonged snow cover leads to high mortality among small-mammal specialists such as barn owls.

Reptiles are rarely taken, but amphibians, especially frogs and toads which are nocturnal, noisy and easy to catch, are caught in moderate numbers. However, barn owls do not seem to exploit temporary abundances because owlets appear to reject frogs. There are reliable accounts of freshwater fish being taken, the owl dropping perpendicularly into the water to catch them, but such captures are exceptional. Invertebrates such as grasshoppers, beetles and earwigs are taken, but are mostly positively avoided — they constitute only a tiny part of the diet, and abundances are not exploited even when staple prey items are scarce.

The majority of barn owls hunt chiefly by night and only occasionally by day in response to changing conditions; however, some are almost exclusively nocturnal, and others habitually hunt by day throughout the year irrespective of weather and prey supply. Not surprisingly, human disturbance and also concerted mobbing by other birds both inhibit daytime emergence. There is also some correlation between daylight hunting and local peak prey activity.

The barn owl's long, broad wings enable it to hunt slowly a few metres above the ground with scarcely a sound; it prefers open areas with little or no cover. The head turns constantly this way and that as the owl scans the grass, its silence not only avoiding detection but also enabling it to listen intently for prey; it will frequently rise and fall, jinking and hovering as every sound or movement is investigated. Sometimes it performs amazing aerobatics to position itself for a headlong plunge towards its victim. At the last moment the head is withdrawn, the feet are

OPPOSITE
Barn owl and young. Some two-thirds of nests are in buildings

147

swung forward into the position formerly occupied by the head, and the eyes are closed — presumably to protect them. If emitting frequencies over 5kHz, prey can be located with astonishing accuracy — less than 1° in both horizontal and vertical planes — in total darkness. Apparently the binocular vision is also important, because a wild bird blind in one eye had great difficulty in hunting. Hunting from perches is less common. Mammals up to the size of a young rat are mostly swallowed whole, but birds are usually decapitated and eaten piecemeal, sometimes with the head rejected and the larger feathers roughly plucked. Hunting barn owls do not screech to frighten their prey into movement. Prey is usually carried in one foot, rarely the bill.

Although a pair of barn owls and their young may consume over 1,000 rodents during their three-month nesting period, the barn owl's importance in vermin control is exaggerated. In most cases the majority of prey taken is well away from human habitation, and any damage caused by the prey species to crops or trees is insignificant. On the contrary, many of the rodents would themselves account for pests in the form of invertebrates. Yet there is no doubting the barn owl's importance in a healthy food chain and it is good to know that many farmers are now not only providing homes for barn owls, but also putting food 'dumps' of undressed waste grain and root crops alongside hedgerows and around field headlands to encourage voles and mice. These can be strategically placed on the owls' regular beats, well away from farmsteads to reduce the risk of unwanted pests. Such dumps are especially important during the snow-covered days of winter. Alternatively, trapped prey can be placed on feeding ledges near building roosts.

Migration, Movements and Roosting

The barn owl is resident throughout its range. British birds are largely very sedentary, most adults remaining paired through the winter. During cold weather, movements to lower or milder areas are mostly very local, but severe weather can induce substantial nomadic movements out of regions where prey has temporarily been depleted. In years of normal food supply most dispersing juveniles settle within 20km of their birthplaces, and only a tiny percentage of birds of all ages are found over 100km away from their ringing places. Britain does not seem to have the eruptive dispersal of young as is usual on the Continent — this is governed by cyclical prey supply and snow cover. However, such European movements do bring stragglers of the *guttata* race to eastern Britain.

For roosting, the barn owl almost always uses one well-sheltered site, and this is often used subsequently for nesting; typical sites are in the interiors of buildings, holes in walls, tunnels between bales of hay, hollow trees, and — less frequently — in dense trees and bushes (especially evergreens). Very often not only is the same perch regularly used, but also the same part of the perch, especially in buildings. Alternative roosts in a territory are usually used only after disturbance — and this need only be a single incident. More unusual sites recorded include an alder thickly clad in honeysuckle, low stumps among high reeds (used by two birds), gorse bushes and the ground beneath an overhanging bank.

One point of interest concerns the reports of 'ghost' owls at roost. Such birds appear to have acquired luminosity through using hollow trees harbouring phosphorescent bacteria or the sometimes luminous honey fungus (which feeds on rotten wood). Apparently glowing particles adhere to the birds' plumage.

TAWNY OWL
(*Strix aluco*)

Althrough absent from Ireland, this is the most common and widespread owl in Europe and perhaps the most numerous raptor in Britain. It is the owl of fairy tales, whose voice of the night has become part of our literary heritage: *tu-whit, tu-whoo* is the most familiar rendition, though not strictly accurate in that one owl will not utter the two main calls close together. Woodland duets have probably given rise to this impression.

History and Conservation

Earliest British records are from the Pleistocene, from caves in Derbyshire and the south-west, towards the end of the last glaciation, presumably during periods when trees were present. With subsequent warming of the climate and general afforestation of Britain, this woodland bird would have been widespread and at its most numerous, its numbers decreasing sharply with deforestation in modern times.

Although it is an insignificant predator of game, it suffered greatly through shooting in the 19th century. Morris (1850) wrote:

> Here is another victim of persecution! Were it not for the friendly shelter of the night and the fostering care of some few friends, where is the brown owl that would be able to maintain a place among the feathered tribes of England? Their 'passports' are invariably sent to them in the form of cartridge paper; a double-barrelled gun furnishes a ready 'missive'; their 'congé' is given with a general 'discharge' . . .

Many thousands were shot and trapped indiscriminately and displayed on gamekeepers' gibbets. Even four of the five released near Belfast in 1900 were shot, and the introduction of protective legislation has not completely halted the slaughter.

Fortunately, things improved on several fronts after 1900. First, up to 1950 there was sustained warming of the climate bringing improved prey supply. Second, there was a steady decline in keepering which, moreover, was largely suspended during the two World Wars, enabling the species to make substantial gains. Third, the national afforestation programme started to provide much new habitat. Thus the first thirty years of this century saw a substantial increase in numbers and widespread range expansion, which continued into the early 1950s in northern districts. Unlike the barn owl, the tawny reacted well to environmental changes, its catholic diet and ability to survive severe winters enabling it to exploit the spread of suburbia and the transformation of the countryside. Its physical dominance over other owls has also helped — for example in ousting barn owls from traditional tree nest sites. Furthermore it is relatively long-lived compared with other British owls.

Some expansion is continuing in the uplands, with new habitat provided by conifer forests, but overall the species has not shown any great change since the late 1950s. The era of organochlorine pesticides in the late 50s and early 60s seemed to make relatively little impact, and during the bitter winter of 1962–3 the species suffered less than other owls. A peak appears to have been reached in the

TAWNY OWL
Once known as wood owl, brown owl, common brown owl, ivy owl, wood ullat, beech owl, hoot owl, howlett, Jenny howlett, tawny hooting owl, brown ullert, brown hoolet, golden owl, grey owl, ullet, Jinny yewlet, Billy hooter, Gilly hooter, hollering owl, screech owl, hill hooter, ferny hoolet, *Cailleach oidhche* — Gaelic for old woman of the night

Many of the species' folk names are derived from its calls, the word 'owl' itself going back to the Anglo Saxon *ūle*, which has counterparts all over Europe, all deriving from some ancient root meaning 'to howl'. The Latin specific, too, originates in the call, deriving from the Greek *strizo*, 'to screech'. 'Brown owl' and 'wood owl' were perhaps the two most popular genuine folk names relating to plumage and habitat, but these gradually became secondary when Pennant coined the name 'tawny owl' in 1768, to contrast with white owl – his term for the barn owl.

TAWNY OWL

early 70s, and since then the population appears to have fluctuated around a slightly lower level. Low points in the 80s were probably governed by severe winters and troughs in small-mammal cycles.

The loss of so many nest trees to Dutch elm disease must have had a serious impact, but the species has responded well to widespread provision of nestboxes. Unlike rural tawnies, which may not even attempt to breed in poor prey years, urban tawnies have taken advantage of a more stable food supply to achieve consistent breeding success. In particular, town owls have exploited the bird populations which are increasingly attracted to gardens by owners more aware of conservation needs. Rodents, too, are attracted by dense shrubberies. Some tawnies have even learnt to pick off some of the rats and mice which feed on the fast-food scraps littering the streets in the small hours of the morning, and at least one bird has taken to roosting by day on a street light. However, man's environment is not all good news. Many tawny owls, especially juveniles, are killed in collision with road traffic, trains and overhead wires, and there are also recent reports of contamination with organic biocides, mercury compounds and other heavy metals used in farming and forestry.

Distribution, Habitat and Population

The latest estimate of the breeding population for Britain (Sharrock, 1976) is 50,000–100,000 pairs, probably nearer the higher figure. Glue (1986) suggested a midwinter population of up to 350,000 individuals.

The tawny owl is resident in the warmer boreal to warm temperate zones of Eurasia, from Britain to Korea, from Fennoscandia and Russia, south to the more wooded parts of North Africa and the Caucasus. There is no breeding record at all for Ireland, only one for the Isle of Man, and it is absent from the Northern Isles and Outer Hebrides. In the north-west Highlands the tawny is very local, and on the Inner Hebrides and Clyde Islands it is relatively scarce; in fact the sea bars the species from most islands, although some do winter on Skye and Anglesey, and just a few on the Isle of Wight. Its distribution is sparse in the fens of eastern England, along rocky coastlines, and in some upland regions (mostly above 550m) where there are few or no trees for nesting. However, elsewhere on the UK mainland this highly sedentary species is widely distributed.

The British stronghold was always in deciduous or mixed woodland, but the species has adapted well to tree-dotted farmland — there is a strong correlation with the density of farmsteads around which trees and hedges tend to be preserved; it also frequents parkland, churchyards, large gardens and even urban areas (including inner London). The afforestation of recently treeless upland areas (especially in Northumberland and southern Scotland) has enabled it to increase its range significantly this century, but whereas long-eared owls occur chiefly in young conifer plantations, tawnies arrive when the canopy has closed and gaps appear through thinning, clear felling and windblow. Densities are low in parts of eastern England where crop monocultures have led to the removal of most trees and hedges.

Field Characters and Anatomy

OPPOSITE
The tawny owl's eyes are conspicuous and extraordinarily sensitive

Considering how common it is and how well it has adapted to the urban environment, it is surprising that the tawny owl is not seen more often. It is one of the most nocturnal of European owls, although it does occasionally fly by day, mostly when it has been flushed from its roost. Daytime hooting is said to be rare, yet I have heard it on many occasions before sunset and several times in mid-afternoon. This

TAWNY OWL

Length 37–39cm (14.6–15.4in), wingspan 94–104cm (37–41in), wing 26.2–27.4cm (10.3–10.8in), tail 14.8–17.1cm (5.8–6.7in). Males of the British race, *S.a.sylvatica*, are about 20g lighter, and females up to 100g lighter than the nominate race, males weighing 0.33–0.47kg (0.71–1.04lb) and females 0.39–0.58kg (0.85–1.27lb), but significantly less during starvation periods. Females are 20–40 per cent heavier than males and their wings 5–10 per cent longer.

The adult tawny owl has at least ten basic calls, and the young five, their variety being surpassed only by the long-eared owl. Not only is there some variation between male and female, but also individuals can be recognised by their own tremolo and constant pitch. The familiar *hoo* is first uttered as a protracted monosyllable, followed by a long pause, then a faint monosyllable, a short pause, and finally a long, soft quaver, falling in pitch. The common *ke-wick* call is heard mostly in spring and summer.

owl is mostly seen as a silhouette in a tree or on a chimney pot, when it is easily recognised by its top-heavy appearance, with large, round head and short tail. Its wings are broad and rounded for manoeuvrability in woodland, whereas those of the long-eared and barn owl are relatively long and slender. Although these three owls look much the same in size and wingspan, the tawny is about 70 per cent heavier than the long-eared and 60 per cent heavier than the barn. The sexes are similar, with a more-or-less uniform brown plumage; grey and rufous-brown forms occur in most regions of its range, with intermediate phases throughout. The most northerly birds are of a cold grey colour, but greys are the least common in Britain. Scandinavian birds are about 12 per cent larger and 40 per cent heavier than those in Britain and on the Continent; British birds are among the smallest. Up to September, the juvenile has noticeably loose or shaggy body plumage, with more finely barred feathers.

Flight is medium-paced with level glides, at a greater height than other owls and very direct, with measured, relatively even wingbeats and less flapping than the barn owl, only occasionally interrupted by wheels and tilts.

The large, dark eyes are very conspicuous and vision is extraordinarily sensitive, the ability to hunt in darkness being enhanced by this very sedentary owl's know-

A tawny owl looks up as a plane passes overhead. The species is sometimes active by daylight

152

ledge of local topography. Directional hearing is also highly developed, but less so than that of the long-eared owl and much less than that of the barn owl, though more so than that of the little owl.

Though apparently very meek when mobbed by diurnal birds at roost, tawny owls can be furious in defence of their nests and will readily attack passers-by at any time of day. Throughout Europe there are records of humans, dogs and cats being terrorised; some public parks have been temporarily closed because of un-provoked attacks. Although most assaults are from behind, some are right in the face of the intruder, concentrating on the eyes. At least two people in Britain have lost an eye to a tawny owl, including the famous bird photographer, the late Eric Hosking.

Breeding

A small number of males are bigamous, but generally the mating system is monogamous, the pair-bond lifelong and maintained all year. Established pairs defend their territories continuously, from year to year. Most birds are 2–3 years old at first breeding, but some are just one year. Although territories may have many different owners over several decades, their boundaries are remarkably stable, especially at high densities. Their size varies with habitat, ranging from an average 18.2ha in deciduous woodland to 37.4ha on mixed farmland and 46.1ha in mature spruce forest. Some territories where prey is particularly abundant and accessible, such as in parkland, may be as small as 7ha, but these are not viable for breeding. Nests are usually at least 100m apart.

Pair formation and strengthening of existing pair-bonds starts in early autumn, when territories are established or re-asserted with plenty of hooting and *kewick* contact calls. Courtship includes wing-clapping and a spiralling flight by the male, and when he chases the female he utters all sorts of strange noises including screeches, mewing, groans and rattles, which have been the source of many ghost stories. When perched near the female he sways from side to side and bobs up and down, raising his wings alternately and then together. He also puffs out and com-presses his plumage, grunting softly, sometimes edging back and forth along his perch.

Most nests are in spacious tree holes 1–3m deep, but the tawny is very adapt-able and readily takes to nestboxes, especially where natural sites are scarce, as well as holes in buildings (sometimes displacing barn owls) or cliff ledges. Disused nests of other birds are often used, especially those of carrion and hooded crow, magpie, sparrowhawk and buzzard, in that order of frequency. Sometimes it nests on the ground, in the entrance to a rabbit burrow, among tree roots or in bracken and heather. Squirrel dreys are also used. There is no actual nest-building, but a hole may be cleaned out and a slight scrape formed by the female, pellets acting as a nest lining. Perhaps the most unusual of sites recorded was under the back seat of an old Morris, dumped on a Scottish rubbish tip.

Incubation is by the female alone and apparently starts with the first or second egg; it takes 28–30 days, the first egg laid not always being the one to hatch first. Hatching is asynchronous, but the size difference between chicks is not so marked as in barn and long-eared owls.

The male provisions the sitting female, who broods the chicks for about the first fifteen days, though she may leave them to hunt after seven days, or earlier if food is short. After three weeks the young can feed themselves; they fledge at 32–37

TAWNY OWL

In Britain the single clutch (occasionally replaced after loss) of 2–3 (range 1–8, varying with food supply), eggs, average size 47 × 39mm (1.8 × 1.5in), is laid at 2 to 3-day intervals. The tawny consistently lays earlier than other British owls, with a mean first-egg date of 25 March, and often before this in towns where the ambient temperature is higher and the prey supply more stable.

days, but generally leave the nest at 25–30 days and hide nearby. Independence is achieved after a further 2–3 months. Mortality is high as the young owls learn to fend for themselves and try to establish territories.

As the tawny is relatively long-lived and sedentary, and vacant territories are hard to find, productivity is low. Over ten years, an average 44.6 per cent of pairs did not breed in any one year. Of 562 British eggs, 44 per cent were lost before hatching, and 2 per cent of 314 hatchlings were lost before fledging.

Diet and Feeding Behaviour

The diet of the tawny owl has been well studied but, as with other owls, the proportion of invertebrate prey is very difficult to determine as little is known about differential digestion — the non-appearance in pellets of various prey. Food varies considerably with the habitat and local prey abundance, rural owls generally taking more small rodents (often 30–60 per cent of the diet) than urban owls, which often concentrate on birds (up to 96 per cent in Kensington, London, for example). The most important rodents are voles and mice, especially woodland species — bank vole and woodmouse, but also short-tailed vole, water vole, yellow-necked mouse, harvest mouse, housemouse and dormouse. Other mammals taken include black rat, brown rat, shrews, mole, hedgehog, bats, young rabbit, young brown hare, red squirrel, stoat and weasel. The wide range of bird prey varies from the tiny goldcrest to an adult mallard, but concentrates on those species which roost or feed in trees or are associated with man, especially starlings, tits, thrushes, sparrows and finches.

Less important prey includes reptiles (lizard, slow-worm, grass snake), amphibians (frogs, toads and great-crested newt), fish (trout, goldfish, perch, roach, miller's thumb), insects (mostly beetles, but also dragonflies, crickets, grasshoppers, earwig, shieldbug, horsefly, wasps, bees), snails, slugs, earthworms, cockles, crayfish, spiders and carrion (rat, hare, polecat, lamb, trout). Invertebrates generally form a greater proportion of the diet than in that of other native owls.

Most hunting takes place between dusk and dawn, but occasionally in full daylight, especially with young to feed. As hearing is important in prey detection, bad weather (especially wind and rain) reduces success through noise interference. Much hunting is from a perch, the owl gliding or dropping onto prey; and when perch hunting, it usually makes a short flight every few minutes, returning to the same perch or another nearby. In more open habitat the owl hunts on the wing, flying slowly at a height of two or three metres, with frequent glides, sometimes hovering or zig-zagging over a small area in a thorough search. Most birds are taken from roosts (especially communal), the owl diving into trees or bushes or driving birds out by beating its wings against the twigs, or making them call by wing-clapping, sometimes after hovering briefly to investigate the sites. Bats are taken in flight, and adult and young birds from open nests (one owl took an entire brood of three hobby fledglings), nest-holes and nestboxes. Apparently fish are taken by wading in the shallows, or are snatched from the surface while the owl is in flight. Insects are seized in flight and beetles taken from trees or on the ground, in the foot or bill.

The tawny owl owes much of its success to its catholic diet and great adaptability. For example, some birds visit nestboxes regularly. One was seen to wait in a hedge while a field was being ploughed, then fly out each time the plough passed

to search the fresh furrows for invertebrates along with the gulls. It is a powerful bird, and will also take other raptors — including little owl, long-eared owl, goshawk, sparrowhawk and its own kind — using its high initial speed and manoeuvrability among trees to great advantage. Surplus food may be cached in or on a tree. Such flexibility in feeding enables the tawny owl to remain in a relatively small territory throughout the year. One or two pellets are cast daily, usually before going to roost, which explains why relatively few are found beneath roosts. They are mostly located below trees which act as special pellet-dropping stations, these often being changed with the season. The diet, too, alters with the season so that the appearance of pellets varies considerably.

A young tawny owl eagerly awaits supper. Most nests are in spacious tree holes

Migration, Movements and Roosting

The tawny owl is strictly resident, and even the post-breeding dispersal of young is generally limited to about 10km (maximum known distance 133km) in Britain. However, in parts of its range where winters are more severe, young birds may wander further afield. Dispersal is usually complete by November, by which time juveniles are either established in territory or have died. Winter and summer ranges overlap considerably because this highly territorial owl relies on great familiarity with local topography for winter survival.

Because its hearing is so acute, it is almost impossible to surprise a tawny owl at roost. It may look asleep, but it will be watching closely through half-closed eyes, swivelling its neck constantly to face any intruder without moving its feet or body position. It roosts by day, mostly in trees — in a hole or on a side branch close to the trunk — but also in chimneys and sometimes in holes in buildings. From July to October it usually roosts alone and changes site frequently, but thereafter up to the breeding season sites become fewer and paired birds increasingly roost together. Paired birds also often roost together at a former nest site outside the breeding season. Roosting in pairs decreases after February, with continual occupation of the nest site by the female. However, males with poor cover may continue to share the nest site. Most males roost nearby while the female incubates. About two weeks after fledging, the young start to roost together, often in the dense crown of a tree, but just before dispersal they start to roost apart. Although tawny owls kill and eat birds, they never attack those which are mobbing them at roost. If a mobbed owl remains still, the molestors soon tire of it and go away, but should it fly off then it will be followed by the mob, whose noisy alarms will intensify.

LITTLE OWL
(Athene noctua)

LITTLE OWL
Once known as little night owl, little grey owl, little spotted owl, Lilford's owl, sparrow owl, Dutch owl, Belgian owl, French owl, Indian owl, Spanish owl and little Dutch owl

IN the first half of the 19th century, this smallest of British owls was but a rare vagrant to the British Isles from the near Continent, but subsequent introductions were surprisingly successful and it is now a species familiar to countrymen throughout the land. Yet despite its late arrival, this is the bird from which Britain and the western world first derived the idea of the 'wise old owl', because in Greek mythology it was sacred to Pallas Athene, the goddess of wisdom.

History and Conservation

The earliest British record is from the Mendips, in an interglacial about 500,000 years ago. Thereafter, there are only odd records of vagrants up to the introductions of the 19th century. It is likely that even in central and western Europe it was scarce in relatively recent times, because it appears to have evolved as a semi-terrestrial species which shuns woods and forests, and may only have arrived after the destruction of lowland forests in the Middle Ages.

Bewick included the species in the supplement of rarities published with the 1821 edition of his *History of British Birds*, his drawing being based on a specimen shot in Northumberland in January, 1813. Three years later, the first recorded introduction — into Yorkshire — failed. At the time, this owl was a popular cagebird on the Continent, where, according to Bechstein, it was 'much used as a decoy to entrap small birds'.

In 1842 that father of conservationists, Charles Waterton, unsuccessfully released five birds at Walton Park (Yorkshire); at that time the species appeared to be no more common than it was in the Middle Ages, and in fact it was rare enough for Morris (1850) to detail individual records. For example:

Two were taken in chimneys many years ago, in the parish of Lambeth. One was seen in Wiltshire, nailed up against a barn door, and probably many another has adorned the 'gamekeeper's museum'. Three are recorded to have been met with in Devonshire; one in Flintshire; one near Bristol; a pair bred in Norwich, and two other specimens have been authenticated in Norfolk. One was on sale in July, 1842, in the Brighton market, and said to have been shot in an orchard at Sheffield Park, near Fletching: it was believed from the light colour of its plumage to have been a young bird. One was caught near Derby, which lived a long time in captivity, becoming so far tame as to know those who fed it: it used to drink much. In Ireland it has not hitherto been known to have occurred.

Introductions in Norfolk and Sussex in the 1870s failed, but forty released in Kent by E.B. Meade-Waldo during 1874–80 had some success. During 1889–90 Lord Lilford carried out extensive introductions of Dutch little owls near Oundle, Northamptonshire, which led to breeding in Rutland by 1891 and Bedfordshire by 1892. Indeed, his efforts were so significant that the species was often called 'Lilford's owl' or 'Dutch owl'. There were further introductions in Yorkshire, Hampshire and Hertfordshire, and by 1910 the owl was breeding through the East Midlands and south-east, from Hampshire to Cambridgeshire, and by 1930 was into the south-west peninsula, Wales, northern England, and across the Scottish border. But not everyone welcomed the bird's progress. There was, as Coward said in 1928, 'No small alarm among game preservers, for the bird is spreading in all directions'. Although birds were reported in Scotland from 1925, it was not known to breed there till 1958, and remains extremely rare, not having penetrated north of the Edinburgh–Glasgow line.

By the mid-1930s the initial explosive phase had slowed, and was followed by reports of decreases in parts of central and southern England. This has been attributed to various factors such as colder winters in the 1940s, organochlorine pesticides in the 1950s, further cold winters 1961–3, loss of tree nest-holes with continuing hedgerow removal, persistent crop spraying and related prey reduction. However, it would appear that the effect of persecution has been underestimated, since a very large number of birds were shot and killed by gamekeepers right up to the early 1980s.

The population pattern since regular censusing began has been unusual, with fairly regular spacing of peaks (average every four years) and troughs, which appears to be cyclical. There has been simultaneous peaking of tawny owl and kestrel populations in some years, so it could be that there is a link with small-mammal cycles, even though the little owl eats many invertebrates all year round. There is no clear recent trend, but the population is probably still increasing.

Like other raptors, little owls have suffered extensively through man's persecution and control of the environment. In 1971, Glue estimated that road casualties and collisions with trains accounted for at least 22 per cent of known mortality cases in Britain, with a further 3 per cent due to collision with overhead wires, and 5 per cent to trapping or shooting. In 1980 Glue and Scott found that 14 of 52 breeding failures were due to egg theft by man. On the other hand, there is no doubt that much of the species' success this century has been due to the cultivation of large areas of temperate Europe, which has boosted prey supply. Also, in Europe this owl has responded well to the provision of artificial roosting and nesting places, to compensate for the felling of natural sites. But nestboxes

LITTLE OWL

Athens revered the little owl – hence the Latin *Athene*, regarding it as the epitome of calmness and moderation, in direct contrast to Dionysus, the god of revelry and ecstacy. Consequently, the owl was used in many recipes to counteract evils such as drunkenness, alcoholism, epilepsy and madness; perhaps most bizarre was taking salted owl for gout, a condition believed to be the result of excess alcohol. The other part of its Latin name – *noctua*, meaning night-owl – is less appropriate, because in fact this is the least nocturnal of our owls.

Before its introduction to Britain ornithologists in this country used simple translations of the Latin name: for example, 'night owl' (Merrett, 1667). Ray coined the more appropriate 'little owl' in 1678, and this was used by most writers thereafter.

In 1976 the *Breeding Atlas* estimated the British population at 7,000–14,000 pairs, and in 1986 the *Winter Atlas* suggested a mid-winter population of 19,000–38,000 individuals.

Length 21–23cm (8.3–9.0in), wingspan 54–58cm (21.3–22.8in), wing 15.8–17.3cm (6.2–6.8in), tail 7.4–8.3cm (2.9–3.3in), weight 0.15–0.23kg (0.32–0.50lb). The female is usually only a few per cent heavier than the male, and its wing about 3 per cent longer.

At least eight calls are recognised, all far-reaching and penetrating. The two main ones are a ringing, plaintive *kiew, kiew,* repeated every few seconds, and a loud, rapidly repeated, yelping *wherrow,* with the emphasis on the first syllable. The courting male utters a loud *hooo-oo, hooo-oo.* Some of the more unusual rattling, laughing and snorting calls are often uttered fiercely from rooftops, reinforcing the superstition which surrounds the species. It often calls by day, particularly to proclaim territory, from February onwards.

The little owl takes most prey from the ground, usually launching from a low look-out post

should be carefully designed and positioned to exclude predators, including tawny owls. The most successful have been made in Switzerland, consisting of a pipe 80–100cm long, hung parallel with a horizontal branch of a low tree, and ending in a spacious nest-chamber.

Distribution, Habitat and Population

The little owl is on the north-western edge of its range in Britain, being resident in temperate to warm temperate zones, from the Atlantic to the Pacific, and south into the subtropical zone in Africa and Arabia. In Britain it is widely distributed throughout well-timbered, low-lying areas of southern, central and northern England, and the borders of central and south Wales. Only a small number breed in Scotland, in border districts, and it is absent from most upland areas of Wales, the south-west peninsula and northern England, where there is a lack of tree cover and prolonged periods of ice and snow cover. However, a milder coastal climate allows occupation of coastal headlands, cliffs and quarries in parts of Wales and south-west England. Although there have been four confirmed sightings in Ireland, there has been no nesting there.

The preferred habitat is more open country and it avoids tall and dense stands of trees and vegetation, such as in wetlands and croplands. In Britain it favours agricultural land with plenty of hedgerow trees and farm buildings, parkland, old orchards, drained fenland with pollard willows, as well as marginal land such as sand-dunes, moorland edge, industrial waste ground, inshore islands and settlements, though it rarely penetrates inner cities. The essential elements of habitat are open ground rich in small prey, hunting perches, nest holes, day-roosts and a fairly mild climate.

Field Characters and Anatomy

There is little likelihood of confusing this species with any other bird in Britain. Small (about the size of a song thrush), compact and tubby, with spotted upperparts, streaked underparts, relatively long legs, rounded wings, bright yellow eyes and pale 'eyebrows', it has a disapproving expression. The race found in Britain and western Europe, *A.n. vidalii,* is much darker than that found in dry, sandy areas of the eastern Mediterranean. The facial disc is less well defined than that of our other owls. The sexes are similar, but the juvenile may be distinguished by its distinctly paler or greyer colour, and it is much more uniformly patterned, with buff rather than white spots and narrower, paler streaking.

The little owl is well suited to ground hunting, its long legs allowing nimble walking, hopping and a fast, loping run. The flight is undulating, with alternate bouts of flapping and closing wings reminiscent of a large woodpecker, and as the species is partly diurnal it is often seen flying low from perch to perch. Flight is less silent than that of the other owls, presumably because hunting by day, especially taking invertebrates, is less demanding. In fact it is among the least specialised of owls, with small, almost circular and uncomplicated ear openings, the outer ear tubes without spacious cavities. For an owl, the number of auditory nerve cells is small, so its hearing is not significantly different from that of other diurnal birds. Neither is its visual acuity; and its colour vision, which is probably of no use to nocturnal birds, appears to be as good as in the song thrush.

Breeding

First breeding occurs at one year old and the monogamous pair-bond often persists all year for several years, probably until one partner dies. In Britain, nests are usually at least 200–300m apart, and in southern England the average territory was found to be 35ha on water meadows and 38ha on mixed farmland. Non-breeding or unpaired birds often hold territory through the breeding season.

Proclamation of territory usually begins at the beginning of February, when the male sings from a favourite perch, but the main courtship starts in March, when the female shrieks and yelps in answer to the male's hoot. The male calls to entice the female into a nest hole, and in a very variable pre-copulation display he bobs up and down and from side to side while she may solicit by crouching low with shivering wings. Sometimes they chase each other, with great flying skills, the male occasionally hovering above the sitting female. There is also courtship feeding and mutual preening.

Nest sites may be changed every year, but successive use up to five years is known. The most common sites are tree holes: of 482 British nests, 24 per cent were in oak, 23 per cent in ash, 18 per cent in fruit trees and 15 per cent in willows. Of 267 nests, 37 per cent were in the main trunk, 23 per cent in a lateral branch, and 14 per cent in a pollarded tree, 0.3–12.2m above ground. Holes in buildings and walls are used, as well as holes in the ground (including rabbit burrows), also old birds' nests and haystacks, and nestboxes. Sand- and gravel-pit tunnels and

The single clutch (only one record of two broods) of 3–5 (1–8) eggs, average size 36 × 30mm (1.4 × 1.2in), sometimes replaced after loss, is usually laid at one- or two-day intervals from mid-March to mid-June, but there may be up to a week between eggs, especially the last two, most clutches being started in late April and early May. Laying has been recorded as late as September.

The little owl: once a rare visitor, now common following widespread introductions

moorland peat-stacks are more unusual sites. There is no actual nest-building, but the female may clear the chamber and form a scrape in the bottom.

Incubation is by the female alone, and begins with the first or second egg (more rarely when the clutch is complete), and takes 27–28 days (23–35), exceptionally less. Some males remain in the nest chamber with the female during laying.

In contrast to most owls, hatching is usually synchronous, or nearly so. During incubation and the first two weeks of the nestling phase the male does all the hunting, but thereafter, when the young can tear off pieces of food for themselves, the female often helps to provision the family. After three weeks, the young clamber to the nest entrance and may sometimes venture outside, hiding among surrounding branches or vegetation, before fledging at 30–35 days (individuals 0–5 days apart), exceptionally to 43 days. They are fed by the parents for a further month or so. Adults sometimes attack intruders near the nest, flying at the head of man, perhaps clawing and biting. The little owl has the shortest breeding season of any European owl.

In a study of breeding success, 56.4 per cent of 477 British eggs hatched, and 49 per cent fledged. Of 156 clutches, 28 per cent failed during incubation or before completion of egg-lying, 26 per cent failed during fledging, and 26 per cent yielded flying young. A dismal 54 per cent of 52 failures were due to man taking eggs or young, destroying nests or shooting parents. Only 16 per cent were predated. Of 241 broods at fledging, 21 per cent had 1 young, 32 per cent 2, 36 per cent 3, 8 per cent 4, and 3 per cent 5, giving an average of 2.4.

Diet and Feeding Behaviour

Although it is itself often preyed upon by the tawny owl, and to a lesser extent by the barn and long-eared owls, peregrine, sparrowhawk and goshawk, the little owl is a powerful and formidable predator, often taking prey larger than itself. Yet it is also substantially insectivorous, and appears to be the only European owl which regularly takes plant food. Rodents and invertebrates are its staple diet throughout the year, with birds important only in the breeding season, perhaps because the young of other species are then so abundant and easily taken, along with sitting adult songbirds. Because its diet is so catholic its population fluctuates little with rodent numbers and it easily shifts to other prey when small mammals are scarce. However, it is significantly affected by severe winters, and when cold or snow cover is extreme it is more likely to starve to death than move.

When the bird was relatively new to this country and little was known about it, gamekeepers hounded it mercilessly, believing that it was a substantial predator of gamebirds. Who could blame them for refusing to believe that this 'hookbeak' was an eater of worms? The truth is that the number of young gamebirds taken is insignificant. The little owl will take birds as large as magpie, moorhen, wood-pigeon, lapwing, jay and tern, but more common prey are songbirds of open grassland, especially the starling and skylark. One pair on Skokholm Island (Pembrokeshire) fed largely on storm petrels. Birds may be taken from water and roosts as well as from nests and nest holes.

Mammal prey includes rabbit (up to three-quarters grown), hedgehog, mole, bats, shrews, mice and voles, and even the tricky weasel and adult rat. Reptile food includes the slow-worm and snakes, and amphibian prey features frogs, toads and newts. Fish are rarer morsels, carp and minnow being among those recorded.

The invertebrate menu is extensive, with the emphasis on beetles, earwigs and

LITTLE OWL

The owl is well adapted to taking the majority of its prey from the ground, usually by surprise, launching from low lookout posts. It may hover briefly, though awkwardly, but its long legs make running over flat ground relatively easy. The main hunting periods are from shortly before to a few hours after sunset, and from late in the second half of the night to just after dawn. Although primarily nocturnal, with young in the nest it may be seen hunting at any time of day.

earthworms, but it also includes crickets, grasshoppers, moths (larvae and adults), cockroaches, lacewings, craneflies, sawflies, wasps, bees, millipedes, woodlice, snails and slugs. It will also eat small berries and fruits as well as grass and other leaves, and in England at least plant material is taken throughout the year. Its relatively small, grey pellets are usually rounded at both ends, but sometimes they are tapered at one end, and may be confused with those of the kestrel.

Migration, Movements and Roosting

This resident bird is very sedentary. The pair-bond is strong and many adults roost at or close to the nesting place in winter, though outside the breeding season some wander further afield; however, only 2 per cent of British-ringed birds were found over 100km from the ringing place, and most ringed adults are recovered within 10km. Stragglers which have crossed the Irish Sea to eastern Ireland and the Isle of Man are exceptional. Dispersal of juveniles is mostly very short-range, too, the majority settling in random directions within 20km of the birthplace.

Roosts are in trees, bushes, rock crevices, lofts or other cavities, and most provide a clear view as well as cover; but in the breeding season it is not unusual to encounter a little owl by day at an exposed site. However, such birds soon fly off when approached.

LONG-EARED OWL
(Asio otus)

ALTHOUGH the 'horned' owl is one of the most popular effigies of English literature, this is the least known and most mysterious of British owls. Being the most nocturnal and strongly arboreal, it is rarely seen by day and easily escapes attention, especially in winter, when it is generally silent. Also, it is more of a nomad than our other widespread owls, and occasionally Britain hosts considerable invasions.

Morris (1850) wrote:

It is readily tamed, and affords much amusement by the many grotesque attitudes it assumes, to which ears and eyes give piquancy. It may often be detected with a small orifice left through which it is peeping when its eyes would seem to be shut; and it has the singular faculty of being able to close one eye while the other is not shut.

Much earlier, the Athenians had used the name *otus* synonymously with 'simpleton' as a term of derision. Their dislike of the horned owl (which suffered through the little owl cult) inspired the superstition that if someone were to walk right round one at roost it would turn its head to the extent that it wrung its own neck.

History and Conservation

The earliest British record is from the Pleistocene, from the end of the last glaciation in Somerset, when it was probably prey to some animal or bird. Thereafter it

LONG-EARED OWL
Once known as horn-owl, long-horned owl, horned owl, horn coot, hornie hoolet, long ears, long-horned ullat, tufted owl, and cat owl

OPPOSITE
A little owl with a moth for its young. Insects form an important part of the diet

The Latin specific *otus* is derived from the Greek for 'ear', but the name is probably ill-founded because the so-called ear tufts appear to have nothing to do with hearing. The first English record seems to be Turner's 1544 reference to the 'hornoul'. Willughby continued with horn-owl in 1676, but in 1768 Pennant coined 'long-eared owl', as an obvious contrast to its short-eared 'cousin'.

Since Sharrock (1976) suggested 3,000–10,000 pairs for the British Isles, there has not been any attempt to assess breeding numbers. The *Winter Atlas* (1986) estimated the midwinter population at 10,000–35,000 individuals, including Continental visitors.

Length 35–37cm (13.8–14.6in), wingspan 90–100cm (35.4–39.4in), wing 28.2–31.0cm (11.1–12.2in), tail 13.0–14.9cm (5.1–5.9in), weight 0.2–0.4kg (0.45–0.96lb), the female generally being about 14 per cent heavier than the male, a fact reflected in the bone measurements. The female also has much stronger and heavier talons.

was almost certainly widespread and common, varying in abundance with the amount of woodland and woodland edge. During the 19th and 20th centuries it suffered along with other raptors at the hands of gamekeepers. Although its relatively secret lifestyle made it difficult to shoot, it was taken extensively in indiscriminate traps. Also, its cat-like face made it very popular as a stuffed, indoor decoration.

The casual observations of 19th-century naturalists mean little in assessing the owl's former status, not only bcause the bird is hard to detect, but also because of its nomadic habit — undoubtedly it has been consistently under-recorded. Nonetheless, much of the patchy distribution is thought to be the result of a substantial decline this century, coinciding with the tawny owl's ascendancy. By 1930 this was noticeable in southern England and Wales, and by the 1950s the decrease in northern England was clear. However, there has been no evidence of decline in Ireland, where the species remains widespread, and where there are no tawny owls, which frequently prey on and compete with long-eared owls. Indeed, there have been local increases in Ireland, where the long-eared is the commoner of the two breeding owls (the other being the declining barn owl); these gains are thought to be directly related to the additional habitat provided as many relatively recent forestry plantations mature. Moreover, it is likely that a high proportion of long-eared owls are now associated with commercial forestry plantations throughout the British Isles, especially as developing programmes of felling and replanting provide the ideal patchwork of clear foraging areas as well as secure tree nest sites. However, we have much to learn about distribution in new forests, including why the species is rare in the middle of most mature plantations.

Because this owl is not usually a hole-nester, it does not take to standard nestboxes; yet it has accepted wicker baskets put up for duck in trees and bushes, as well as open-sided nestboxes chiefly designed for kestrels. However, experiments in Border forests have already shown that it is worthwhile erecting artificial nest platforms in areas where old crows nests and other natural breeding bases are scarce.

Because they do not eat carrion, long-eared owls have not suffered from environmental poisoning to the extent that other raptors have. However, where they feed close to human habitation, which is common, there has been lethal contamination with organic biocides, insecticides, fungicides, rodenticides, PCBs and heavy metals such as mercury. It must not be forgotten that many toxins occur in remote areas, too, especially in the plantations with which long-eared owls are increasingly associated. The rodenticide warfarin, for example, is used extensively to kill grey squirrels, yet it commonly kills non-target species as well, such as the small rodents on which long-eared owls prey. Although few herbicides and insecticides are used widely in forests, local use can be alarming. For example, Fenitrothion was used extensively in aerial spraying 1977–87 and, while no harm could be detected among small passerines, the cumulative effects on predators such as the long-eared owl are unknown. As small birds can form a substantial part of the owl's diet in the British Isles, such application must be closely monitored, especially in upland areas which have hitherto been largely free of contaminants.

Distribution, Habitat and Population

The long-eared owl is widespread throughout North America (where its plumage differs) and Eurasia, from Ireland to Japan. It breeds from mid-boreal to warm temperate zones and winters in warmer boreal to warm temperate zones, being migratory in the more northerly parts of its range. Britain lies in the zone where birds are found all year, but it also hosts substantial numbers of winter visitors. Throughout its range, distribution is constantly changing and imperfectly known, and is especially patchy in the British Isles, where the species occurs widely. Areas of greatest scarcity are south-west England, Wales and west Scotland, but even elsewhere the breeding distribution is mostly very irregular. Unlike mainland Britain, Ireland has not suffered general decline this century and the species still occurs widely there, with concentrations in Ulster and the south-west. This owl is even harder to locate in winter, when the majority are recorded in eastern Britain, with concentrations in many coastal areas. Our winter and breeding ranges overlap considerably, the overall picture being confused by widely varying numbers of winter immigrants.

In habitat choice, the supposed close competition with the tawny owl is open to question, in that the long-eared seems to be satisfied with small patches of woodland, particularly conifer plantations. It is also less restricted in that it readily uses the old nests of other birds. Other habitats used are wide-ranging, including farmland, low bushes on marshes and sand-dunes, hawthorn and elder scrub, tree-dotted moorland, rough grazing, open parkland, urban wastes and large gardens. In Ireland there is no clear concentration on conifers, all types of woodland being used. Some studies have cast doubt on the significance of tawny owl competition, having found that the two species may use different ages of plantation in the same area — this is determined by the considerable dietary differences between them. What is certain is that the long-eared's optimal habitat includes ample cover with plenty of old nests near open ground with short herbage and prolific prey. Thus the interiors of large, unbroken forests are mostly avoided.

Field Characters and Anatomy

Slightly smaller than the tawny and short-eared owls, the long-eared owl has a very effective cryptic plumage which makes it difficult to see when perched, motionless, against the lichen-covered bark of a tree or in dense foliage during daytime. With hunched posture, ruffled plumage, raised ear-tufts, narrowed eyes and slightly elongated face, it has a distinctly cat-like appearance. But its size can be very confusing as its bulk alters markedly with attitude: when at ease it is more squat and fluffed out, its face rounded, but when alarmed it is noticeably long and slender, an escaping bird looking much slimmer than the rounded bird spotted at roost. It also alters its posture according to its surroundings, being more upright on an open perch or among trees near its nest, and more hunched in thicker cover.

Seen clearly, the adult is unmistakable, with its complex, striking plumage and orange eyes, the ear-tufts usually conspicuous, although sometimes they are flattened, mostly in flight. The markedly uniform ground colour of the plumage shows great colour variation throughout the world range, from deep chestnut-brown nearing black, to golden-buff or fawn, but this seems to be related to the age and sex of individuals rather than to geographical variation. The sexes are similar, and the juvenile has loose, greyer plumage with dominant barring, downy ear-tufts, and a smaller, darker facial disc with black smudges beside the bill. It is best distinguished from the short-eared owl by its larger head and longer ears, more uniform and less streaked plumage, broader and more rounded wings, evenly barred outer primaries which do not form a dark wing-tip, longer face,

LONG-EARED OWL

Though its calls often appear to lack penetration, the vocabulary of the long-eared owl is probably more varied and richer than that of any other owl in the northern hemisphere, even though the bird is mostly silent outside the breeding season. Not only is there great variation between individuals but also between the calls of each bird. The hoot is distinct from that of the tawny, the male's territorial proclamation being a relatively quiet, long, drawn-out, quavering *hoo-hoo-hoo-hoo*, repeated every few seconds. The female's main call is a soft *shoo-oogh*, which fades away softly, like a heavy sigh. Both sexes sometimes hiss like a cat when passing food and intruders may be greeted with *oo-ack, oo-ack*, sometimes following a barking *woof-woof*. Many of the calls can be quite alarming in the darkness of deep countryside, from the 'squeaky-hinge' hunger cry of young to the awful, human-like scream uttered when a bird is disturbed near the nest. Disturbance also encourages bill-snapping, and courtship is the incentive for wing-clapping.

LONG-EARED OWL

heavily barred tail, and lack of pale trailing edge to the inner wing. Apart from its lack of ear-tufts, the tawny owl has a less striking wing pattern, less obviously barred tail, no carpal patch, relatively massive head, greater bulk (40–45 per cent heavier) and more direct flight. The flying long-eared owl imparts a much greater feeling of instability, and its generally low, long-winged, moth-like flight is characterised by short series of wingbeats alternating with long glides, gentle banking and occasional wavering and hovering, all being reminiscent of a harrier. The wings are usually held straight and not raised above body level, only occasionally in a very shallow V.

The purpose of the ear-tufts remains a mystery. Apparently such appendages are not essential for owl life because only about 50 of the world's 130–140 known owl species have them. They do not seem to be significant in display or identification as they are difficult to see at night and owls concentrate on vocal recognition rather than shape. One suggestion is that they mimic mammals, notably cats, and enhance their forbidding attitude in defence. Another is that they are useful in camouflage, but there is no correlation between this and when they are raised. However, their apparent sensitivity suggests that they are more than mere ornaments and probably serve as tactile organs or as a means of emotional expression. Moreover, it would be foolish to rule out any link with hearing, because they are situated in the same plane as the rim of the facial disc, whose feathers do appear to open and close in relation to sound gathering when at rest. At the moment we can only speculate, but there is no denying the long-eared owl's highly developed hearing. Although its total range does not seem to differ greatly from that of the human ear, it can probably hear low- and medium-pitched sounds about ten times better than we can. The outer ear openings are exceptionally large, the slits behind the facial disc being complex and asymmetrical, occupying almost the full height of the skull.

Breeding

In Britain there is usually one clutch of 3–5 (1–6) eggs (average size 40 × 32mm (1.6 × 1.2in), which is occasionally replaced after loss; sometimes two successful broods are raised. Earliest laying is in late February (rarer in Ireland) and the latest in early June, with the bulk from late March to early April. The laying interval is 2 days.

First breeding is at one year. Monogamous mating is the rule, though bigamy has been reported in Holland. The pair-bond is renewed annually, at least among sedentary birds. Males resident on territories all year start calling from late October, but other males do not generally occupy and defend territories before March. As the abundance of food varies so greatly over several years, birds may be forced to find new territories, the proportion of resident but non-breeding pairs complicating estimates of densities. For example, in a Scottish study an average 17 per cent of 9–18 pairs present on 10sq km did not breed each year. Typical density is about 10–50 pairs per 100sq km. Unlike most other owls, the long-eared holds no territorial hunting ground and nesting territories are small, so a single copse may hold more than two breeding pairs per sq km.

The male will occupy a new territory several days before the female, with regular display flights from dusk to dawn, zigzagging and undulating between and sometimes above trees. His wingbeats are deep and slow, with occasional gliding, and wing-claps below the body. Later the pair may fly briefly together and the female will call persistently, flying in circles around the nest site and sitting there for long periods to entice the male down.

Most long-eared owls breed in small patches of wood among open fields, 74 per cent of nests being in conifers in one British study. The majority choose the old tree nest of another bird, especially magpie and crow, but also a wide variety of

OPPOSITE
The true purpose of the long-eared owl's ear tufts remains a mystery

166

Although long-eared owls rarely attack humans, as do tawny owls in defence of their young, they commonly intimidate intruders with an impressive posture, making themselves appear as large and as fearsome as possible. Even the owlets do this. The parents also use broken-wing and other distraction displays.

The long-eared owl is a night hunter, preferring to search along forest edge and in open areas adjacent to its woodland breeding sites and day-roosts, thereby largely avoiding direct confrontation with the more powerful tawny owl, which sometimes preys upon it.

others, ranging from the flimsy platform of the woodpigeon to the more substantial home of the jay and the large structure of the heron. Squirrel dreys are used too, though less often, as are reed nests, tree cavities, rabbit burrows and other ground sites among vegetation such as bramble and heather, and cliff holes. Open-fronted nestboxes, willow baskets and artificial twig platforms have also been accepted. Occasionally, the male may add material to the nest of another species, though this may have courtship rather than practical significance, and on the ground the female often forms a shallow scrape.

Incubation (predominantly by the female) is 25–30 days (beginning with the first egg), and hatching asynchronous.

For the first week the young are brooded continuously by the female, the male bringing decapitated prey which the female dismembers for her charges. Brooding stops at two weeks, but the chicks are still fed by the female with food brought by the male. After about three weeks the owlets leave the nest to climb and jump about neighbouring branches with the aid of bill and wings, whereupon the female joins the hunt and both parents feed the young. Fledging is after 30 days and independence achieved from about 60 days. Although siblings may eat each other, it is not known if fratricide occurs; there is also one case of a parent eating two young, but again it is not known if the mother in fact murdered them.

Breeding success is poor in Britain compared with Continental Europe, where the species is probably better adapted to the environment. In a study of 287 British eggs, only 30 per cent hatched and 24 per cent produced fledged young, while 41 per cent of 78 nests produced at least one fledged young. Over four years, 83 per cent of 58 Scottish pairs laid, 63 per cent hatched young, 57 per cent fledged young, and 23 per cent of completed clutches were deserted. There was an average of 3.2 young per successful nest, but only 1.7 young per nest started.

Diet and Feeding Behaviour

It has longer and narrower wings than the tawny owl, with lower wing-loading and higher aspect-ratio which facilitate the slow flight required when hunting for small mammal prey in short vegetation. However, this specialisation makes it rather vulnerable so that, unlike the tawny owl, when food is short in many areas most birds must leave to breed or winter elsewhere.

In most countries there is an overwhelming reliance on mice and voles — these often comprise over 90 per cent of the diet, necessitating migratory behaviour in cyclical vole-trough years where there is little alternative food. In the British Isles the diet is usually at least two-thirds voles and mice (47 per cent short-tailed voles in one British analysis, but in Ireland the woodmouse is the main prey), with larger mammals (rabbit, young hare, squirrels, rats, mole, bats, stoat, weasel) accounting for some 20 per cent. However, Britain is one of only a few countries in which birds, too, form an important part of the diet. A study of twenty sites found that birds constituted 8 per cent of prey (numerically) in the breeding season, but 23 per cent for the rest of the year (August–February). In particular, the long-eared owl exploits communal winter roosts of birds which are both abundant and easy to catch, especially house sparrows and starlings, hovering and wing-clapping in front of bushes to provoke the birds into flying out. A wide variety of other birds is taken, ranging from the goldcrest, finch and thrush to (more rarely) larger species such as adult moorhen, nightjar, common snipe, jackdaw, magpie, young kestrel and little owl. Young gamebirds are very rarely taken. This seasonal flexibility in diet explains why so many long-eared owls happily overwinter in Britain, unlike Fennoscandia, where there are insufficient secondary sources of food, such as birds and shrews, when the vole stock collapses.

Other secondary foods include lizards, slow-worms, frogs, toads, fish (very rarely) and invertebrates, especially beetles, crickets and grasshoppers, but also earwigs, adult and larval butterflies and moths, ants, larval and pupal flies, snails, crabs, mussels and earthworms. Pellets (which resemble those of the tawny owl but are paler grey, slightly narrower and much smaller) have also been found to contain yew berries and the bird's own eggshells.

In hunting, the bird flies low and slow over open ground, systematically searching with fairly fast wingbeats and frequent short glides. Sometimes it uses the same technique inside plantations, taking prey in a shallow glide, stalling and plunging feet-first or wheeling about with great skill. Hunting from low perches is more frequent in rough weather. One report describes two birds working each side of a hedge, one taking birds flushed by the other.

Prey is killed in the same way as the barn owl, nipping through the back of the skull. Small birds are mostly decapitated and dismembered and their wings and tail plucked before they are eaten – usually entrails first, then the breast. Small mammals are generally eaten whole, larger ones have the head discarded and are torn apart. Despite distinct sexual dimorphism, no differential prey and hunting niches between male and female long-eared owls have been proved.

Migration, Movements and Roosting

Because their main food — microtine voles — cannot be relied upon, northernmost European populations of long-eared owls must migrate to more temperate climes in most winters; but when food is sufficient, some winter as far as 64°N in Finland. Displaced birds flight to their west European wintering sites over a broad front and in most years some arrive in Britain, but their numbers are as erratic as their prey. Such visitations are often simultaneous with mass appearances of short-eared owls and hen harriers, which are subject to similar dietary constraints. Most occur in eastern Britain and come from Fennoscandia, a few passing as far west as Co Mayo. Smaller numbers arrive from as far afield as eastern USSR and Czechslovakia.

British Isles-bred birds, on the other hand, have a more stable food supply and are largely sedentary, frequently returning to the same wood to breed in successive years. Of 148 ringing recoveries of birds of all ages, only 26 per cent travelled further than 100km, 35 per cent remaining within 10km of the ringing site. Young birds disperse randomly in their first winter, though there is some gravitation towards the south and coastal areas, where prey is easier to obtain.

Long-eared owls usually roost by day in the thickest cover available, preferring trees covered in ivy, conifers and hawthorn, usually settling close to the trunk. Ground roosting is rare. Paired birds which remain on territories throughout the year usually roost near each other outside the nesting season. Most immigrants gather in winter, usually in groups of 6–12, but up to 29 have been recorded in Britain, and up to 150 on the Continent. Such roosts may continue in March and early April, when some local birds are already incubating. Birds remain close together, in a copse or even a single tree, some being relatively conspicuous on the bare branches of deciduous trees, and others in odd places such as town parks and cemeteries.

LONG-EARED OWL

This owl can locate prey with astonishing accuracy in almost total darkness, yet happily hunts by daylight when necessary, such as when young are in the nest, and rain and wind have either halted foraging or reduced attack success.

This species is quite commonly preyed on by other raptors, notably the tawny owl, but also the goshawk, common buzzard, red kite and peregrine.

In some years we experience considerable invasions of several thousands, as happened in 1975–76 and 1978–79. Some of these immigrants temporarily rest on ships and oil rigs around the coast, while others migrate in groups, flocks having been recorded coming from the sea in the Orkneys and Shetlands, and on the north-east English coast.

SHORT-EARED OWL
(*Asio flammeus*)

SHORT-EARED OWL
Once known as mouse hawk, hawk owl, short-horned owl, short-horned howlet, woodcock owl, pilot owl, marsh owl, march owl, fern owl, moor owl, sea owl, cat owl, day owl, brown yogle, grey yogle, grey hullet, and red owl

The origin of the Latin *flammeus* is obscure because neither the bird's plumage nor eyes ever approach flame colour. Willughby (1676) referred to both this species and the long-eared owl as 'horn owl', but Thomas Pennant coined the distinguishing names 'short-eared owl' and 'long-eared owl' in 1768. Some of the bird's folk names refer to its migratory habits. For example, it was known as 'woodcock owl' and 'pilot owl' because it often arrived on the east coast with winter visitors, notably the woodcock.

OPPOSITE
Unlike Britain's other common owls, the short-eared is primarily a bird of open country

UNLIKE our other common owls, this is primarily a bird of open country, which spends long periods away from trees and bushes — throughout its life it is mainly terrestrial, nearly always nesting on the ground. Its nomadic lifestyle has fascinated man for centuries, but only recently have the reasons for its wanderings been clearly understood.

History and Conservation

This bird is a great opportunist whose mobility has always allowed it to take quick advantage of changing conditions. Also, in the long-term its population has undoubtedly fluctuated widely in the British Isles in response to both climatic and habitat change. It does have a long history here, being known from Derbyshire and Somerset caves in the last glaciation of the Pleistocene (where it was probably the prey of a larger bird such as the eagle owl), but we know little of its progress. During early times it would have been restricted to a relatively small amount of moorland and marsh, but would have gained considerably through the extensive creation of rough pasture and further moorland following forest clearances. Thus numbers probably peaked in the 18th and 19th centuries when forest cover was at a low, when marginal land was still abundant, and most agricultural land was still largely unimproved and rich in prey.

One of the major setbacks of the 19th century came with the rising popularity of grouse shooting, for then considerable numbers of short-eared owls were killed by upland gamekeepers. In more recent decades, however, with greater protection for birds of prey, sporting estates are almost certainly of nett benefit to the short-eared owl in that they maintain vast acreages of heather moorland, much of which provides suitable nesting and foraging habitat and would otherwise have been lost to overgrazing.

But even in the last century this owl does not appear to have been common anywhere, even allowing for the fact that it was found chiefly in relatively remote districts where observations were few. Indeed, Bewick (1799) referred to it as 'rare', and he lived in the Northumberland stronghold. So even then, cyclical influxes caused quite a stir: 'It flies by day and is sometimes seen in companies: 28 were once counted in a turnip-field in November (by Thomas Penrice of Yarmouth).'

Throughout its range, it has steadily decreased in numbers through habitat destruction, especially drainage and cultivation of marshes and natural wet grasslands. However, during this century there have been local increases which have been attributed to fortuitous afforestation. When grazing animals are excluded and fertilisers applied prior to tree-planting, there is usually a great increase in numbers of the short-eared owl's main prey, microtine rodents, as well as an increase in suitable nest-sites. In optimum conditions the owls' territories may shrink to a seventh of their previous size, and clutch and brood sizes increase greatly; this is particularly true where afforestation has occurred in predominantly grassland areas. However, it is also significant that as the forests grow they become increasingly useless to short-eared owls; we can only hope that by the time most of them have matured there will be a nett overall gain for this raptor. There is

SHORT-EARED OWL

no doubting their immediate benefit, which has probably led to the short-eared owl now being more firmly established in the British Isles than at any time this century. Breeding reports show notable gains in north Norfolk and the Brecklands, which were colonised from the 1930s; Yorkshire, which became a regular breeding haunt in the 1940s, as did the Suffolk, Essex and Kent coastal marshes in the 1940s–50s; and the Wash region from the 1960s.

In modern times, breeding in Ireland has been rare and sporadic, perhaps partly because of the absence of voles. However, bank voles have been recorded in south-west Ireland since the 1960s, and as they have spread significantly since then short-eared owls and other raptors may benefit in the future. Although primarily a woodland and scrub species, the bank vole is sometimes abundant in grassland and other open habitats, and it is interesting to note that its Irish distribution coincides with one of the short-eared owl's winter concentrations. In Shetland, where there are no voles, there have been no breeding records at all since the 19th century.

The short-eared owl's flight behaviour and preferred habitat have saved the species from significant mortality caused by man through road traffic, overhead wires and pesticides. However, the species has discovered the prey-rich grasslands surrounding airports, and in some countries this has led to a considerable number of deaths through collision with aircraft.

Distribution, Habitat and Population

The short-eared owl is both resident and migrant: it breeds in subarctic to temperate zones, widely across central and northern Eurasia and northern North America, with a discontinuous population in South America, and it winters in temperate to subtropical zones. However, the northern and southern limits of the breeding range fluctuate considerably with the food supply.

The preferred habitat is open country rich in rodents, so in Britain the main breeding areas are the moorlands and heaths, areas of rough grazing and newly afforested hillsides, and the marshes and bogs of Scotland, northern England and central Wales; there are further centres around eastern England's coastal heaths, marshes and sand-dunes as well as in north Norfolk and on the Brecks. Breeding records are few from southern and central England, and there are only a handful from Ireland. There is little or no nesting in much of western Scotland and on many of the islands.

In winter, distribution is much wider over Britain and parts of Ireland, but with significant gravitation towards the south and east, where numbers are swollen by irregular invasions. Many of the nesting areas of central and northern Scotland are vacated, as is high ground with protracted snow cover elsewhere. High numbers are usually found on many of the chalk downlands of southern England, as well as on the estuaries and coastal marshes. But the picture is constantly changing as this very nomadic bird ranges widely in search of sufficient food. Farmland is used more extensively in winter, including harvested fields, stubbles and some standing crops.

With such an irregular pattern of movement, the population is hard to gauge accurately, but there is thought to be some stability in Britain as the provision of new habitat through afforestation counteracts continuing drainage and destruction of preferred habitat.

It has been suggested (Sharrock, 1976) that Britain may hold less than 1,000 pairs in poor vole years, but perhaps 10,000 pairs during rodent peaks. The *Winter Atlas* (1986) estimated a British Isles midwinter population of 5,000–50,000 individuals, including visitors; this represents only a small fraction of the world population.

Length 37–39cm (14.6–15.3in), wingspan 95–100cm (37.4–39.4in), wing 30.4–33.1cm (12.0–13.0in), tail 13.4–15.4cm (5.3–6.1in), weight (0.26–0.42kg (0.57–0.94lb), the female averaging 17 per cent heavier than the male.

Field Characters and Anatomy

The shortness and general inconspicuousness of this species' ear-tufts suggest that they are relatively unimportant in terrestrial life, but their true function remains a mystery. The ears proper are as large, complicated and asymmetrical as those of the long-eared owl, but the short-eared seems to be less dependent on its hearing, even though it can hear much better than the hen harrier, with which it is often compared. Its eyesight by day appears to rival that of any diurnal bird.

It is the same length as the tawny owl and about the same size as the long-eared owl, but is considerably heavier (20–25 per cent) than the latter, and even more harrier-like in being adapted to open-country life. The short-eared owl may be distinguished from the long-eared by its much longer, narrower wings and its smaller head; its paler, less striking and more uniform plumage; more prominent, dark carpal patch at the 'wrist' of the wing, which is more pointed; and the longer, wedge-shaped tail. The broadly streaked chest is usually conspicuous, and the bulging facial disc with black patches around glaring yellow eyes imparts a baleful expression. The sexes differ only slightly, the male being generally paler and less heavily marked, but there is wide individual variation, sometimes through age (old birds being whiter), so sexing in the field is unreliable. Some authorities attribute the whiter birds to summer bleaching. The juvenile is generally darker, with ill-defined streaking, cream tips forming loose bars on the upperparts, and looser plumage generally.

Flight seems more buoyant and moth-like than that of the long-eared owl, but also more uncertain and wandering, with a distinct 'rowing' action; at low speed the wings are set stiffly forward and up in a shallow V, with frequent wavering glides, side-slipping and sudden banking, all usually at a greater height than the long-eared owl. Migrating birds travel at a much greater height, with more regular wingbeats. Sometimes it hovers slowly in search of food; on the ground it adopts a rather horizontal posture, whereas on a perch (mostly low) it is more upright.

This rather quiet owl has a small vocabulary; certainly it lacks the rich variety of the long-eared, perhaps reflecting its vulnerability in open habitat. The main calls are the male's oft-repeated, low-pitched territorial and courtship hoot *voo-hoo-hoo-hoo-hoo* or *boo-boo-boo-boo*; a *chef-chef-chef* alarm call; the female's harsh *ree-yow* or *kee-ow*; and an antagonistic *wak-wak-wak*. Wing-clapping by the male in threat and display sounds like quiet handclapping, and is produced by rapid, successive strikes of the wingtips below the body before the upward stroke is made.

Breeding

First breeding is at one year; the predominantly monogamous pair-bonding begins in late winter but is of seasonal duration only, and probably not renewed between the same individuals in successive years. In courtship the male wing-claps while chasing the female in a flight pattern which may be either low and rapid or high and exaggerated; he hovers and hoots into the wind, and performs a spectacular sky-dance in which he climbs rapidly with rhythmic 'bouncing' wingbeats, ascending in tight circles, sometimes dropping like a stone while wing-clapping, sometimes hovering, and finally stooping almost vertically in rocking and rolling flight, occasionally interrupted by short, rapid glides.

Successful nesting requires substantial tracts of open country free from continued human disturbance and with a good rodent prey supply. The size of the territory varies considerably with the food available; for example, at one time in a Scottish conifer plantation there were seven averaging 17.8ha, but later in the same year the food supply had dwindled to such an extent that the area supported only two pairs, with an average territory size of 137.2ha. In view of such uncertainty, there is not thought to be any strong site fidelity. However, short-eared owls are vigorous in defence of territory; they are always watching for trespassing

There is usually just one clutch (often replaced after early loss), but two are not unknown in exceptional vole years. The 4–8 (up to 16) eggs, average size 40 x 31mm (1.8 x 1.2in), may be laid as early as March but as late as July if there are two clutches, at 1/2-day intervals.

owls, which they chase with much wing-clapping, sometimes hovering face-to-face or talon-grappling. Although perhaps not so daring as the tawny owl, they have been known to attack men, inflicting serious wounds on the head and neck.

This is the only Palearctic owl which almost regularly builds a nest, even if it is no more than a simple ground scrape; this is lined by the female with whatever vegetation is available, and generally well hidden in tall grass, reeds, heather or other thick cover. A more substantial platform is made in damper areas. Building is usually complete by the end of March or early April. The female usually sits so tightly that the nest is very hard to find, and she will deliberately half close her eyes to conceal the glaring yellow iris – but when confronted closely she can change dramatically, displaying enormously dilated pupils and raised ear-tufts, and adopting an intimidating posture. However, the male's spectacular distraction display, in which he crashes alarmingly to the ground, is a sure sign that a nest is nearby. Where breeding density is high, groups of five or more birds may temporarily forget their differences and circle together over an intruder. Very rarely, a nest is in the old tree-nest of another bird such as a crow, or on a ledge, or in a low stump or other cavity.

The female incubates for 24–29 days, beginning with the first egg, and hatching is asynchronous. Larger clutches are laid in good vole years. Throughout laying, incubation and brooding, the male provisions the female, who rises up to meet him in a spectacular, harrier-like food-pass.

As with other owls, the female takes the dominant share of nest-duties, brooding the chicks closely almost the entire time they are in the nest, providing food is plentiful. However, they do leave the nest exceptionally early, at 12–17 days (before they are able to fly), scattering widely in surrounding vegetation, where they make distinct runs; such behaviour is thought to minimise predation in exposed situations. Nonetheless, losses to foxes and carrion crows are considerable — one Scottish fox den contained the remains of 8 adult and 68 young short-eared owls. When food is short the stronger owlets may eat their weaker siblings, though these are probably already dead. However, there is one record of a chick grabbing its smaller sibling by the head and swallowing it alive. To control such cannibalism, parents will cache food around the nest during times of abundance. Fledging is at 24–27 days and independence achieved at 50–60 days or more, according to food supply.

Productivity is extremely variable. For example, during a period with dwindling vole numbers only five broods were hatched from twenty-four British nests, with just two fledging. However, the species has an extraordinary capacity to respond rapidly to food gluts.

Diet and Feeding Behaviour

The short-eared owl specialises in hunting small mammals which live in open countryside, especially voles, and through its nomadic habit may temporarily concentrate in numbers to exploit local prey abundance. But it is also a very adaptable bird, and will take a wide range of other species when voles are scarce; and as with most raptors, there is some local specialisation by individuals. It is by far the most diurnal of European owls, especially where insufficient food is available at night.

In one British study (Glue, 1977) of eleven sites, the short-tailed vole accounted for 83 per cent of 1,857 prey items, mice 5.1 per cent, common shrew 3.9 per cent, birds 3.8 per cent, and other prey 3.8 per cent. However, the same analyst found

that in the British Isles, for the whole year, during the period 1964–73, mice and voles accounted for 54.6 per cent by weight, with larger mammals 37.3 per cent, shrews 1.2 per cent and birds 7.0 per cent. In the absence of voles, the brown rat and the woodmouse are the chief prey in Ireland, but small flock-feeding birds are also important. There is also notable specialisation on some smaller islands, for instance Rhum in the Inner Hebrides, where in the absence of voles the concentration is on brown rats, pygmy shrews and woodmice. On Skomer, rabbits comprised 42 per cent of the diet by weight, with Skomer voles making up 44 per cent.

Other mammal prey includes hedgehog, mole, pipistrelle bat, water vole, harvest mouse, house mouse, stoat and weasel. Many species of birds are taken, ranging in size from the goldcrest to a moorhen (and once even an adult pheasant was attacked) but mostly open-country species such as finches, pipits, starlings and thrushes. Reptiles and amphibians are rarely eaten, but include lizards and frogs. Other occasional prey of little overall importance includes beetles, craneflies, earwigs, wasps, earthworms and snails. This is one of only a few raptors for which there is evidence of a sense of smell, an injured bird in captivity having consistently refused 'off' liver without even touching it, yet never hesitated in taking fresh liver.

The main hunting method involves quartering with alternate flapping and gliding at an altitude of under 3m. Less frequently the owl hovers, dropping in stages like a kestrel, the speed of descent being governed by the amount the wings are raised. Usually perch hunting is only employed when inclement weather precludes the other methods. Exceptionally, the short-ear watches for prey from the ground, and runs after or ambushes mammals; and some have specialised in the ground capture of young colonial seabirds such as terns. It has also been known to

SHORT-EARED OWL

steal food from kestrels and stoats, and is thought to hover over water, so as to take fish. All its captures are usually taken to another place for consumption, mostly being carried in the feet. Small mammals are swallowed whole (sometimes in flight) and head-first, but larger prey is torn apart.

Migration, Movements and Roosting

In northern parts of its range, the species is migratory, elsewhere partly so. Also, all short-eared owls are highly nomadic at all seasons in response to fluctuating food supplies. Only 28 per cent of 77 recoveries of British-ringed birds of all ages were found within 10km, while 52 per cent travelled beyond 100km, some overseas to Russia, Belgium, France, Spain and Malta. But every year far more visit the British Isles in autumn and winter than leave it. With snow cover usually slight here, a large number of Continental birds (often several thousands) find feeding relatively easy, and flock into eastern Britain from late August to November. Within the British Isles, winter gravitation of home-bred birds is southward and away from high ground to generally milder areas where prey is more concentrated and obtained relatively easily. Individuals may range very widely during a single winter. Young birds disperse randomly, but with winter concentration in the south. Some birds from Scotland and Northern Ireland winter in southern Ireland.

Outside the breeding season the species is mostly solitary, but migrants often travel in parties and large numbers are found feeding and roosting together where food is abundant. Communal roosts often contain 6–40 birds and are mostly on the ground, or just off it among thick cover such as reeds, scrub, evergreen thickets and tussocks; less frequently they occur in woods. Some are used for many successive years, but even the largest may be suddenly vacated in severe weather. Individual birds may use one or several roosts during a single winter, according to prey supply. In the breeding season the female roosts at the nest site until the young have fledged, the male usually less than 100m away.

SNOWY OWL
Once known as great white owl

SNOWY OWL
(Nyctea scandiaca)

THE true home of this beautiful white bird is the Arctic tundra, so it caused great excitement when, in 1967, it bred in Britain for the first time this century; however, since then its toehold in the far north has been disappointingly tenuous, with no confirmed breeding in most years. It is superbly adapted to withstand extreme cold, and has even been found at the northernmost tip of the Arctic. Experiments have shown that it can survive ambient temperatures below the lowest recorded in the northern hemisphere –62°C. One even withstood five hours in a laboratory at –93°C!

History and Conservation

How and where the snowy owl first became adapted to such climatic extremes remains a mystery, but it is well represented in the world's fossil record. Only two remains are known from Pleistocene Britain, from Devon and Derbyshire in the last glaciation, but it is likely that the species then bred widely during cold periods. Records are more extensive from Continental Europe. For example, cave deposits from the last glaciation in France contained 1,130 snowy owl bones, representing 84 individuals — 90 per cent of all bird bones collected there. Many of these bones were claws and adjacent toe bones, indicating that the tundra people of the time made ornaments of snowy owl claws, or used them for magical purposes. There is also a long tradition of Eskimos and other northern peoples taking snowy owls from their breeding grounds for food, the birds being particularly fat in early winter. Such persecution by man continued into modern times and may have been as significant as the contraction of the arctic habitat in causing the relative rarity of snowy owls in northern Europe.

However, in winter snowy owls do not shun cultivated land when hunting — they will even enter small towns, and may spend much of the day perched on roofs or other artificial prominences. Inexperienced birds are then very tame and are easily shot and trapped; some are accidentally electrocuted. These owls can also cause problems at airports in northern countries, especially Canada, where they are attracted by the high concentrations of rodents in surrounding fields, and sometimes end up striking aircraft and damaging engines. The authorities have trapped many of these birds and released them at a safe distance.

In Britain there have been no such problems because in modern times the snowy owl has been but a very rare visitor to the north. In the 19th century it was just about a regular visitor to the northern isles and adjacent mainland — though it would be surprising if it had not bred at least some time during the period 1550–1850, known as the Little Ice Age. Indeed, Bewick (1821) wrote:

> On the authority of Mr Bullock, of the London Museum, we give this as a new species of British owl. On his tour to the Orkney, Shetland, and the neighbouring isles, in the month of July 1812, he discovered that these birds breed there, and live chiefly upon the rabbits, which it appears are pretty abundant in the warrens on the sea shores. He describes the male bird to be of an immaculate white, but observes that others of them are mottled with brown, and supposes them to be the female, or the young . . .

Also, in 1850 Morris stated that they had bred regularly on Yell, Shetland.

From the end of the 19th century they became increasingly rare visitors to Britain; this was perhaps linked to a warming of the Arctic over the period 1900–1940, which meant that birds were more inclined to stay farther north — but from 1963 they were again seen regularly. Then in 1967 there was great excitement when a nest with three eggs was found on the open hillside on the tiny island of Fetlar, in the Shetlands. Close protection was essential as the crofters' sheep and ponies grazed there, and a regular stream of birdwatchers might have endangered the ground nest. So the RSPB mounted a round-the-clock guard and in the end seven eggs were laid, all of which hatched. Two of the young died, but five flew — a high success rate.

With continued close protection over nine years, what was presumably the same pair of owls raised twenty-one young; but in 1975 the old male disappeared and no owls have fledged there since. The site has continued to be occupied by females, and unfertilised eggs have been laid in some years, but there has been no strong male nearby, though a few have been seen elsewhere in Scotland, including Fair Isle. In 1989 a male was released there, having been found exhausted on an oil tanker at sea, but he soon left.

SNOWY OWL

The Latin *Nyctea*, from the Greek *nukteros* meaning 'by night' is misleading in that the species commonly hunts by day. Similarly, the specific *scandiaca* is only loosely relevant in that the bird is by no means confined to Scandinavia. First use of the English name 'snowy owl' was by Latham in 1781, and not surprisingly it won immediate acceptance. Rarity precluded evolution of many English folk names.

The beautiful snowy owl can survive incredibly low temperatures

The idea of importing males has had considerable support, but I am pleased that this has not come to fruition because it smacks of too much interference with nature. Such an action cannot be compared with the reintroduction of a species such as the white-tailed eagle, which *man* has been responsible for eliminating in modern times — it runs the risk of encouraging the importation of a whole range of exotic species, and thwarting the natural process. Nature alone should determine when the time for colonisation is right.

The main problem seems to be that because the male is considerably smaller than the female it is far less adaptable, and therefore more susceptible to cold, wet conditions when prey is scarce. It appears to have had difficulty in relying on rabbit hunting in Britain: certainly when there were two nests on Fetlar in 1973, the lone male could not provide for both and the younger female deserted her nest and three eggs.

There is no doubt that egg-collecting remains a serious threat to such a tenuously established species, the prospect of a British specimen being a far greater attraction than one from abroad. Also, such a handsome bird has always been at the mercy of trophy hunters. As Morris wrote in 1850: 'Beauty in owls as well as in human beings is a dangerous possession, and often entails damage and destruction'. Among snowy owls shot in Britain, he listed one on the Isle of Uist in August or September, 1812 ('old birds and young together have regularly been seen on that island'), one on Orkney in 1835, one near Selby (Yorks) in 1837, three in Northumberland 1822–3, two in Norfolk (1814 and 1820), one in Kent in 1844, one in Dorset, a number in Ireland, and another 'knocked down with a stick by a boatman, on the bank of the River Tamar (Cornwall) in 1838'.

Distribution, Habitat and Population

With a holarctic distribution, the snowy owl ranges across Eurasia and North America, north of the treeline. It is usually resident, though there are some regular migrations south into the Canadian prairie provinces and the Siberian and Mongolian Steppes, as well as dispersive irruptions southwards in periods of food scarcity. Everywhere — in arctic, subarctic and alpine zones — its occurrence as a breeding bird is irregular, depending on the dramatic population cycles of lemmings and, to a lesser extent, bird prey. It is therefore only a very rare summer and winter visitor to northern Britain, with sporadic breeding related to cold phases in modern times. The regular breeding sites nearest to Britain are in Iceland and the Scandinavian mountains.

Its breeding habitat ranges throughout the tundra of the High and Low Arctic, often at the highest, coldest and most exposed situations, though there is a preference for low tundra, especially near coasts where there is greater variety and concentration of prey. Dry ground is preferred, with plenty of hummocks and rocky outcrops for lookout posts. In winter, individuals wander extensively and often visit farmland, especially grassland and stubbles rich in prey; they may also frequent surprisingly busy places such as airfields, golf courses and beaches.

In recent years the majority of summer visitors have been in the Shetlands, Fair Isle, Orkneys, St Kilda, the Outer Hebrides and the Cairngorms, where they mostly occur on mountains and moorlands with boulders scattered among short, tundra-type vegetation.

Field Characters and Anatomy

Should you be lucky enough to see a snowy owl in Britain, there is little likelihood of confusing it with any other species. The male of this very large owl has some fine black-brown spots and bars, but generally appears wholly white, especially in flight. The female has the same ground colour, but is more heavily marked with dark-brown, her pure white face and centre of breast contrasting starkly with the barred body. Her patterned plumage no doubt has camouflage value when nesting, as does the unusually distinctive plumage of the relatively weak and naive first-year birds. Up to October, juvenile plumage is looser, greyer and downy.

The species is remarkably well adapted to life in extreme cold. Its compact shape minimises heat loss, as does its great bulk – it is five times heavier than the short-eared owl, and larger bodies are better at conserving energy. Importantly, however, the head is relatively small, thus reducing heat loss from one of the hottest parts of the body. The eyes, too, are unusually small, and the bones surrounding the eyes are specially adapted to protect against severe cold and to assist long-distance vision in a relatively featureless landscape. Even though the species is predominantly terrestrial, the legs are relatively short and exceptionally thick, and the claws relatively short, all reducing heat loss. But perhaps most important is the exceptionally dense and insulating plumage, with feathers filled with air pockets and almost completely covering the bill and claws. The undertail coverts

The last confirmed breeding was in 1975. In 1988 there were two females in Shetland up to 3 June, one bird laying four eggs, but again no mate appeared. In 1989 just two birds were seen, bringing the total recorded to ninety-two since 1958. Occasional individuals wander as far afield as southern England and Ireland.

Length 53–66cm (20.8–26.0in), wingspan 142–166cm (60–65.4in), wing 40–46cm (15.7–18.1in), tail 20.6–24.1cm (8.1–9.5in), weight of Eurasian owls (North American birds lighter) 1.3–2.9kg (2.8–6.5lb). Sexual dimorphism is marked in the snowy owl, the female at around 2.1kg (4.6lb) averaging 30 per cent heavier than the average male at 1.75kg (3.8lb), 12 per cent longer in the body, with 8 per cent greater wingspan and 16 per cent longer claws. This size difference appears to be important in defence of winter territory as well as in prey selection.

The male's deep, hollow hoot – *hoo-hooooo*, sometimes ending in a harsh, gull-like *aaow* – is loudest in territorial proclamation, and may travel some 10km in the thin polar air. The female's voice is higher-pitched and includes a mewing. The vocabulary also features loud alarm barks, a harsh *keeea* attack note, whistles, cackles, squeals and hisses.

It is not known if the single clutch of eggs, average size 57 x 45mm (2.2 x 1.8in), is replaced on loss. In a peak prey year a clutch generally contains 8 – 16 eggs (exceptionally large for an owl this big), with high reproductive expectancy; during a prey trough, however, clutches are small and have minimal success rate, or there will be no nest at all. The average of the nine Shetland clutches was 5.4. The eggs are generally laid at 2-day intervals, but this may be as long as 3–5 days during inclement weather, as has happened on Fetlar.

reach the end of the tail, and even the undersides of the toes have a hair-like covering.

In flight the snowy owl is reminiscent of a hawk, sometimes gliding like a buzzard, but with typical owl buoyancy, with frequent side slips. It can also fly very fast and hover in search of prey. It often rests on the ground, less frequently on stumps or higher perches, and walks rather upright, rolling and lurching, often sitting, resting on its breast in a cat-like manner.

Breeding

Age of first breeding is not known. Mating is mostly monogamous, but male bigamy is not rare. As with the short-eared owl, the size of the territory varies tremendously with prey abundance, being anything from about ½sq km to 20sq km.

Because of the constraints of the very short Arctic summer, the breeding cycle does not usually start before the end of April, but then proceeds rapidly. Unlike most owls, the snowy does not attempt to breed every year: instead its cycle coincides with, and therefore profits from, the 'lemming' cycle, with prolific reproduction every 3–5 years.

In territorial and nuptial display, the male has an exaggerated, undulating flight with deep wingbeats, in which the wings are held in a deep V at the top of each upstroke, causing him to drop repeatedly. He also has a dramatic ground display in which he raises his wings in an angelic posture – this can be seen as a flashing white signal over a mile or more away. Inevitably he brings food to the female, hoots and assumes a grotesque posture while cocking his tail, generally on raised ground — apparently this tells the female that he is a good hunter and that there will be enough food to raise a family.

Nest sites often have a long tradition, but there is little evidence that the same individuals use them in successive years. The female does most of the work in forming a shallow scrape, usually on a hummock or rocky outcrop with a commanding view — though if there is a lining it has probably been blown in by the wind. Occasional use is made of the former nest sites of another raptor, such as a roughlegged buzzard. Well-used sites are often surrounded by a rich and diverse flora, the high fertility being the result of owl excrement.

Incubation is by the female alone, starts with the first egg, and averages 20–30 days for a clutch of eleven. With hatching at similar intervals to those of laying, there can be big size differences between the chicks. To accommodate these large clutches, the female has an enormous brood patch — the flabby, featherless area of belly skin rich in blood vessels.

With little time before winter returns, development of the young is rapid. Providing food is plentiful, the female broods the chicks almost continually till they leave the nest at 7–14 days, when they hide in surrounding vegetation. Meanwhile, the male provisions the whole family and uses a broken-wing display against predators. The owlets can fly at 43–50 days and are independent from about 60 days. During gluts, the male caches food around the nest.

In 'lemming' years, breeding success is usually very high, having reached 100 per cent even with the largest clutches, and thus compensating for almost zero reproduction in lean years. Of 49 Shetland eggs, 44 hatched and 23 young fledged, success ranging from 4.8 young hatched per pair and 1.5 young fledged in poor prey years, to 5.3 and 3.1 respectively in years of food abundance. The main cause of chick death was starvation when bad weather prevented hunting.

Diet and Feeding Behaviour

It is now clear that in most places the importance of the lemming to the snowy owl has been overestimated, though exceptionally this highly nutritious rodent can account for over 90 per cent of the diet. A good example of the snowy owl's flexibility comes from Fetlar, where in a survey of 116 prey items 72 per cent were rabbit, and the remainder fledgling birds — mostly oystercatcher, but also curlew or whimbrel, lapwing, arctic skua and four unidentified. Other mammals taken include hares, shrews, voles, mice and weasels; while birds range in size from redpoll to black grouse and goose. Grouse, ptarmigan and colonial seabirds are sometimes locally important. Raptors which are preyed on by the snowy include short-eared owl, gyrfalcon, peregrine and roughlegged buzzard — but the snowy owl itself has been killed by the gyrfalcon and peregrine. Unlike most owls, the snowy readily eats carrion such as walrus, seal and fox. Frogs, fish and beetles are of little importance.

When winter arrives the snowy owl is very fat, so it can fast for as long as forty days in succession if food is short. It also moves as little as possible to conserve energy. Most hunting is conducted at dusk and dawn, but it can be at any time throughout the day; though on Shetland it was seen to be chiefly between 16.00 and 04.00 hrs, and especially 22.00–03.00. Hunting in the darkness is more common in winter. Most prey is spotted from an open perch on the ground or a few metres high. Prey is often approached over a long, low flight, the owl sometimes landing close by and waiting before seizing it. Hovering is also frequent, and the snowy may take small mammals from under snow. Birds on which it is a food-pirate include the short-eared owl and hen harrier. It makes no special attempt to kill large prey before eating it, and generally devours it where taken. Smaller mammals are usually swallowed whole, head-first. The male mostly carries food for his family in his feet, but transfers it to his bill before passing it to his mate.

Migration, Movements and Roosting

Even though it is superbly adapted to withstand extreme cold, the snowy owl cannot rely on its prey supply and as a hunter it is probably inhibited by the sustained darkness in the northern winter. Thus in some parts of its range it regularly migrates south to overwinter, and in other areas it is partially migratory. But it is also highly nomadic and irruptive, and can fluctuate in abundance according to density of prey: when prime prey species (notably lemmings, voles and hares) crash, as they often do on a cyclical basis, then many owls must move out to find sufficient food. Sometimes the weather may be the most important stimulus. But whatever the reason, displaced birds sometimes irrupt in huge numbers, invasions of thousands occurring in certain areas every few years. Some have crossed oceans and have been seen resting on sea ice or ships, a few eventually ending up in the British Isles or as far south as France and Yugoslavia in Europe. Thus the populations are constantly intermingling, inhibiting the evolution of subspecies. However, some geographically isolated populations, such as those which bred in the Shetlands 1967–75, have contained adults which have been resident for up to eight years, while their young have been dispersive.

Little information is available on roosting habits, but it is thought that each bird uses a number of favourite, scattered perches overnight (especially in winter) and for loafing/sleeping by day, either on the ground or on an exposed perch.

VAGRANTS TO THE BRITISH ISLES

SCOPS OWL

In addition to the species described in the preceding main accounts, there is a small number of raptors whose presence in these islands is very irregular or accidental. Most of these so-called vagrants are Palearctic migrants which leave Eurasia to winter farther south, some of them — especially inexperienced first-year birds — wandering way off-course during their seasonal travels, to the delight of British birdwatchers. Others arrive here through exceptional irruptive response to cyclical prey abundance. An even smaller number are Nearctic or transatlantic vagrants, arriving here only after remarkable ocean crossings of up to 5,000km, though some are ship-assisted. The most interesting raptor vagrants are listed below. However, it should be noted that a considerable number of raptor sightings have been attributed to escapes. Also, the apparent increase in the number of vagrants to these islands in recent decades is probably largely accounted for by the ever-increasing army of birdwatchers whose expertise is sufficient to make positive identification.

American Kestrel (*Falco sparverius*): First record from Fair Isle, in May, 1976.

Black Kite (*Milvus migrans*): A breeding bird of central and southern Europe and north-west Africa, mostly seen here in May–June when mostly young birds overshoot in returning to their breeding grounds. By 1976 there had been only 12 records, but there were 134 to 1989, increasing incidence being linked with European range expansion. This is a potential British breeder.

Eagle Owl (*Bubo bubo*): Morris (1850) noted a small number shot or caught throughout the British Isles during the first half of the 19th century, as well as four in Donegal 'after a great snow-storm from the north-east'. Although he was probably misinformed in saying that 'In the Orkney islands it is considered to be a permanent resident', we do know that this species did once breed here. Some English records have been of escaped birds, the species having long been an aviary favourite, but those occurring in Scotland and the northern isles are wanderers from Scandinavia. Although the bird is virtually sedentary, in years of food scarcity it can travel long distances.

Egyptian Vulture (*Neophron percnopterus*): One of two birds seen in 1825 was killed in Somerset. Another occurred in Essex in 1868. This is a scarce breeder in the Mediterranean Basin, but more abundant in the Tropics. The small number of British reports involves mostly young birds returning and wandering north of the European breeding area.

Eleonora's Falcon (*Falco eleonorae*): This bird breeds in the Mediterranean area and Morocco, and was new to the British list in 1977.

Griffon Vulture (*Gyps fulvus*): The very small number of this southern European breeder recorded in Britain include one captured near Cork in 1843, one near Southampton in the same year, and two in Derbyshire in 1927.

Hawk Owl (*Surnia ulula*): It is said that both the American and European subspecies have occurred here, though identification of the former has been questioned. In Britain there were only eight records 1830–1903, two 1959–72, and none between. Undoubtedly, the majority of our records concern Fennoscandian birds of northern coniferous forests, which carry out remarkable invasions into central Europe in peak vole years, stragglers crossing the North Sea.

The vagrant red-footed falcon has been recorded in Britain with increasing frequency

Lanner Falcon (*Falco biarmicus*): Only a few records over the last 200 years, though its range was once much more extensive. In 1799 Bewick claimed that it bred in Ireland, but now the closest breeding birds are in Italy and Yugoslavia.

Lesser Kestrel (*Falco naumanni*): This bird breeds in the Mediterranean Basin and winters in tropical Africa. On returning, it frequently wanders north and west in Europe, some coming to the British Isles, including Scotland and Ireland. They are mostly seen in spring and autumn, with a few late birds in Oct/Nov. Most records are of males, so it is likely that many females have been overlooked as they are hard to identify. Twelve records to 1976, but only one 1926–76.

Mottled Owl (*Strix virgata*): Morris records one of a pair shot in Yorkshire in 1852, which is rather surprising as this is a bird of tropical America, occurring north to Mexico.

Pallid Harrier (*Circus macrourus*): Although it breeds only in the eastern part of the west Palearctic, this migratory bird sometimes wanders well to the west, giving a small number of British records — all since 1931.

Pygmy Owl (*Glaucidium passerinum*): Although mostly resident, very occasionally Fennoscandian irruptions have brought birds of the Eurasian race to Britain.

Red-Footed Falcon (*Falco vespertinus*): 19th-century British records mostly refer to the orange-legged hobby or red-legged falcon. This migrant is a summer visitor to the west Palearctic, the entire population breeding from the Baltic to Mongolia and wintering in southern Africa. However, every few years substantial numbers occur in western Europe, where exceptional breeding may be the result of such irruptions. Although there has been worldwide decline this century, sorties to the north and west of the main breeding range have occurred with increasing frequency in recent years. Indeed, it has been of annual occurrence in Britain since the 1960s, the 31 recorded throughout these islands in 1989 bringing the all-time total to 446. Many are spotted in southern and eastern England in spring, and the males are easily recognised with their slate-grey plumage and red thighs and legs.

Red-Shouldered Hawk (*Buteo lineatus*): The 1863 Inverness record of this American bird was not accepted for the national list.

Saker (*Falco cherrug*): The small number of records of this Central European, Asian and North African species are suspect as there is a risk of escaped hybrids from disreputable falconry centres. The bird has a great tradition in Arab sport.

Scops Owl (*Otus scops*): Mostly a summer visitor to Europe and once much more numerous, this long-distance migrant sometimes wanders as far as the British Isles. In 1989 there was just one bird, bringing the total recorded to 81.

Short-Toed Eagle (*Circaetus gallicus*): If the bird seen on the Isle of Wight in May 1990 is accepted, it will be the first record for the British Isles.

Spotted Eagle (Greater) (*Aquila clanga*): It is suggested that this very irregular visitor from eastern Europe may once have bred here, the closest breeding birds now being in Germany. Most records are from the 19th and early 20th centuries, totalling 14 by 1976.

Swallow-Tailed Kite (*Elanoides forficatus*): This beautiful, migratory and nomadic American bird has been recorded only a few times, one being killed in Argyllshire in 1772 and another caught in Yorkshire in 1805.

Tengmalm's Owl (*Aegolius funereus*): Irruptions of Scandinavian birds sometimes bring stragglers to our shores, most records being from eastern counties. European records have suggested range extension, and in 1977 there was a British breeding record.

FLIGHT SILHOUETTES

In *Hamlet* (Act II, Scene 2), Shakespeare said:

I am but mad north-north-west: when the wind is
southerly, I know a hawk from a handsaw.

And even today most people would find little difficulty in distinguishing a hawk
from a handsaw – a corruption of hernshaw, the old name for a heron. But many
folk now have problems in telling one bird of prey from another, partly because

Golden
Eagle

Sea
Eagle

Osprey

Red Kite

Hen Harrier

Marsh
Harrier

Montagu's Harrier

FLIGHT SILHOUETTES

Common Buzzard

*Honey
Buzzard*

Roughlegged Buzzard

Peregrine Falcon

Hobby

Gyrfalcon

Merlin

Kestrel

*Red-footed
Falcon*

Goshawk

Sparrowhawk

we see so few to practise identification on. Positive naming of a species is also complicated by the fact that raptors often display significant plumage variation between individuals, with distinct colour phases, juvenile plumages, immature plumages and different patterns between male and female. Furthermore, these birds are generally seen at long distance and often only fleetingly or in poor light. But the task of identification can be much easier if an effort is made to study the birds' plumage profile, flight characteristics, body proportions and relative size. Therefore, the flight silhouettes reproduced here should be studied in conjunction with the characteristics which are given within each species account. Try to remember a few key points, such as the red kite's long, forked tail or the subtle differences in flight pattern. Take note of any call and the habitat where a bird is spotted, and put these facts together with the visual clues to solve the puzzle. It will rarely be easy, but with persistence the average observer should attain a fair degree of proficiency.

Barn Owl

Tawny Owl

Little Owl

Long-eared Owl

Short-eared Owl

Snowy Owl

FURTHER READING AND REFERENCES

Albin, E. *A Natural History of Birds, 1731–38.*

Aldrovandi, U. Aldrovandus *Ornithologia, 1599–1603.*

Arnold, E. *Bird Life in England* (Chatto & Windus, 1887).

Atkinson, Rev. J. *British Birds' Eggs and Nests* (Routledge, 1886).

Avery, M. and Leslie, R. *Birds and Forestry* (Poyser, 1990).

Batten, L., Bibby, C., Clement, P., Elliott, G., and Porter, R. *Red Data Birds in Britain* (Poyser, 1990).

Baxter, E., and Rintoul, L. *The Birds of Scotland* (Oliver & Boyd, 1953).

Bechstein, J. *The Natural History of Cage Birds* (Groombridge, 1837).

Beven, G. 'The Food of Tawny Owls in Surrey' *Surrey Bird Report 1966.*

Bewick, T. *A History of British Birds* (Walker, 1799 and 1821).

Bewick, T. *Supplement of Rarer Species to the History of British Birds* (Walker, 1821).

Bibby, C., Robinson, P., and Bland, E. 'The Impact of Egg Collecting on Scarce Breeding Birds' (*RSPB Conservation Review, 1990*).

Blaker, G. *The Barn Owl in England and Wales* (RSPB, 1934).

Brazil, M., and Shawyer, C. *The Barn Owl — The Farmer's Friend needs a helping Hand* (The Hawk Trust, 1989).

Brown, L., and Amadon, D. *Eagles, Hawks & Falcons of the World* (Hamlyn, 1968).

Brown, L., and Watson, A. 'The Golden Eagle in relation to its food supply' (*Ibis 106, 1964*).

Brown, L. *Birds of Prey: their Biology and Ecology* (Hamlyn, 1986).

Brown, L. *British Birds of Prey* (Collins, New Naturalist, 1976).

Brown, P., and Waterston, G. *The Return of the Osprey* (Collins, 1962).

Bunn, D., Warburton, A., and Wilson, P. *The Barn Owl* (Poyser, 1982).

Burton, J. (ed) *Owls of the World* (Eurobooks, 1973).

Burton, P. *Birds of Prey of the World* (Dragon's World, 1989).

Cadbury, C., Elliott, G., and Harbard, P. 'Birds of Prey Conservation in the UK' (*RSPB Conservation Review, 1990*).

Cade, T. *The Falcons of the World* (Collins, 1982).

Campbell, B., and Lack, E. (eds) *A Dictionary of Birds* (Poyser, 1985).

Chancellor, R. (ed) *World Conference on Birds of Prey 1975* (ICBP, 1977).

Chaucer, G. *Parlement of Foules* (c. 1381).

Coward, T. *The Birds of the British Isles and their Eggs* (Series 1, 1928 and Series 3, 1947).

Cramp, S. (ed) *Birds of the Western Palearctic* vols II (1980) and IV (1985) (Oxford Univ Press).

Cummins, J. *The Hound and the Hawk* (Weidenfeld & Nicholson, 1988).

Davenport, D. 'Influxes into Britain of Hen Harriers, Long-Eared Owls and Short-Eared Owls in Winter 1978–79 (*British Birds 75, 1982*).

Day, J. 'Marsh Harriers in Britain' (*RSPB Conservation Review, 1988*).

Edwards, G. *Gleanings of Natural History 1758–64.*

Edwards, G. *Natural History of Uncommon Birds, 1743–51.*

Elkins, N. *Weather and Bird Behaviour* (Poyser, 1983).

Elliott, G. 'Montagu's Harrier Conservation' (*RSPB Conservation Review, 1988*).

Everett, M. *A Natural History of Owls* (Hamlyn, 1977).

Eyton, H. *History of the Rarer British Birds, 1836.*

Fairley, J. 'An Indication of the Food of the Short-Eared Owl in Ireland' (*British Birds 59, 1966*).

Finn, F. *Eggs and Nests of British Birds* (Hutchinson, 1910).

Fuller, R. *Bird Habitats in Britain* (Poyser, 1982).

Gardiner, L. *Rare, Vanishing and Lost British Birds* (compiled from notes by W.H. Hudson, Dent, 1923).

Gaza, T. *Aristotelis de Natura Animalium* (Latin translation of Aristotle), 1476.

Gensbol, B. *Birds of Prey of Britain & Europe* (Collins, 1984).

Gesner (C. Gesnerus) *Historia Animalium Liber 111 quis est de Avium Natura, 1555.*

Glue, D., and Scott, D. 'Breeding Biology of the Little Owl' (*British Birds 73, 1980*).

Glue, D. 'Bird Prey taken by British Owls' (*Bird Study 19, 1972*).

Glue, D. 'Breeding Biology of Long-Eared Owls' (*British Birds 70, 1977*).

Glue, D. 'Prey taken by the Barn Owl in England & Wales' (*Bird Study 14, 1967*).

Gooders, J. *Bird Seeker's Guide* (Deutsch, 1980).

Gooders, J. *Birds That Came Back* (Deutsch, 1983).

Gordon, S. *The Golden Eagle, King of Birds* (1955).

'Goshawks, Breeding Biology of in Lowland Britain', anon, (*British Birds*, Dec 1990).

Greenoak, F. *All the Birds of the Air* (Deutsch, 1979).

Harrison, C. *An Atlas of the Birds of the Western Palearctic* (Collins, 1982).

Harrison, C. *The History of the Birds of Britain* (Collins/ Witherby, 1988).

Harting, J. *The Ornithology of Shakespeare* (Gresham, 1864, reprinted 1978).

Hosking, E., and Newberry, C. *Birds of the Night* (Collins, 1945).

Johnson, P. 'Town Owls, Country Owls' (*Country Life 22.3.90, p 184*).

Knox, A. *Game Birds & Wild Fowl: their Friends and Foes* (John van Voorst, 1850).

Lack, P. (ed) *The Atlas of Wintering Birds in Britain & Ireland* (Poyser, 1986).

Latham, J. *General Synopsis of Birds, 1781–85* supplement 1787.

Lockie, J. 'The Breeding Habits and Food of Short-Eared Owls after a Vole Plague' (*Bird Study 2*, 1955).

Lockwood, W. *The Oxford Book of British Bird Names* (OUP, 1984).

Love, J. *The Reintroduction of the White-tailed Eagle to Scotland 1975–87* (NCC, 1988).

Love, J. *The Return of the Sea Eagle* (CUP, 1983).

Lovegrove, R., Elliott, G., and Smith, K. 'The Red Kite in Britain' (RSPB *Conservation Review 1990*).

Lovegrove, R. *The Kite's Tale* (RSPB, 1990).

MacGillivray, W. *History of British Birds, 1837–52.*

Madders, M., and Welstead, J. *Where to Watch Birds In Scotland* (Helm, 1989).

Marquis, M., and Newton, I. 'The Goshawk in Britain' (*British Birds 75*, 1982).

Martin, B. *The Glorious Grouse — A Natural and Unnatural History* (David & Charles, 1990).

Martin, B. *World Birds* (Guinness, 1987).

Martin, G., and Gordon, I. 'Visual Acuity in the Tawny Owl' (*Vision Res. 14*, 1974).

Mead, C. 'Movements of British Raptors' (*Bird Study 20*, 1973).

Mearns, R., and Newton, I. *Turnover and Dispersal in a Peregrine Population* (Ibis 126, 1984).

Meinertzhagen, R. *Pirates & Predators* (Oliver & Boyd, 1959).

Merrett, C. *Pinax Rerum Naturalium Britannicarum 1667.*

Mikkola, H. *Owls of Europe* (Poyser, 1983).

Mitchell, W. *Birdwatch Around Scotland* (Hale, 1983).

Montagu, G. *Ornithological Dictionary, 1802, Supplement 1813.*

Moore, N., 'The Past and Present Status of the Buzzard in the British Isles' (*British Birds 50*, 1957).

Mudie, R. *British Birds, 1834.*

Newton, I., and Haas, M. 'The Return of the Sparrowhawk' (*British Birds 77*, 1984).

Newton, I. (ed) *Birds of Prey (of the world)* (Merehurst, 1990).

Newton, I. *Population Ecology of Raptors* (Poyser, 1979).

Newton, I. Raptors in Britain — a Review of the last 150 Years' (*BTO News 131*, 1984).

Newton, I. *The Sparrowhawk* (Poyser, 1986).

Norris, D., and Wilson, H. *Survey of the Peregrine in Ireland 1981* (Bird Study 1983).

Ogilvie, M. 'Birds in Ireland 1970–74' (*British Birds 69*, 1976).

Parslow, J. *Breeding Birds of Britain & Ireland: a historical Survey* (Poyser, 1973).

Pennant, T. *Genera of Birds, 1773.*

Petty, S. 'A Study of Tawny Owls in an Upland Spruce Forest' (*Ibis 125*, 1983).

Petty, S. 'Goshawks: their Status, Requirements and Management' (*Forestry Commission Bulletin 81*, HMSO, 1989).

Picozzi, N. 'Dispersion, Breeding and Prey of the Hen Harrier in Glen Dye, Kincardineshire' (*Ibis 120*, 1978).

Portenko, L. *Die Schnee-eule* [snowy owl] (N.Brehm-Buch 454, A. Ziemsen Verlag Wittenberg, 1972).

Porter, R. *Flight Identification of European Raptors* (Poyser, 1981).

Ratcliffe, D. *The Peregrine Falcon* (Poyser, 1980).

Ray, J. *The Ornithology of Francis Willughby, 1678.*

RSPB *Conservation Review 1988* (ed) Cadbury, C., and Everett, H.

Selby, P. *Illustrations of British Ornithology: 1) Land Birds, 1825, 2) Water Birds, 1833.*

Sharrock, J. (ed) *The Atlas of Breeding Birds in Britain & Ireland* (Poyser, 1976).

Sharrock, J. 'Rare Breeding Birds in the UK in 1981' (*British Birds 1-25* 1981).

Shaw, G., and Dowell, A. 'Barn Owl Conservation in Forests' (*Forestry Commission Bulletin 90*, 1990).

Shawyer, C. *The Barn Owl in the British Isles — Its Past, Present and Future* (The Hawk Trust, 1987).

Southern, H. *Tawny Owls and their Prey* (Ibis 96, 1954).

Sparks, J., and Soper, T. *Owls: their Natural and Unnatural History* (David & Charles, 1970).

Swainson, C. *Provincial Names & Folk Lore of British Birds, 1885.*

Swann, H. *A Dictionary of English and Folk Names of British Birds, 1913.*

Taylor, K. 'Buzzard — Gaining Lost Ground' (*Birds* (RSPB) 9, 1983).

Thom, V. *Birds in Scotland* (Poyser, 1986).

Tubbs, C. *The Buzzard* (David & Charles, 1974).

Tulloch, R. 'Fetlar's Snowies' (*Birds 5*, 1975).

Tulloch, R. 'Snowy Owls Breeding in Shetland' (*Scottish Birds 5*, 1967).

Turner, W. *Avium precipuarum, quarum apud Plinium et Aristotelem mentio est brevis et succincta historia, 1544.*

Village, A. 'The Diet and Breeding of Long-Eared Owls in relation to Vole Numbers' (*Bird Study 28*, 1981).

Village, A. *The Kestrel* (Poyser, 1990).

Voous, K. *Owls of the Northern Hemisphere* (Collins, 1988).

Walcot, J. *Synopsis of British Birds, 1789.*

Watson, D. *The Hen Harrier* (Poyser, 1977).

Watson, J. 'Food of Merlins nesting in Young Conifer Forest' (*Bird Study 26*, 1979).

Yarrell, W. *History of British Birds, 1843.*

ACKNOWLEDGEMENTS

My very special thanks to Alastair Proud, whose great artistic ability and expert knowledge of raptors has produced the best set of British bird-of-prey paintings I have ever seen. He has also provided the excellent egg paintings and flight silhouettes. Thanks also to artist Robert Gilmoor, who suggested Alastair Proud for this project, and to the expert photographers listed below, whose superb work has further embellished these pages. Of the people who have helped provide information for the text I would specially like to thank the staffs and honorary officers of the RSPB, BTO and Hawk and Owl Trust, who always give so unstintingly of their time. My thanks to publishers David & Charles, whose idea this book was and whose quality production can always be relied on; to my editor Sue Hall, and to my family for accepting my many long absences from family life while slaving over a hot typewriter.

PICTURE CREDITS

Hugh Clark, page 155; R. V. Collier, pages 40, 42; D. N. Dalton, page 152; R. Davies/RSPB, page 26; Forestry Commission, page 145; C. H. Gomershall/RSPB, page 95; Dennis Green, pages 11, 33, 34, 60, 111, 116, 146, 162, 175; Ian Grindy, page 17; Eric and David Hosking, pages 53, 121; E. A. Janes/ZAP, pages 103 (adult only), 123, 138, 142; Paul Johnson, pages 15, 18; Lea MacNally, pages 21, 78, 96; F. G. Rippingale, page 160; Tony Waddell, pages 13, 54, 70, 101, 102-3 (except adult), 129; Robin Williams, page 65.

INDEX